ADAPTIVE 2017

The Ninth International Conference on Adaptive and Self-Adaptive Systems and Applications

February 19 - 23, 2017

Athens, Greece

ADAPTIVE 2017 Editors

Andrei Alexandru Enescu, EOS Electronic Systems, Romania

Andreas Rausch, TU Clausthal, Department of Computer Science, Software Systems Engineering, Clausthal-Zellerfeld, Germany

Printed from e-media with permission by:

Curran Associates, Inc.
57 Morehouse Lane
Red Hook, NY 12571

Some format issues inherent in the e-media version may also appear in this print version.

Printed by Curran Associates, Inc. (2017)

International Academy, Research, and Industry Association (IARIA)
412 Derby Way
Wilmington, DE 19810

Phone: (408) 893-6407
Fax: (408) 527-6351

petre@iaria.org

Additional copies of this publication are available from:

Curran Associates, Inc.
57 Morehouse Lane
Red Hook, NY 12571 USA
Phone: 845-758-0400
Fax: 845-758-2633
Email: curran@proceedings.com
Web: www.proceedings.com

Table of Contents

ADAPTIVE 2017

Forward

The Ninth International Conference on Adaptive and Self-Adaptive Systems and Applications (ADAPTIVE 2017), held between February 19-23, 2017 in Athens, Greece, continued a series of events targeting advanced system and application design paradigms driven by adaptiveness and self-adaptiveness. With the current tendencies in developing and deploying complex systems, and under the continuous changes of system and application requirements, adaptation is a key feature. Speed and scalability of changes require self-adaptation for special cases. How to build systems to be easily adaptive and self-adaptive, what constraints and what mechanisms must be used, and how to evaluate a stable state in such systems are challenging duties. Context-aware and user-aware are major situations where environment and user feedback is considered for further adaptation.

The conference had the following tracks:

- Fundamentals and design of adaptive systems
- Adaptive mechanisms
- Managed Adaptive Automotive Product Line Development

We take here the opportunity to warmly thank all the members of the ADAPTIVE 2017 technical program committee, as well as all the reviewers. The creation of such a high quality conference program would not have been possible without their involvement. We also kindly thank all the authors that dedicated much of their time and effort to contribute to ADAPTIVE 2017. We truly believe that, thanks to all these efforts, the final conference program consisted of top quality contributions.

Also, this event could not have been a reality without the support of many individuals, organizations and sponsors. We also gratefully thank the members of the ADAPTIVE 2017 organizing committee for their help in handling the logistics and for their work that made this professional meeting a success.

We hope that ADAPTIVE 2017 was a successful international forum for the exchange of ideas and results between academia and industry and to promote further progress in the area of adaptive and non-adaptive system applications. We also hope that Athens, Greece provided a pleasant environment during the conference and everyone saved some time to enjoy the charm of the city.

ADAPTIVE 2017 Committee

ADAPTIVE 2017 Steering Committee

Roy Sterritt, Ulster University, UK
Constantin Paleologu, University Politehnica of Bucharest, Romania
Claudia Raibulet, University of Milano-Bicocca, Italy

Radu Calinescu, University of York, UK
Po-Hsun Cheng, National Kaohsiung Normal University, Taiwan
Marc-Philippe Huget, Polytech Annecy-Chambery-LISTIC | University of Savoie, France
Ryotaro Kamimura, Tokai Univerisity, Japan
Valérie Camps, Paul Sabatier University – IRIT, Toulouse, France

ADAPTIVE 2017 Industry/Research Advisory Committee

Weirong Jiang, Google, USA
Jessie Y.C. Chen, U.S. Army Research Laboratory, USA
Sherif Abdelwahed, Distributed Analytics and Security Institute (DASI), USA
Gregor Grambow, AristaFlow GmbH, Ulm, Germany
Marc Kurz, ecx.io austria GmbH - An IBM company, Wels, Austria
Habtamu Abie, Norwegian Computing Center/Norsk Regnesentral-Blindern, Norway

ADAPTIVE 2017

Committee

ADAPTIVE Steering Committee

Roy Sterritt, Ulster University, UK
Constantin Paleologu, University Politehnica of Bucharest, Romania
Claudia Raibulet, University of Milano-Bicocca, Italy
Radu Calinescu, University of York, UK
Po-Hsun Cheng, National Kaohsiung Normal University, Taiwan
Marc-Philippe Huget, Polytech Annecy-Chambery-LISTIC | University of Savoie, France
Ryotaro Kamimura, Tokai Univerisity, Japan
Valérie Camps, Paul Sabatier University – IRIT, Toulouse, France

ADAPTIVE Industry/Research Advisory Committee

Weirong Jiang, Google, USA
Jessie Y.C. Chen, U.S. Army Research Laboratory, USA
Sherif Abdelwahed, Distributed Analytics and Security Institute (DASI), USA
Gregor Grambow, AristaFlow GmbH, Ulm, Germany
Marc Kurz, ecx.io austria GmbH - An IBM company, Wels, Austria
Habtamu Abie, Norwegian Computing Center/Norsk Regnesentral-Blindern, Norway

ADAPTIVE 2017 Technical Program Committee

Sherif Abdelwahed, Distributed Analytics and Security Institute (DASI), USA
Habtamu Abie, Norwegian Computing Center/Norsk Regnesentral-Blindern, Norway
Nadia Acbchiche-Mimouni, University of Evry, France
Jose M. Alcaraz Calero, University of the West of Scotland, UK
Harvey Alférez, Universidad de Montemorelos, Mexico
Richard Anthony, University of Greenwich, UK
Charles K. Ayo, Covenant University, Ogun State, Nigeria
Antonio Brogi, University of Pisa, Italy
Radu Calinescu, University of York, UK
Valérie Camps, Paul Sabatier University – IRIT, Toulouse, France
Carlos Carrascosa, Universidad Politécnica de Valencia, Spain
Jessie Y.C. Chen, U.S. Army Research Laboratory, USA
Po-Hsun Cheng, National Kaohsiung Normal University, Taiwan
Enrique Chirivella Perez, University of the West of Scotland, UK
Jose Alfredo F. Costa, Federal University - UFRN, Brazil
Anderson da Silva Soares, Professor at Federal University of Goiás, Brazil
Baudouin Dafflon, Université de Lyon, Université Lyon 1, France
Mihaela Dinsoreanu, Technical University of Cluj-Napoca, Romania

Copyright Information

4T Loadless SRAMs for Low Power FPGA LUT Optimization

Karol Niewiadomski, Carsten Gremzow, Dietmar Tutsch
University of Wuppertal
Chair of Automation and Computer Science
Wuppertal, Germany
Email: {niewiadomski, gremzow, tutsch}@uni-wuppertal.de

Abstract—**The adaptiveness of Field Programmable Gate Arrays (FPGAs) is a key aspect in many mobile applications. Modern vehicles contain up to 100 "Electronic Control Units" (ECUs) in order to implement all necessary functions for autonomous driving. Due to the limited power resources of mobile applications, an appropriate implementation of power reduction measures is crucial for achieving an acceptable amount of power savings. Commercial Electronic Design Automation (EDA) tools support the designers to implement low-power circuits on architectural level. However, effective power reduction mechanisms have to be applied to the backbone of each FPGA: the look-up table (LUT). In this paper, we describe the implementation and comparison of various LUTs based on different Static Random Access Memory (SRAM) cells. All SRAM cells have been analyzed in order to evaluate feasible modifications for the sake of lowering leakage currents and modified in order to minimize static and dynamic power consumption. Followed by a comparison of different LUT implementations based on the optimized SRAM cell designs, we derive further optimization approaches to achieve effective power savings for the usage in environments like vehicles, smartphones, etc. with limited power.**

Keywords–FPGA; LUT architecture; SRAM cell optimization; low-power; leakage-current reduction; power reduction measures.

I. Introduction

During the last years, the number of classic desktop computers used in domestic homes has constantly decreased. The reason behind this phenomenon is the rising number of mobile devices such as smartphones and tablets, taking over most of the functionalities provided by desktop computers before. Furthermore, upcoming features like highly automated driving cars or fully autonomous vehicles require a high demand for computing power. Whilst the computing performance of mobile devices is improved constantly to face the challenges of complex applications like video processing for adaptive cruise control on long distance highway drives, the capacities of batteries providing the needed energy resources have not been extended in the same way. A modern, upper-class vehicle contains more than 70 ECUs to provide all features desired by consumers these days [1]. On-board communication networks like Controller Area Network (CAN), FlexRay and ethernet ensure the communication between these devices, but also introduce a remarkable amount of additional weight of approximately up to 30% (depending on the used technology). In order to counter the limits set by power consumption and overall weight, a significant reduction of the ECU number would be an efficient approach. This could lead to the application of more powerful processors, taking over many of the functionalities from the large number of slower ECUs used before. The downside of this approach would be a higher power consumption due to higher clock frequencies. A more comprehensive approach focuses on the massive usage of FPGAs in mobile applications. FPGAs offer various advantages compared to processors and Application Specific Integrated Circuits (ASICs). Being fully configurable, FPGAs are well-suited for the execution of various functions which have been spread over several ECUs before, either purely by hardware implementations or software execution running on a softcore processor implemented on the FPGA's fabric. However, FPGAs don't offer similar power saving mechanisms implemented on microprocessors and lack of of a substantial power management system. Power consumption saving mechanisms shall be applied to series production passenger cars, which is a cost-sensitive market, hence we choose the Xilinx Spartan-3 low-cost FPGA as a baseline architecture for all further considerations [2]. FPGAs play a major role for the realization of adaptive systems. Partial, dynamic reconfiguration [3], supported by various FPGA designs, offer a vast potential for fast adaption of the implemented functional range within a vehicle, e.g., realizing a requested function by the driver and disengaging a previously implemented vehicle function which is not required any more [4].

In this paper, we evaluate selected SRAM cell designs on their suitability for a low-leakage LUT implementation, which are the elementar computational elements. Since the overhead of reconfigurability leads to unused parts within the FPGA, both static and dynamic power consumption are analyzed for each cell design. In Section II, we give an overview about a selection of existing designs and our motivation for improvements. In Section III, we describe a number of leakage reduction techniques and evaluate the feasible adaption on current designs. In Section IV, we investigate the SRAM cell designs on their assets and drawbacks and compare the simulation results. In Section V circuit improvement methods for standby and active currents reduction are introduced. All investigated SRAM cells are enhanced with these additional improvements and compared again. In Section VI, we use each modified SRAM cell to implement a 4-input LUT reference design and explore the power consumption during the idle and active state. The advantages of reasonable SRAM cell design modifications are presented based upon the simulation results. In Section VII, all previous discussions are summarized and concluded.

II. Related work

Various SRAM cell designs have been under research over the years. Compared to dynamic RAM (DRAM), which is widely used as main memory in many applications, SRAM offers numerous advantages like quick read & write-cycles, cell stability, data retention without refresh cycles, differential outputs and many more. During the pre-Complementary Metal-Oxide-Semiconductor (CMOS) era, the 4T cell [5] was commonly used for cache memories. Considering the additional effort in terms of process variations for implementing the resistor load and weaker signal to noise (SNM) margin, this cell type was replaced by the 6T cell [6]. This design depicts the mostly used approach for combining reliable functionality with a proven in use fabrication process due to its CMOS structure. Being the starting point for benchmarking, cell variations like the 5T SRAM [5] design were developed to eliminate the parasitic capacitance penalties of two bitlines. Further derivations like the 7T cell implementation [7] inherit the characteristics of the reference 6T design and provide power savings by exploiting an effective writing mechanism, putting no further requirements on adaptions to auxiliary circuitry. Features like soft error rate robustness during low-power operation have been explored in a 10T design variation [8]. All of these cell types have been designed during research without applying additional, commonly used power reduction measures. LUT designs have been evaluated and improved on architectural level [9] for power reduction by power gating mechanisms. New FPGA designs were presented and compared to commercial products, by adding structural improvements [10].

Our approach goes one step further and is based on circuit level improvements to a LUT by reasonable selection of a suitable SRAM cell design and substantial modification of the cell circuitry to achieve better leakage reduction and power savings. The improvements achieved on that level are essential for important leakage current suppression and are an inevitable step to be combined with architectural amendments.

III. LEAKAGE REDUCTION

Three major components of leakage currents can be identified for a Metal-Oxide-Semiconductor (MOS) transistor of gate lengths in nanometer scales:

- Subthreshold leakage
- Direct tunneling gate leakageshown in
- Reverse biased p-n BTBT leakage

Whilst the band-to-band tunneling (BTBT) leakage currents can be neglected for devices exceeding 50nm gate lengths, subthreshold and direct tunneling gate leakage currents come into consideration for our design. Tunneling electrons through gates oxides can be countermeasured by carefully setting an adequate oxide thickness of each transistor. This dependency can be seen in (1):

$$J_{DT} \propto A(\frac{V_{ox}}{T_{ox}})^2 \tag{1}$$

where

$$A = \mu_o C_{ox} \frac{W}{L_{eff}} (\frac{kT}{q})^2 e^{1.8}$$

By increasing the oxide thickness T_{ox}, the direct tunneling current density J_{DT} can be efficiently lowered to a minimum stage [11]. Increasing the gate length L_{eff} would have a similar effect, but lead to higher effort in the manufacturing process due to a change in one of the basic technology parameters like the gate length of a transistor. Therefore, this option should be avoided. However, the usage of multi-oxide thicknesses is a technology dependent parameter and requires awareness for the selection of a suitable multi-oxide technology.

Subthreshold currents can be expressed by the following equation:

$$I_{sub} \propto \frac{W}{L_{eff}} e^{(V_{GS} - V_{t0} - \gamma V_{SB} + \eta V_{DS})/nV_t)(1 - e^{-\frac{V_{DS}}{V_t}})} \tag{2}$$

Equation (2) shows the parameters which contribute to the overall weak-inversion current, flowing below the threshold voltage V_{th} of each MOS transistor in the circuit. Several leakage reduction measures can be applied by utilizing these parameters to design a low leakage circuit:

- W: setting the width of a transistor as small as possible leads to a higher resistance of it and therefore to smaller leakage currents
- V_{gs}: Gate biasing is done by applying a V_{gs} voltage lower than Gnd, which turns the transistor deeply off
- V_{sb}: Body biasing by tweaking the body voltage of a turned off transistor
- V_{dd}: Lowering the supply voltage mitigates or even completely removes the DIBL (drain-induced barrier lowering) effect, represented by η in (2)

In general, we can distinguish between two classes of leakage reduction techniques [12]. Some can be applied during the design, whereas others can be used during operation time of the circuit. A reasonable extract of these techniques is shown in Table I:

TABLE I. LEAKAGE REDUCTION TECHNIQUES

Design leakage reduction	*Static leakage reduction*	*Active leakage reduction*
Dual-V_{th}	Stacking	DVS
Multi-V_{dd}	Sleep mode	
	VTCMOS	DVTS

Energy efficient circuits should feature multiple supply voltages and at least a dual threshold approach. As shown in Table I, these characteristics need to be added during the development phase. Furthermore, additional techniques working during operation of the circuit can help to continuously reduce the overall power consumption. Dynamic (threshold) voltage scaling (DVS & DVTS), as well as variable threshold CMOS (VTCMOS) circuitry are powerful methods to overcome the side-effects like subthreshold leakage due to progressive scaling to smaller technology nodes.

We analyze the techniques listed in Table I on their careful combination and application to volatile (SRAM) memory cells and therefore automatically to LUTs.

IV. SRAM CELL DESIGNS

The backbone of each computational activity within an FPGA is the LUT [13]. Depending on the number of the LUT's inputs, a LUT can contain numerous SRAM cells. For example, in case of a 4-input LUT, 16 SRAM cells are necessary for the realization of all possible input value combinations. Since the memory cells are used for configuration, they are also called configuration RAM (CRAM). Once configured during the start-up phase, the content of these memory cells won't be changed until the next reconfiguration cycle. In consequence, the static leakage current reduction is of higher significance for the overall power consumption.

The selection of a low-power SRAM cell design is crucial for an appropriate energy-efficient implementation of integrated circuits. Many memory cell designs have been introduced in the past. The common 6 transistor cell can be found in most FPGAs nowadays [14]. In principle, this memory cell consists of two cross-coupled inverter and two access transistors, connecting the inverters to the bitlines, as shown in Figure 1.

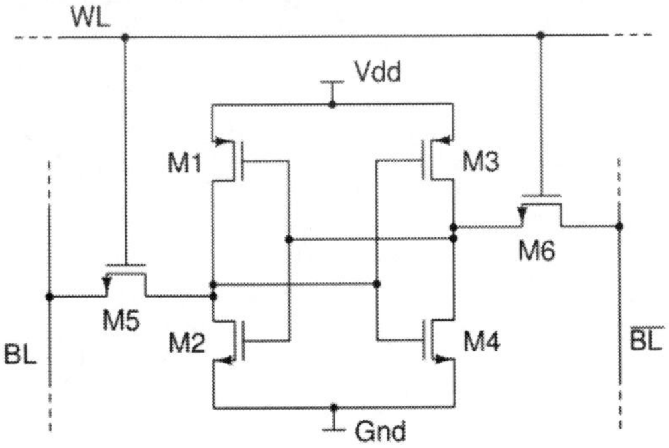

Figure 1. 6T SRAM cell

As long as $M5$ and $M6$ are in cut-off mode, the cross-coupled inverters are isolated from the bitlines and store the complementary data value at the output nodes of each inverter. Data retention is ensured as long as a sufficient supply voltage V_{dd} is applied. Before reading the stored data, both bitlines BL and $\overline{BL}$ are precharged to V_{dd} by a special precharge circuit and the access transistors $M5$ and $M6$ are turned on. One of the bitlines will be discharged to Gnd, whereas the other bitline will remain on V_{dd}. The voltage drop between BL and $\overline{BL}$ will be sensed and evaluated by a sense amplifier. For writing data into the cell, one of the bitlines is kept at V_{dd}, whereas the other bitline is kept at Gnd. By turning the access transistors on, the desired value is written. For this purpose, a suitable bitline driver circuit is needed to ensure the propoer execution of the writing cycle. Careful transistor sizing is required for avoiding the cell to flip during, e.g., a read cycle. This cell design is well-elaborated and used for years in integrated circuits. Its stability and reliability is well-known and therefore used in various applications. However, the power consumption of the 6T SRAM cell can be further optimized by some modifications resulting in the SRAM cells described in the following paragraphs:

1) 4T SRAM cell: A typical implementation of a four transistor SRAM cell is shown in Figure 2. In comparison to the 6T cell, a smaller are of approximately 30% can be achieved [15]. Due to the replacement of all pMOS transistors by polysilicon resistors, only nMOS transistors are used for the pure functionality of this cell. Despite of the space-savings, which could lead to a higher yield after the manufacturing process, the realization of high-resistivity polysilicon resistor adds additional technological steps to the manufacturing process, resulting in higher costs.

The 4T (polysilicon) SRAM is a predecessor of all CMOS-based SRAM cells. Lower stability, lower tolerance against

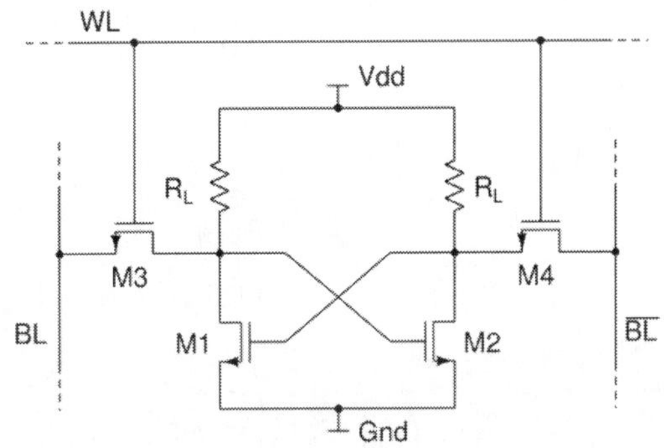

Figure 2. 4T SRAM cell

soft-errors and a more technically demanding manufacturing process exclude this cell type from further considerations [5].

2) 5T SRAM cell: The circuitry of a five transistor SRAM cell is shown in Figure 3. The advantage of this cell design compared to the 6T reference cell is the availability of just one access transistor $M5$ and therefore only one bitline BL [16]. The connecting bitlines in each slice of an FPGA add undesired parasitic capacitances, which underly the process of charging and discharging during each read- and write-cycle and lead subsequently to higher power consumption. A cell design working with just one access transistor adds space-savings. For a proper and stable functionality of this cell, asymmetric transistor sizing is required, which may complicate the manufacturing process and to modifications of auxiliary circuitry like sense amplifiers, precharge circuits, etc..

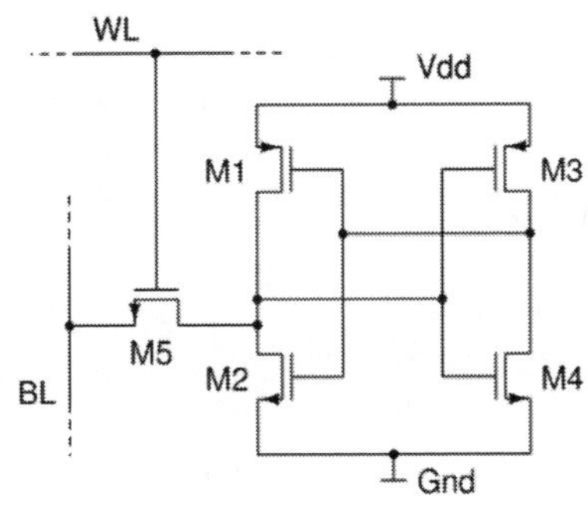

Figure 3. 5T SRAM cell

3) 7T SRAM cell: The seven transistor SRAM cell is shown in Figure 4, which enhances the 6T reference cell design by an additional feedback transistor $M7$ and 2 signal lines R and W. The idea behind this design is a write mechanism, which depends only on one of the two bitlines in order to execute a write operation. This can be also expressed in equation 3 [11].

While the activity factor α equals 1 in conventional memory cells, the 7T SRAM cell reduces this factor to less than 0.5 by exploiting the fact, that most of the bits in memories and caches are zeros [7]. The main asset of this implementation is the reduction of the switching activity and therefore a reduction of charging and discharging cycles of parasitic capacitances. The drawback is the required additional control logic and

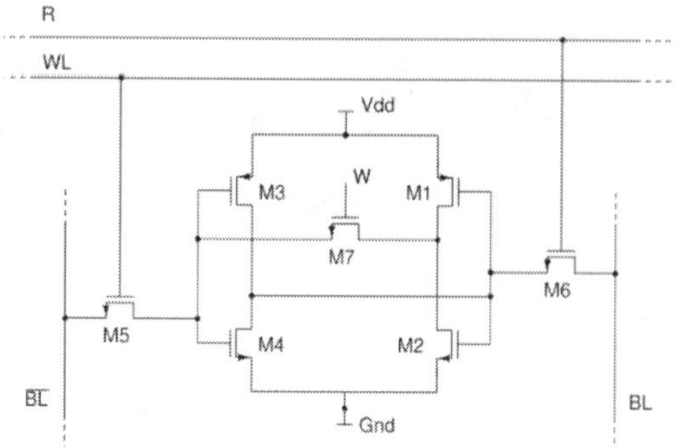

Figure 4. 7T SRAM cell

the loopback transistor, which lead to higher complexity and required space.

$$P = \alpha C_{BL} V^2 F_{write} \quad (3)$$

V. SRAM Cell design modifications

The simulation results showed that the choice of a suitable SRAM cell design leads to a significant impact on power consumption of a LUT. In this section we present further improvements on each cell design in order to achieve even better power savings in this essential component. Since Xilinx' Spartan 3(A) is manufactured in a 90nm process and has a recommended internal supply voltage of $1.2V$, we choose a 90nm TSMC technology library at an comparable operating voltage of $1.2V$.

Coming back to the proposed cell designs in Section IV, we refer to the 4T SRAM cell since its compact design is of interest for further considerations and performance comparison to other design. The major drawback of the 4T SRAM cell is the high-resistive polysilicon resistor, which should be replaced or completely omitted in an improved cell. A possibility how to bypass this drawback is shown in Figure 5.

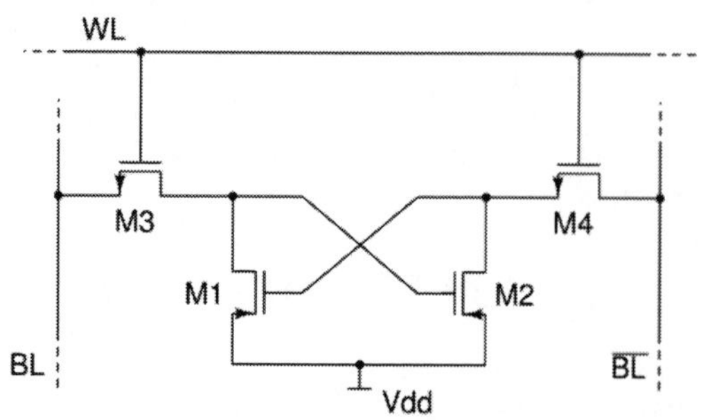

Figure 5. 4T loadless SRAM cell

The previous pull-down network (PDN) consisting of two nMOS transistors is replaced by a pull-up network of two pMOS $M1$ and $M2$ transistors [17]. In combination with both nMOS access transistors $M3$ and $M4$ a stable and power saving functionality is achieved. Instead of precharging both bitlines to V_{dd} as a pre-step of the reading-phase, the bitlines are "precharged" to Gnd, due to the fact, that pMOS transistor are used as drivers in this cell. This saves power and ensures compatibility with CMOS logic processes. Nevertheless, minor adaptions to the auxiliary circuitry around the cell have to be done, e.g., modifying the bitline drivers.

A. Test results

All SRAM cells have been designed and simulated by usage of the Cadence toolchain and a $90nm$ technology provided by TSMC at an ambient temperature of 27°C. The main challenge to achieve comparable results was to develop suitable bitline drivers, precharge circuitry and a sense amplfier. Careful design of the bitline drivers is crucial for avoiding the cell to flip during a read cycle. All simulations are performed with a clock frequency of $200MHz$ and a load of $600aF$. Configuration memory cells used in a LUT are not supposed to be written and read at high frequencies, like e.g., memory arrays in a microprocessor's cache (up to $4GHz$). Therefore, we choose a lower frequency, nevertheless all cells have also been successfully tested with a higher clock frequency of $500MHz$.

For the first step, the determination of the best SRAM cell design in terms of power consumption without any further improvements, is done. The simulation results of the 6T cell design are shown in Figure 6:

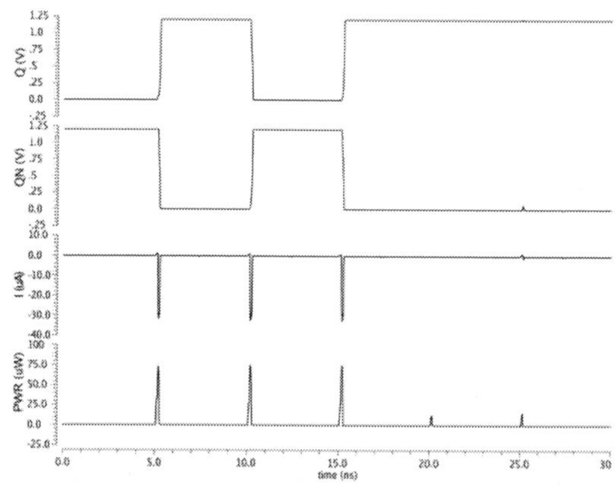

Figure 6. Power dissipation and I_{Leak} of 6T SRAM cell

The average power consumption, the maximum and minimum power consumption during simulation time were traced and summarized in Table II:

TABLE II. SIMULATION RESULTS WITHOUT MODIFICATIONS

SRAM cell	*Average Power nW*	*Max. Power uW*	*Min. Power pW*
4T	334.5	35.07	161.7
5T	587.2	61.26	217.34
6T	927	75.39	250.8
7T	491	49.19	221.7

Compared to the other designs, Table II shows clearly the drawbacks of the reference 6T SRAM cell. Substantial power savings can be achieved by the choice of alternative cell design. For example, the average power consumption of the 6T SRAM reference cell design is $927nW$ and about 3 times higher than the average power consumption of the 4T loadless SRAM cell, which is only $334.5nW$. That results in power savings of approximately 65%.

B. Dual Threshold CMOS

Further optimizations can be achieved by the introduction of high threshold voltage (V_{th}) transistors. High V_{th} transistors require a higher V_{GS} voltage at the gate in order to turn the transistor on, which can lead to an increase of the propagation delay within a signal path. Therefore, high V_{th} should be only used in applications which are not timing-critical. However, the SRAM cells in a LUT are used as configuration RAM (CRAM) and are pertinent for use with high threshold voltage transistors. All cell designs have been modified and the simulations were performed again. These modifications are limited to the core cell only, the precharge circuitry, the sense amplifier and the bitline drivers have not been modified. The results are summed up in Table III.

TABLE III. SIMULATION RESULTS WITH HIGH THRESHOLD VOLTAGE TRANSISTORS (hvt)

SRAM cell	*Average Power nW*	*Max. Power uW*	*Min. Power pW*
4T hvt	324	31.83	74.99
5T hvt	541.78	54.9	130.5
6T hvt	695.1	64.46	158.3
7T hvt	427	36.21	161.9

In comparison to the reference design of the 6T SRAM cell, the introduction of the high V_{th} transistors adds power savings of about 25%. The performance of the high V_{th} 4T loadless SRAM cell is slightly improved and leads to energy savings of approximately $10nW$.

C. Transistor Stacking

Transistor stacking, shown in Figure 7, which is also known as self-reverse biasing, is a strong technique to reduce subthreshold leakage current by raising the voltage at the source terminal of each transistor. By constantly increasing the source voltage V_S and keeping the gate voltage V_G at the same level, V_{GS} becomes negative at a certain point of time, which leads the transistor into super cut-off mode and turns it deeply off. Subthreshold currents are exponentially reduced.

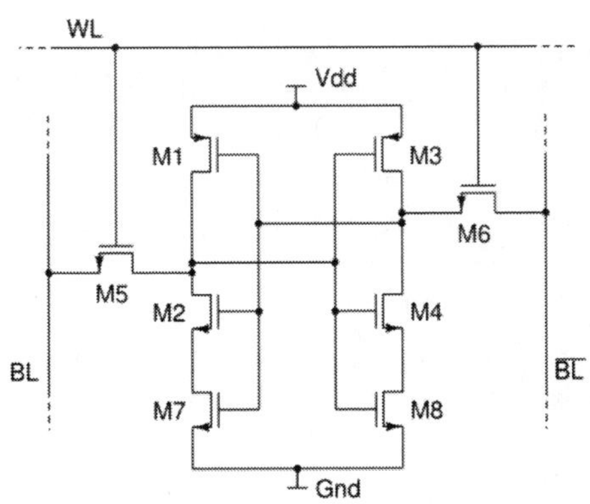

Figure 7. 6T SRAM cell with stacking

At the same time, the body to source potential V_{SB} also becomes negative, since the body terminal of a nMOS transistor is usually kept at Gnd. In consequence, the body effect is intensified, thus V_{th} is tuned by that effect to a higher level. This fact can be further exploited by continuing stacking transistors in series, but the effect of subthreshold current reduction becomes diminished with a rising number of transistors.This technique implies a trade-off between power savings and size ratio of the chip. Despite the gradual technology shrink up to $16nm$ FinFET, on-chip space is not an unlimited resource and should be used carefully. Therefore, we choose to add two stacking transistors only in order to have a reasonable compromise between leakage current reduction and size-ratio of the cells. The simulation results are shown in Table IV and Table V.

TABLE IV. SIMULATION RESULTS WITH STANDARD TRANSISTORS AND STACKING

SRAM cell	*Average Power nW*	*Max. Power uW*	*Min. Power pW*
4T	346.8	35.31	137.6
5T	327.4	25.1	189.4
6T	826.6	72.05	274
7T	540.4	31.64	168.3

If the used manufacturing process doesn't support dual-threshold CMOS technology, Table IV shows that a noteworthy reduction of leakage currents within the 4T SRAM cell is achieved by approximately 90%. Even the standard 6T SRAM cell features important amendments in terms of power savings ($\approx 12\%$) and leakage currents.

TABLE V. SIMULATION RESULTS WITH hvt TRANSISTORS AND STACKING

SRAM cell	*Average Power nW*	*Max. Power uW*	*Min. Power pW*
4T hvt	336.6	32.79	70.42
5T hvt	327.4	25.1	189.4
6T hvt	672.4	61.28	167.4
7T hvt	461.8	30.84	523.9

The combination of both techniques, dual-threshold CMOS and transistor stacking, puts additional improvements to the overall power savings parameters. Since most of the currently available technologies feature dual-threshold CMOS, the feasibility of this combination is high.

D. Dynamic Voltage Scaling

The higher the supply voltage is, the faster the operation of the integrated circuit will be, since high V_{dd} allows fast charging and discharging of parasitic capacitances. In case of low demand on performance such as for CRAMs, the supply voltage can be lowered while still ensuring data retention within the cell. Dynamic voltage scaling (DVS) depends usually at least on an operating system and a regulation loop to recognize the circuit speed and to cover a wide range of operating voltages. Our approach simplifies this principle by introducing two additional transistors, shown in Figure 8.

Both transistors $M9$ and $M10$ are used to connect the SRAM cell to two different supply voltages, V_{dd} and V_{ddL}, whereas V_{dd} equals the primary $1.2V$. On the one hand, the prerequisite of this method is a dual-V_{dd} setup, representing a simple alternative to the mentioned operating system driven regulation loop, and on the other hand a modified power gating approach is implemented. Since the 4T SRAM cell has no connection to Gnd in its core, power gating is achieved by the possibility to fully cut-off the supply voltage, if needed. However, power gating should be introduced at a coarse-grain level, e.g., by powering or switching off groups of cells at a higher abstraction layer. By lowering the supply voltage

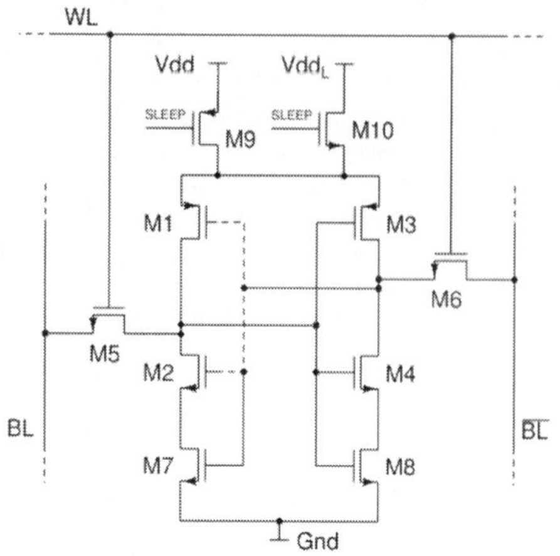

Figure 8. 6T SRAM cell with hvt transistors, stacking and DVS

to V_{ddL}, which equals $1V$, we can further reduce leakage power consumption. Experimental results have shown, that data retention will still be ensured at supply voltages down to $400mV$. A combination of all three power saving mechanisms in a 6T SRAM cell is shown in Figure 8.

TABLE VI. SIMULATION RESULTS WITH hvt TRANSISTORS, STACKING AND DVS

SRAM cell	*Average Power nW*	*Max. Power uW*	*Min. Power pW*
4T hvt	232.9	21.27	49.59
5T hvt	327.4	25.1	189.4
6T hvt	458.7	44.67	166.1
7T hvt	368.3	26.53	167

In order to achieve an average power consumption of $232.9nW$ at a clock requency of $200MHz$ and full data retention like shown in Table VI, we combined all three power saving methods introduced in the chapters before with careful transistor sizing of an efficient memory cell design. We present the modified, loadless 4T SRAM cell in Figure 9.

The simulation was done by injecting a $1 \rightarrow 0 \rightarrow 1$ sequence and one read cycle at the end of the simulation time, which can be seen in Figure 10. By comparing the results of Figure 10 with the outputs shown in Figure 6, we see a reduction in both, power and current spikes. Looking back on the continuous improvements added to each cell type, we see the benefits in reduction of average power consumption in Figure 11.

VI. LUT SIMULATIONS

The LUT was implemented with each cell type investigated in the previous chapters. In order to achieve an equal distribution of bits, all memory cells have alternating bits stored and are not connected to the bitlines by switching off all access transistors. As a matter of lucidity, we present a comparison between the 6T SRAM- and 4T SRAM LUT implementation. As expected, the 4T SRAM cell design shows a better performance in terms of power savings and leakage current reduction than the 6T SRAM cell design does. By comparing a LUT implementation with a standard 6T SRAM cell and our modified 4T SRAM design, Table VII summarizes the results and highlights the improvements in power dissipation, which

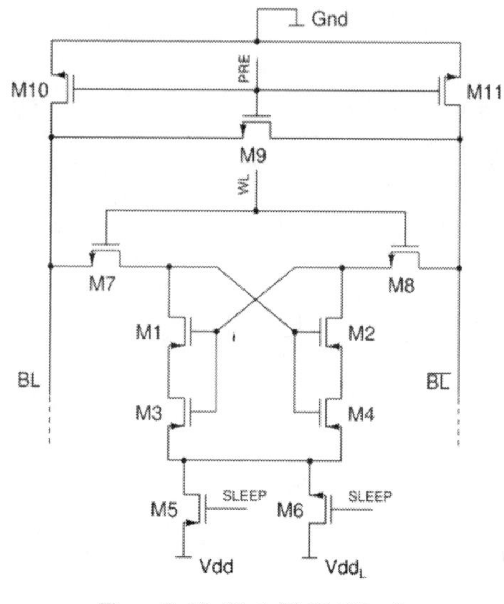

Figure 9. Modified 4T SRAM cell

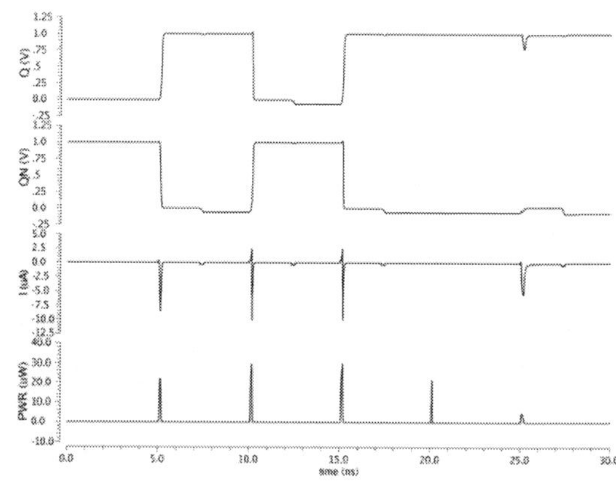

Figure 10. Power dissipation and I_{Leak} of a modified 4T SRAM cell

equals power savings of approximately 16%. Figure 12 shows the related leakage current of the 4T SRAM based LUT.

TABLE VII. LUT COMPARISON

SRAM cell	*Average PWR nW*	*Max. PWR uW*	*Min. PWR nW*	*Energy aJ*
4T hvt	424.2	40.94	0.24	127
6T	500	42.99	2.8	150

It should be mentioned that either the precharge circuit nor the sense amplifier have been optimized for power efficiency. Optimizing these parts will lead to even better results and raise the duration of a battery charge, independent of the target application. Further optimization can be achieved by coarse-grain power gating of CRAM blocks within the LUT architecture. Unused CRAMs should be completely powered off by adding additional, thick-oxide transistors, cutting off the cell from V_{dd} and Gnd.

The modified 4T memory cell design introduced in Figure 9 is superior in terms of low power aspects compared to all other investigated cell designs. However, this solution requires

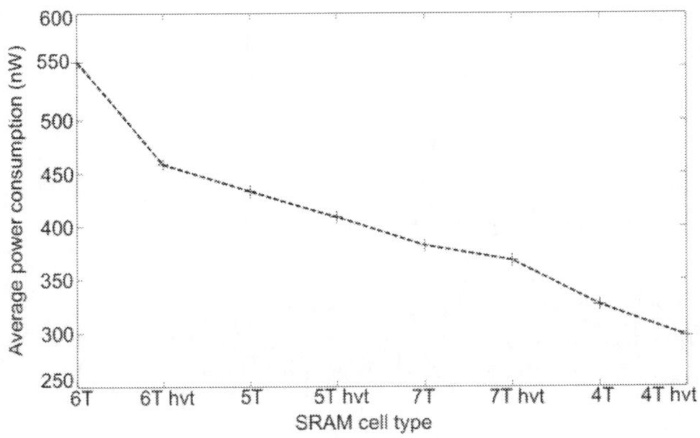

Figure 11. Power dissipation reduction

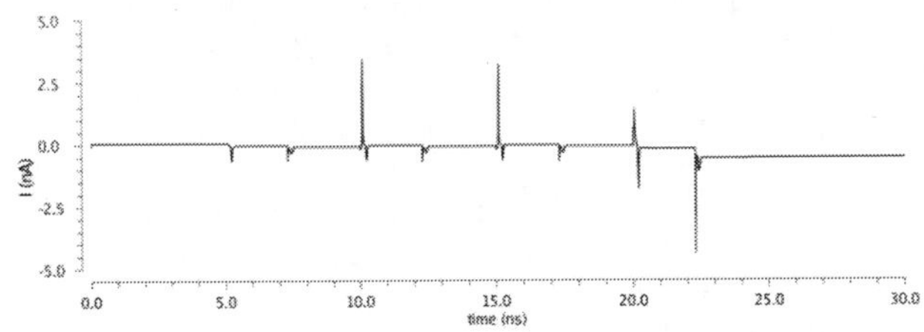

Figure 12. Leakage current of an improved 4T SRAM based LUT

additional space, since it requires at least four additional transistors to achieve its intended power-efficient functionality.

VII. Conclusion

We analyzed a typical LUT structure of an FPGA in terms of power dissipation and leakage current. Our approach was to integrate power savings mechanisms at the basic circuit level before heading for further optimizations on architectural level. Different SRAM cell structures have been investigated on their power characteristics in order to evaluate the best design for implementing a LUT, which features inherent low-power characteristics. Simulations have shown that the 4T loadless SRAM cell features the required properties. We applied various low-power techniques and enhanced this cell for standby leakage current mitigation. Hence, we presented a modified 4T loadless SRAM cell design. By combining dedicated techniques during design time and during operating time, we achieved a reduction of the average power consumption within the LUT of 16% during simulation time. Subsequently, this leads to overall energy savings of $127aJ$ compared to the origin $150aJ$ of a 6T SRAM cell based LUT implementation. The leakage current I_{leak} is reduced dramatically from $1.741nA$ to approximately $0.2nA$, showing the strong impact of leakage reduction methods on power-critical circuitry. FPGAs support adaptiveness of whole systems by re-configuration abilities on demand of the application. The presented low-power cell design reduces power consumption significantly during the charging and discharging cycles of re-configuration tasks within an FPGA.

Acknowledgment

The authors thank Amit Majumdar, from Xilinx, for his support and interesting discussions on FPGA architectures. Also, we want to give credit to Ray Chiang, from TSMC, for his explanations and suggestions on the used technology. We are grateful to Andreas Ullrich, from University of Wuppertal, for his restless dedication in PDK compilation and tool maintenance.

References

[1] S. Fürst, "Challenges in the design of automotive software," in Proceedings of the Conference on Design, Automation and Test in Europe, ser. DATE '10. 3001 Leuven, Belgium, Belgium: European Design and Automation Association, 2010, pp. 256–258. [Online]. Available: http://dl.acm.org/citation.cfm?id=1870926.1870987

[2] XA Spartan-3A Automotive FPGA Family Data Sheet, Xilinx, 04 2011, rev. 2.0.

[3] M. Ullmann, M. Hübner, B. Grimm, and J. Becker, "An fpga run-time system for dynamical on-demand reconfiguration," in Parallel and Distributed Processing Symposium, 2004. Proceedings. 18th International. IEEE, 2004, p. 135.

[4] R. Anthony, A. Rettberg, D. Chen, I. Jahnich, G. de Boer, and C. Ekelin, "Towards a dynamically reconfigurable automotive control system architecture," in Embedded System Design: Topics, Techniques and Trends. Springer, 2007, pp. 71–84.

[5] A. S. Pavlov, "Design and Test of Embedded SRAMs," Ph.D. dissertation, University of Waterloo, Ontario, May 2005.

[6] J. P. Uyemura, CMOS Logic Circuit Design. Norwell, MA, USA: Kluwer Academic Publishers, 1999.

[7] R. E. Aly, M. I. Faisal, and M. A. Bayoumi, "Novel 7t sram cell for low power cache design," in Proceedings 2005 IEEE International SOC Conference, Sept 2005, pp. 171–174.

[8] S. M. Jahinuzzaman, D. J. Rennie, and M. Sachdev, "A soft error tolerant 10t sram bit-cell with differential read capability," IEEE Transactions on Nuclear Science, vol. 56, no. 6, Dec 2009, pp. 3768–3773.

[9] A. Lodi, L. Ciccarelli, D. Loparco, R. Canegallo, and R. Guerrieri, "Low leakage design of lut-based fpgas," in Proceedings of the 31st European Solid-State Circuits Conference, 2005. ESSCIRC 2005., Sept 2005, pp. 153–156.

[10] T. Tuan, S. Kao, A. Rahman, S. Das, and S. Trimberger, "A 90nm low-power fpga for battery-powered applications," in Proceedings of the 2006 ACM/SIGDA 14th international symposium on Field programmable gate arrays. ACM, 2006, pp. 3–11.

[11] J. M. Rabaey, A. Chandrakasan, and B. Nikolic, Digital integrated circuits- A design perspective, 2nd ed. Prentice Hall, 2004.

[12] C. Piguet, Low-power processors and systems on chips. CRC Press, 2005.

[13] C. Maxfield, The Design Warrior's Guide to FPGAs: Devices, Tools and Flows, 1st ed. Newton, MA, USA: Newnes, 2004.

[14] K. Itoh, VLSI Memory Chip Design, ser. Springer Series in Advanced Microelectronics. Springer Berlin Heidelberg, 2001. [Online]. Available: https://books.google.de/books?id=p2FsQgAACAAJ

[15] A. Bellaouar and M. I. Elmasry, Low-Power Digital VLSI Design Circuits and Systems, 1st ed., J. Allen, Ed. Norwell, MA, USA: Kluwer Academic Publishers, 1995.

[16] I. Carlson, S. Andersson, S. Natarajan, and A. Alvandpour, "A high density, low leakage, 5t sram for embedded caches," in Solid-State Circuits Conference, 2004. ESSCIRC 2004. Proceeding of the 30th European, Sept 2004, pp. 215–218.

[17] J. Yang and L. Chen, "A new loadless 4-transistor sram cell with a 0.18 m cmos technology," in 2007 Canadian Conference on Electrical and Computer Engineering, April 2007, pp. 538–541.

Design Patterns for Addition of Adaptive Behavior in Graphical User Interfaces

Samuel Longchamps, Ruben Gonzalez-Rubio

Sherbrooke University,
Sherbrooke, Québec, Canada
Email: {samuel.longchamps, ruben.gonzalez-rubio}@usherbrooke.ca

Abstract—**Graphical user interfaces (GUI) in modern software are increasingly required to adapt themselves to various situations and users, rendering their development more complex. To handle complexity, we present in this paper three design patterns, *Monitor*, *Proxy router* and *Adaptive component*, as solutions to the gradual implementation of adaptive behavior in GUI and general component-based software. Rather than proposing new adaptation mechanisms, we aim at formalizing a basic structure for progressive addition of different mechanisms throughout the development cycle. To do so, previous work on the subject of design patterns oriented toward adaptation is explored and concepts related to similar concerns are extracted and generalized in the new patterns. These patterns are implemented in a reference Python library called AdaptivePy and used in a GUI application case study. This case study shows concrete usage of the patterns and is compared to a functionally equivalent *ad hoc* implementation. We observe that separation of concerns is promoted by the patterns and testability potential is improved. Moreover, adaptation of widgets can be previewed within a graphical editor. This approach is closer to the standard workflow for GUI development which is not possible with the *ad hoc* solution.**

Keywords–adaptive; design pattern; graphical user interface; context; library.

I. Introduction

As applications become increasingly complex and distributed, adaptive software has become a research subject of great interest to tackle related challenges. One area of modern applications where adaptation requirements have flourished is graphical user interfaces (GUI). Because they are generally engineered using a descriptive language and oriented toward specific platforms, it is hard to produce a single GUI which automatically adapts itself to its multiple usage contexts.

Many researchers have proposed models and frameworks to implement adaptive behavior in a generic manner for components-based software [1]–[4]. These solutions typically require significant effort to modify an existing software architecture and make many technological choices and assumptions. They are limited both in terms of gradual integration to the software and in portability, for a framework usually targets a certain application domain (e.g. distributed client-server systems). As a more portable approach, we propose to use design patterns for formalizing structures of components which can be easily composed to produce specialized adaptive mechanisms. While some work has been done to propose design patterns for the implementation of common adaptive mechanisms [5]–[8], the present work aims at generalizing widespread concepts used in these patterns. In doing so, their integration in existing software is expected to be easier and more predictable.

As a proof-of-concept, a reference implementation of the design patterns has been done as a Python library called AdaptivePy. An application was built as a case study using the library to validate the gains provided by the patterns compared to an *ad hoc* solution. Special attention was paid to the compatibility to modern GUI design workflow. In fact, rather than create a specialized toolkit or create a custom designer tool which would include the design patterns' artifacts, the Qt cross-platform toolkit along with the Qt Designer graphical editor was used. The application workflow is presented and compared to original methods and advantages are highlighted. We expect that through the case study, the patterns' usage and advantages will be clearer and offer hints on how to structure an adaptive GUI.

The remainder of this paper is organized as follows. Fundamental concepts of software adaptation extracted from previous work are described in Section II. The design patterns inspired from the concepts are presented in Section III. The prototype application with adaptive GUI is presented in Section IV and an analysis of the gains procured by the use of the proposed design patterns are presented in Section V. The paper concludes with Section VI and some future work is discussed.

II. Concepts of Software Adaptation

This section presents major concepts of adaptation from related work classified in three concerns: data monitoring, adaptation schemes and adaptation strategies.

A. Adaptation Data Monitoring

Contextual data on which customization control rely, referred to as *adaptation data* in this paper, can come from various sources, both internal (for "self-aware" applications [9]) and external (for "self-situated" [9] or "context-aware" applications). The acquisition of contextual data to be used as adaptation data is part of a primitive level, which is necessary for other more complex adaptation capabilities to be implemented [10]. Contextual data is usually acquired by a monitoring entity (sensors/probes/monitors) responsible for quantizing properties of the physical world or internal state of an application [7], [11]–[15]. Multiple simple sensors can be composed to form a complex sensor, which provide higher-level contextual data (Sensor Factory pattern [15]). Internal contextual data can be acquired simply by using a component's interface, but when the interface does not provide the necessary methods, introspection can be used (Reflective Monitoring

[15]). When a variety of adaptation data is monitored, it provides a modeled view of the software context, sometimes shared within a group of components. Some event-based mechanism with registry entities can be used to propagate adaptation data to interested components (Content-based Routing [15]). Quantization can be done on multiple abstraction levels and thresholds can be used to trigger adaptation events (Adaptation Detector [15]).

B. Adaptation Schemes in Components

Many researchers aimed at defining a design pattern for an adaptive component that would allow for various schemes of adaptation in a generic way. Two main approaches can be extracted from previous work: component substitution and parametric adaptation.

a) ***Component substitution:*** The underlying principle of component substitution is to replace a component by a functionally equivalent one with regard to a certain set of features. This can also be done by adding an indirection level to the dispatching of requests and forwarding them to the appropriate component. The first pattern applying this concept is probably the Virtual Component pattern by Corsaro, Schmidt, Klefstad, *et al.* [5]. It is similar to the adaptive component proposed by Chen, Hiltunen, and Schlichting [16], but adds the principle of dynamic (un)loading of substitution candidates. In both cases, an abstract proxy is used to dispatch requests to a concrete component, which is kept hidden from the client. This approach is also used by Menasce, Sousa, Malek, *et al.* [17], who proposed architectural patterns to improve quality of service on a by-request dispatch to one or many components. To maintain the software in a valid state before, during and after the substitution, many techniques have been proposed, such as transiting a component to a quiescent state [18], [19] and buffering requests [20]. State transfer between components can be used when possible, otherwise the computing job must be restarted [16], [19].

b) ***Parametric adaptation:*** Rather than substituting a whole component by a more appropriate one, parametric adaptation is when a component can adapt itself to be more appropriate to a situation. This is usually done by tuning *knobs*, configurable units in a component (e.g. variables used in a computation). Knobs can be exposed in a *tunability interface* [1] for use by external control components, either included by design or automatically generated at the meta-programming level (e.g. with special language constructs, such as annotations [10]). The tunability domain of each knob is explicit and may vary over time. For example, if a new algorithm is discovered in the middle of a large computing job, an adaptation mechanism that is kept aware of the knob's possible values is able to switch to it if it judges that it will perform better overall [21].

C. Adaptation Strategies

No single adaptation strategy is universal for all software. Most past work has been done on applying component substitution using various strategies. For example, many researchers have explored rule-based constraints along with an optimization engine to devise architectural reconfiguration plans [1], [13]. This popular approach has tainted proposed frameworks that tend to be limited to this strategy only. An important principle is that strategies are separate from the component's implementation and can be easily changed. In fact, it is desirable to externalize adaptation strategies in order to be able to easily develop, modify and test them separately. Ramirez [7] calls this class of design patterns "decision-making", since they relate to when and how adaptation is performed. Because these design patterns are concrete adaptation strategies, their artifacts are mainly related to specific strategies (e.g. inference engines, rules, satisfaction evaluation functions). The approach of this class of patterns is typically related to rule-based constraints solving, but a more general goal is to select which plan or components from a set to reconfigure the system with.

III. Design Patterns

This section presents design patterns which realize the concepts presented in Section II with some improvements. When used together, we believe they provide the sought structure for adaptive software. Unified modeling language (UML) diagrams are used to show the structure of the patterns in a standardized way.

A. Monitor Pattern

Classification: Monitor and analyze.
Intent: A monitor provides a value for one type of adaptation data to interested entities.
Motivation: There is a need to quantize raw contextual data as parameters of adaptation data with explicitly defined domain and in specialized modules decoupled from the rest of the application. Adaptation data needs to be reasoned about in arbitrarily high abstraction level and be proactive in the adaptation detection process. Agreement for monitored data should be implied by design in order to allow for safe information sharing among interacting components.
Structure: Fig. 1 shows the structure of the monitor pattern as a UML diagram.

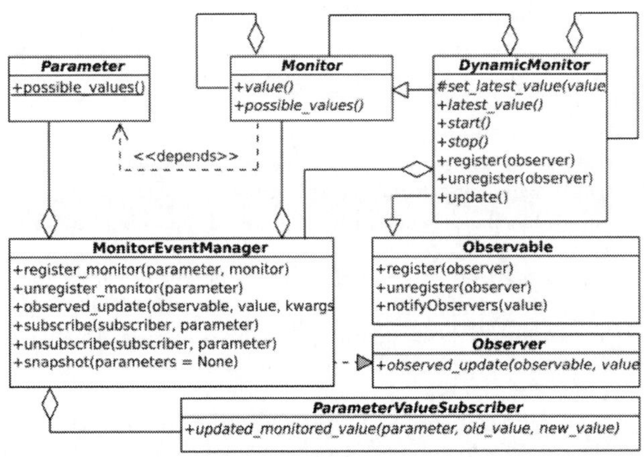

Figure 1. Monitor pattern UML diagram

Participants:

- **Parameter:** A parameter is one type of adaptation data as defined in Section II-A. Its possible values domain is explicitly defined and forms a state space. Many range types can be used to model a parameter's domain.
- **(Static) Monitor:** Provides a stateless (further referred to as "static") means of acquiring a value within

a subset of a certain parameter's domain. Formally, $\Omega_M \subseteq \Omega_P$ for possible values Ω of monitor M and parameter P. A monitor can be an aggregation of other static monitors, but not of dynamic monitors.

- **Dynamic monitor:** Additionally to providing a value for a parameter, schedules the acquisition of the value and alerts an observer that a new value has been acquired. Some form of polling or interrupt-based thread awakening needs to be employed along with a previous value to know if the value has changed compared to the latest value, in which case an event notification is triggered to interested entities. This makes it inherently stateful. Like a static monitor, it can be an aggregation of other monitors. The particularity is that it can aggregate both static and dynamic monitors.
- **Monitor event manager:** Registry entity which allows for a client component to subscribe to a parameter and be alerted when a new value is acquired. Similarly, a dynamic monitor can be registered within the manager and provide a value to any subscriber of the corresponding parameter. In such manager, monitors and parameters are related by a one-to-one relationship; a given parameter can only be monitored by a single monitor.
- **Observable/Observer:** See Gang of Four observer pattern [22]. Used for monitor registering mechanism.
- **Parameter value subscriber:** Provides a means to be notified when a new value of a parameter it has subscribed to has been acquired.

Behavior: An adaptation data type can be formalized as a parameter in terms of the quantized values the system expects to use. A static monitor provides a means to concretely quantize raw contextual data from a sensor or introspection to a value within a defined domain expected by the system. The quantization can be done using fixed or variable thresholds. A dynamic monitor adds scheduling behavior, which allows to provide a value based on accumulated data over time and apply filtering. The monitor event manager is alerted by monitors and dispatches the new value to related subscribers. The dependency regarding subscribers is with the parameters for which they requested to be notified, but actual monitoring is done separately.
Consequences: As monitors are hierarchically built, higher-level abstraction information can be provided. This pattern allows the analysis step of a MAPE-K loop [12] to be done through hierarchical construction of monitors: a parameter can define high-level domain values which are provided by a monitor composed from lower-level ones and components can use this to simplify their adaptation strategies. High-level adaptivity logic is reusable in that parameters are abstract and can easily be shared among projects. Monitors can be chained such that only the concrete data acquisition has to be redone between projects, keeping scheduling and filtering as reusable entities.
Constraints: To assure agreement between interacting components, it is necessary for adaptive components which depend on a common parameter to also subscribe to the same monitor event manager. These components are therefore part of the same *monitoring group*. This can be checked statically or be assumed by contract. The need for a one-to-one relationship between a monitor and a parameter within a monitoring group is based on this agreement requirement. A monitoring group can be thought of as a single entity that cannot have duplicate or contradicting attributes, e.g., it cannot be at two positions at once. In this example, an attribute is a parameter and a monitor is the entity providing the value for this attribute.
Related patterns: Sensor factory, reflective monitoring, content-based routing, adaptation detector [7], information sharing, observer [22].

B. Proxy Router Pattern

Classification: Plan and execute.
Intent: A proxy router allows to route calls of a proxy to a component chosen among a set of candidates using a designated strategy.
Motivation: When implementing component substitution, a way to clearly separate concerns relating to the adaptation logic (substitution by which component) and the execution of substitution (replacing a component or forwarding calls to it) are difficult to implement in an extensible way. The proxy pattern [22] allows to forward calls to a designated instance, but does not specify how control of the routing process should be implemented. Candidate components need to be specified in a way that does not necessitate immediate loading or instantiation and which is mutable (to allow runtime discovery). To maximize reusability, strategies should be devised externally.
Structure: Fig. 2 shows the structure of the proxy router pattern as a UML diagram.

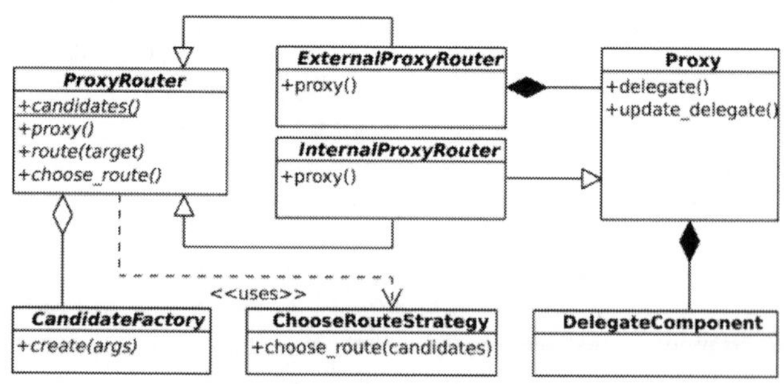

Figure 2. Proxy router pattern UML diagram

Participants:

- **Proxy:** Gang of Four [22] proxy pattern, with the exception that the interface is not necessarily specified (e.g. forwarding to introspected methods). It is responsible for making sure no calls are lost when a new delegate is set.
- **Delegate component:** Concrete component which is proxied. It must be specified as part of the proxy router's candidates set.
- **Proxy router:** Keeps a set of component candidates and allows to control the routing of the calls a proxy receives to the appropriate candidate chosen by some strategy. The proxy router is responsible for ensuring any state transfer and initialization of candidate instances.
- **Candidate factory:** Gang of Four [22] factory pattern for a candidate. Used as part of candidates definition.

Can do local loading/unloading for external candidates.

- **Choose route strategy:** Concrete strategy to choose which candidate among a set to use, based on Gang of Four [22] strategy pattern. It uses accessible information from the application, candidates (e.g. adaptation space, descriptor, static methods) or any inference engine available to make a choice.
- **External/Internal proxy router:** Depending on the use, a proxy router can *use* an external proxy (as a member) or internally *be* a proxy (through inheritance). To allow for both schemes, a means to acquire the proxy is provided and returns either the member object (external) or a reference to the proxy router itself (internal).

Behavior: A set of candidates is either statically specified or discovered at runtime (e.g. looking for libraries providing candidates). The proxy router is then initialized by choosing a candidate using the strategy and controls the proxy to set an instance of the chosen candidate as active delegate. At any time, a new candidate can be chosen and set as active delegate of the proxy.
Consequences: The proxy router pattern allows for flexible and extensible specification of component substitution. The strategies to choose a candidate to route to can be reused in any project with consistent information acquisition infrastructure, such as the one provided by the monitor pattern. Candidates need not be specified statically and control related to routing can be done both internally and externally.
Constraints: Strategies might rely on certain project specific information which is not portable. Separating specific from generally applicable strategies and composing them should help with this constraint.
Related patterns: Adaptive component [16], virtual component [5], master-slave [23], component insertion/removal, server reconfiguration [7], proxy [22].

C. Adaptive Component Pattern

Classification: Analyze and plan.
Intent: Use monitored adaptation data to control parametric adaptation and component substitution by making adaptation spaces explicit.
Motivation: A basic structure is needed to easily add adaptive behavior in the form of parametrization or substitution. Components need a way to explicitly provide means for adaptation strategies to reason about their adaptation space in order to formulate plans. This information should be external to a base component if the adaptation is to be added gradually. Most importantly, an adaptive component must behave like any non-adaptive component and be used among them without any impact on the rest of the system.
Participants:

- **Adaptive:** An adaptive component which defines means for acquiring the adaptation space. It can be used as a subscriber to a parameter value provider.
- **Monitor event manager:** Parameter value provider realized with the monitor pattern (see Section III-A).
- **Parameter value subscriber:** Provides a means to be notified when a new value of a parameter it has subscribed to has been acquired (see Section III-A).
- **Proxy router:** Proxy router pattern (see Section III-B)
- **Adaptive proxy router:** Adaptive version of a proxy router allowing to drive the routing process (substitution) using monitored data.

Structure: Fig. 3 shows the structure of the adaptive component pattern as a UML diagram.

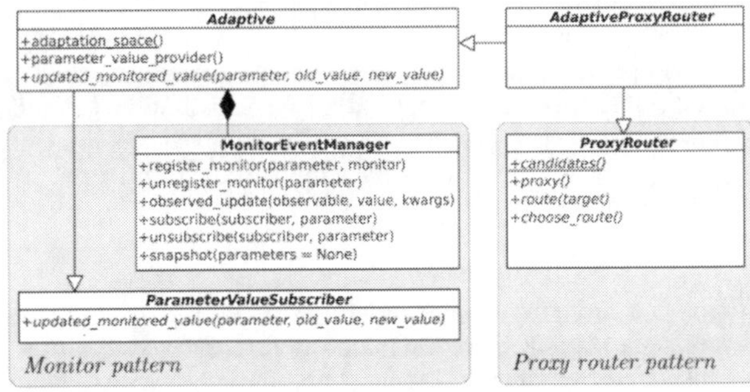

Figure 3. Adaptive component pattern UML diagram

Behavior: A component to be made adaptive can inherit the adaptive interface or a specific decorator can be created if the component's code should remain unchanged. The adaptive implementation defines what base adaptation space it will support. Then, knobs can be defined within the component and used as variables to compute, for example, its size or lay outing specifications. Tuning can be done when an updated parameter value is received. For substitution, the process is the same, but uses the AdaptiveProxyRouter interface. Specific strategies can be created, using as many generic filters as possible (e.g. filter out candidates which adaptation space does not overlap with a snapshot of the current state).
Consequences: Because of the explicit declaration of adaptation space, strategies can easily reason about how a component can behave in a situation. For example, a strategy can use the fact that a component's space is too specific or too wide. Any component can be made adaptive and does not require modifications to other components. Because of the support for both parametric adaptation and component substitution, the basic structure proposed in this pattern is suitable for virtually any adaptive mechanism based on monitored data and components adaptation spaces.
Constraints: Like stated in Section III-A, interacting adaptive components must subscribe to the same monitor event manager to assure consistency in decision-making processes. While arbitrarily large hierarchies of adaptive components can be composed, there is an inherent overhead induced in the adaptation and routing process. Because a component subscribing to some parameter value provider such as the monitor event manager has no guarantee that this parameter is being actively monitored, adaptive components need to define a default behavior or immediately request a snapshot of the current state. To minimize this effect, it is preferable to register monitors prior to creating any adaptive component.
Related patterns: Monitor (III-A), proxy router (III-B), adaptive component [16], virtual component [5].

IV. Prototype

This section presents AdaptivePy, a reference library implementing the three design patterns presented in this paper, along with a prototype as a case study for analyzing the gains they procure compared to an *ad hoc* implementation.

A. *AdaptivePy*

AdaptivePy implements artifacts from all three design patterns described in this paper. The Python language was chosen because it is reflective, dynamically typed and many toolkit bindings are freely available. Beyond the patterns, AdaptivePy provides some useful implementations, such as enum-based discrete-value parameters, push/pull dynamic monitor decorators, operations over adaptation spaces (extend, union, filter) and an adaptation strategy based on substitution candidates' adaptation space restrictiveness. The library is freely available from the PyPi repository under the name "adaptivepy" and is distributed under LiLiQ-P v1.1 license.

B. *Case Study Application*

The case study application is a special poll designed to favor polarization. Five yes/no questions are asked to a user and answered by selecting the most appropriate response among a list of options. The options provided include yes, no, mostly yes, mostly no and 50/50. To favor polarization, statistics from the previous answers are used to restrict the range of options provided to the user. If the polarization is judged insufficient because of mixed responses (low polarization), fewer options are provided. On the contrary, if virtually all users have answered yes (high polarization), more options in between will be given. The workflow of the application is to start the "quiz" using a Start button, choose appropriate options and send the form using a Submit button. If some options remain unselected, a prompt alerting the user is shown and the form can be submitted again once all options are selected.

The adaptation type used is a form of *alternative elements* [24]. The GUI is made plastic by replacing control widgets displaying the available options at runtime, conserving the option selection feature in any resulting interface. Because there is a varied number of options, some widgets are more appropriate than others to display them, while some cannot display certain amounts of options. A checkbox can handle two options, radio buttons could be used for ranges of two to four options and a combo box for five and more options. Of course, radio buttons can hold more options and the combo box less, but the amounts suggested represent the ranges they are subjectively considered most appropriate for. These can be chosen by a designer and further refined through user testing, which means they must be easy to edit.

Polarization levels act as adaptation data to drive adaptation. An appropriate solution would allow to design the GUI within Qt's graphical editor "Qt Designer" and to preview of the adaptation directly, rather than having to add the business logic beforehand. It would also allow for gradual addition and modification of control widget types without necessitating changes in unaffected modules.

The toolkit used for this application is Qt 5 through the PyQt5 wrapper library. It is a cross-platform toolkit library which provides implementations of widgets like checkboxes, combo boxes are radio buttons groups. The concrete work is therefore limited to implementing how these components can replace each other at the appropriate time and how they are included in a main user interface. We are therefore more interested in the underlying structure of adaptation within the

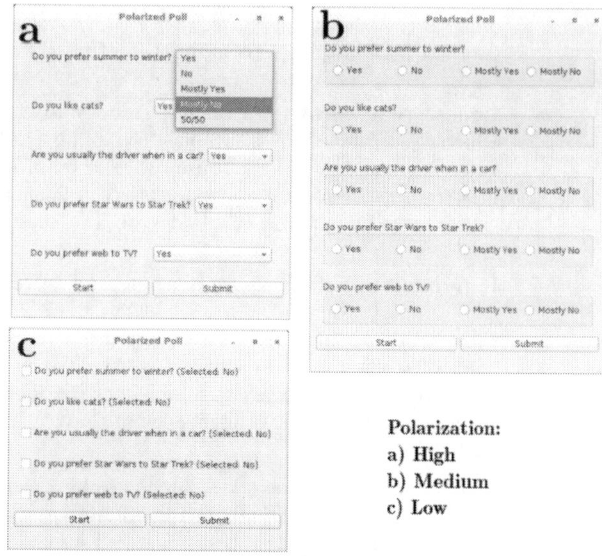

Figure 4. Adaptive case study application "Polarized Poll"

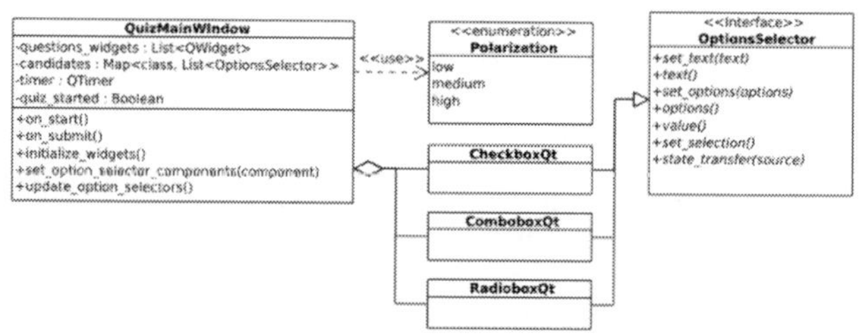

Figure 5. Simplified UML diagram of *ad hoc* implementation of case study application

application than specific adaptation strategies and their user-perceived effectiveness. Once an appropriate structure is in place, we expect these can be more easily devised, tested and improved.

V. RESULTS

The windows shown on Fig. 4 are the resulted GUI for the application in all three polarization states. Because this case study's focus is on GUI, the monitoring of past responses was simulated and a random monitor is used instead which updates its value by means of a polling dynamic monitor every second, allowing to easily observe adaptation.

A. Ad hoc *Application*

A simplified UML diagram of the *ad hoc* implementation is shown on Fig. 5. The chosen approach is to add placeholder widgets in QuizMainWindow which will be substituted by an appropriate component instance at runtime: CheckboxQt, ComboboxQt or RadioboxQt. A polarization level defined in the enum Polarization is bound to each of these types. A timer within QuizMainWindow polls the polarization value and calls `set_options_selector_components` with the appropriate type. Adaptation control, along with any customization necessary, is entirely done in QuizMainWindow.

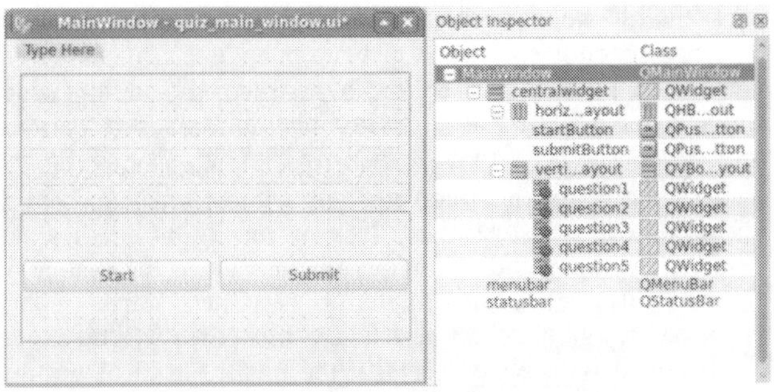

Figure 6. Qt Designer using plain widgets as placeholder for *ad hoc* implementation

Fig. 6 shows Qt Designer as the main window is created for the *ad hoc* implementation. Notice that because placeholder components are blank, no feedback is given to the designer. It is therefore not possible to test the controls or set the question label. This makes the approach incompatible with the usual GUI design workflow, which involves previewing the application in the graphical editor before adding business logic.

When analyzing the *ad hoc* code, it is obvious that separation of concerns is not respected since the option selection logic is tangled to its owner element, the main window. Concerns such as scheduling for recomputing polarization and component substitution are mixed with GUI setup and handling of the business flow. This leads to a lack of extensibility, a tangling of concerns and limits unit testing of components. A method is used to select which control component to use based on the polarization, but this solution remains inflexible. The knowledge of adaptation is hidden and cannot be used to devise portable strategies.

One of our goals is to gradually add adaptation mechanisms to GUI implementations, but this is difficult since modification of important classes will add risk of introducing defects. Also, there is no easy way to work on adaptation mechanisms separately from the application. In fact, we cannot separately test the adaptation logic and integrate it after. Generally, the lack of cohesion induced by the inadequate separation of concerns is a sign of low code quality. Because no adaptation mechanism can easily be introduced, modified and reused in other projects, the *ad hoc* implementation works for its specific application case, but is subject to major efforts in refactoring when requirements and features will be added throughout its development cycle.

B. Application Using AdaptivePy

A simplified UML diagram of the application is shown on Fig. 7. From it, we see that the polarization is a discrete parameter and is used by AdaptiveOptionsSelector, specifically to define its adaptation space based on the ones provided by its substitution candidates: CheckboxQt, ComboboxQt and RadioboxQt. Additionally to adaptation by substitution, RadioboxQt can parametrically adapt to changes of polarization levels {low, medium}, since they respectively correspond to 2 and 4 options. Its behavior is that the appropriate number of options is shown depending on the polarization level. AdaptiveQuizMainWindow is free of adaptation implementation

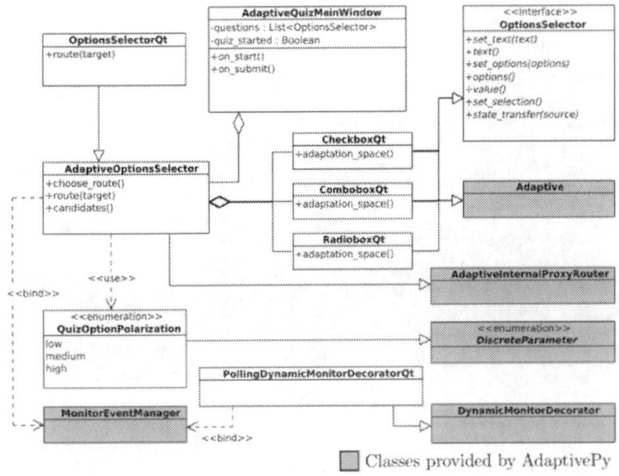

Figure 7. Simplified UML diagram of case study application implementation using AdaptivePy

details and simply uses the AdaptiveOptionsSelector instances as a normal OptionsSelector. OptionsSelectorQt is a subclass to AdaptiveOptionsSelector which is used as a graphical proxy to candidate widgets. It also defines properties used in Qt's graphical editor Qt Designer, in this case the question label.

Every AdaptiveOptionsSelector instance is made a subscriber to the QuizOptionPolarization parameter at initialization. They are updated when a change in the monitored value is detected, i.e., when a monitor detects a value is different from the previous one. This is because identical subsequent parameter values are expected by default to lead to the same state, so they are filtered out. In the case of AdaptiveOptionsSelector, because it is a proxy router, `choose_route` is called to determine which substitution candidate to route to. Prior to using an adaptation strategy to select the most appropriate candidate, inappropriate ones can be filtered out using `filter_by_adaptation_space`. This function, provided by AdaptivePy, takes a list of candidates along with a snapshot of the current monitoring state and only returns those with adaptation space supporting the current context. Then, a strategy like `choose_most_restricted` is used to choose among valid components. If no component is valid, an exception is raised. With a candidate chosen, all that remains is configuring the proxy router by calling the `route` method with the chosen candidate. This method must also take care of state transfer between the previous and new proxied components. This feature is already defined in the common interface OptionsSelector as `state_transfer`.

Fig. 8 shows Qt Designer as the main window is created with the AdaptivePy-based implementation. When compared to Fig. 6, we notice that the designer has a full view of how the application will look. Moreover, the currently displayed adaptation can be controlled through the setup of the monitors. For example, it is possible to replace the random value by one acquired from a configuration file and trigger adaptation manually. Also, each question is simply a OptionsSelectorQt component rather than a placeholder component and the question is entered directly from the graphical editor using the label property (bottom-right). A major advantage is that adaptive

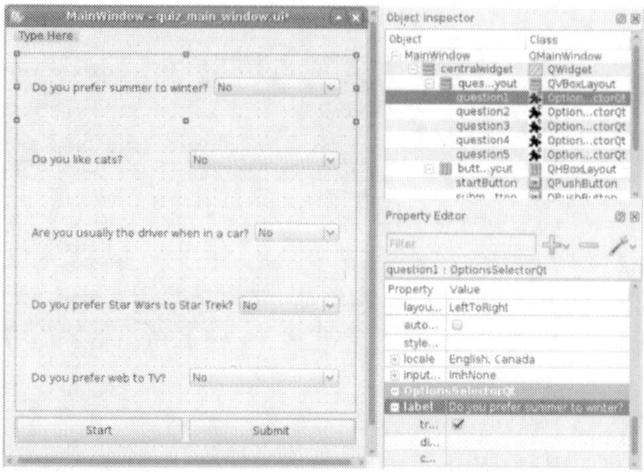

Figure 8. Qt Designer using adaptive components developed with AdaptivePy

components can be reused in other interfaces because they are provided as standalone components. The need for easy edition of adaptation spaces is also addressed by modifying or overriding the `adaptation_space` method of adaptive components.

The adaptation logic is essentially located in the adaptive proxy router class: AdaptiveOptionsSelector. Because adaptation is separated from the rest of the business logic, the main window class can use the adaptive components without the knowledge of adaptation. The only logic remaining is with regard to buttons handling (Start and Submit buttons). It is clear in this implementation that the knowledge of adaptation space which was hidden in the *ad hoc* implementation is used to efficiently choose a substitution candidate. Self-healing action such as replacing a failing component can be easily realized by monitoring the components and including this logic as a strategy. This is not easily realizable in the *ad hoc* implementation. In the prototype, a radio box could safely replace a checkbox since it parametrically covers its full adaptation space, overlapping on {low} polarization. Also, from this case study, we can see that arbitrarily large hierarchies of adaptive and non-adaptive components can be built without tangling code or affecting other components when adding new adaptive behavior.

VI. Conclusion and Future Work

Design patterns presented in this paper can be used as a basic structure to accomplish various levels of adaptation in GUI. Adaptive components can be used with other modules such as recommendation engines to provide more or less automation and proactive adaptation. Monitors can also be extended and even implemented as adaptive components themselves, relying on other more primitive monitors. Proxy routers allow to simplify hierarchical development of arbitrarily large sequences of component substitutions. The patterns form together an effective approach for the integration of various adaptation mechanisms and, in the case of GUI, can be used to provide a more usual workflow than the *ad hoc* implementation. AdaptivePy, as a reference library, is an example of the viability of the patterns when used in a concrete implementation. Even though a simple application was used to observe gains, the solution is applicable to more complex scenarios where multiple parameters, monitoring groups and large hierarchies of adaptive components. The patterns are general enough that they can be used for adding adaptive behavior based on user, environment and platform variations.

Future work will focus on exploring parameters types with more complex value domains and try to formalize a structure to express them. Also, the lack of adaptation quality metrics for verification and validation methods limits the evaluation of gains. To alleviate this limitation, new metrics using concepts of the design patterns presented in this paper will be explored. The goal is to better quantify the quality level of prototypes with regard to adaptation.

References

[1] F. Chang and V. Karamcheti, "A framework for automatic adaptation of tunable distributed applications," *Cluster Computing*, vol. 4, no. 1, pp. 49–62, 2001, ISSN: 1573-7543.

[2] E. Bruneton, T. Coupaye, M. Leclercq, V. Quéma, and J.-B. Stefani, "The fractal component model and its support in java," *Software: Practice and Experience*, vol. 36, no. 11-12, pp. 1257–1284, 2006.

[3] Y. Maurel, A. Diaconescu, and P. Lalanda, "Ceylon: A service-oriented framework for building autonomic managers," in *2010 Seventh IEEE International Conference and Workshops on Engineering of Autonomic and Autonomous Systems*, Mar. 2010, pp. 3–11.

[4] M. Peissner, A. Schuller, and D. Spath, "A design patterns approach to adaptive user interfaces for users with special needs," in *Proceedings of the 14th International Conference on Human-computer Interaction: Design and Development Approaches - Volume Part I*, ser. HCII'11, Orlando, FL: Springer-Verlag, 2011, pp. 268–277.

[5] A. Corsaro, D. C. Schmidt, R. Klefstad, and C. O'Ryan, "Virtual component - a design pattern for memory-constrained embedded applications," in *In Proceedings of the Ninth Conference on Pattern Language of Programs (PLoP*, 2002.

[6] G. Rossi, S. Gordillo, and F. Lyardet, "Design patterns for context-aware adaptation," in *2005 Symposium on Applications and the Internet Workshops (SAINT 2005 Workshops)*, Jan. 2005, pp. 170–173.

[7] A. J. Ramirez, "Design patterns for developing dynamically adaptive systems," Master's thesis, Michigan State University, 2008.

[8] T. Holvoet, D. Weyns, and P. Valckenaers, "Patterns of delegate mas," in *2009 Third IEEE International Conference on Self-Adaptive and Self-Organizing Systems*, Sep. 2009, pp. 1–9.

[9] M. G. Hinchey and R. Sterritt, "Self-managing software," *Computer*, vol. 39, no. 2, pp. 107–109, 2006.

[10] M. Salehie and L. Tahvildari, "Self-adaptive software: Landscape and research challenges," *ACM Transactions on Autonomous and Adaptive Systems (TAAS)*, vol. 4, no. 2, p. 14, 2009.

[11] M. L. Berkane, L. Seinturier, and M. Boufaida, "Using variability modelling and design patterns for self-adaptive system engineering: Application to smart-home," *Int. J. Web Eng. Technol.*, vol. 10, no. 1, pp. 65–93, May 2015, ISSN: 1476-1289.

[12] IBM, "An architectural blueprint for autonomic computing," IBM Corporation, Tech. Rep., 2005.
[13] S. Malek, N. Beckman, M. Mikic-Rakic, and N. Medvidovic, "A framework for ensuring and improving dependability in highly distributed systems," in *Architecting Dependable Systems III*, R. de Lemos, C. Gacek, and A. Romanovsky, Eds. Berlin, Heidelberg: Springer Berlin Heidelberg, 2005, pp. 173–193.
[14] V. Mannava and T. Ramesh, "Multimodal pattern-oriented software architecture for self-optimization and self-configuration in autonomic computing system using multi objective evolutionary algorithms," in *Proceedings of the International Conference on Advances in Computing, Communications and Informatics*, ser. ICACCI '12, Chennai, India: ACM, 2012, pp. 1236–1243.
[15] A. J. Ramirez and B. H. Cheng, "Design patterns for developing dynamically adaptive systems," in *Proceedings of the 2010 ICSE Workshop on Software Engineering for Adaptive and Self-Managing Systems*, ACM, 2010, pp. 49–58.
[16] W.-K. Chen, M. A. Hiltunen, and R. D. Schlichting, "Constructing adaptive software in distributed systems," in *Distributed Computing Systems, 2001. 21st International Conference on.*, Apr. 2001, pp. 635–643.
[17] D. A. Menasce, J. P. Sousa, S. Malek, and H. Gomaa, "Qos architectural patterns for self-architecting software systems," in *Proceedings of the 7th International Conference on Autonomic Computing*, ser. ICAC '10, Washington, DC, USA: ACM, 2010, pp. 195–204.
[18] H. Liu and M. Parashar, "Accord: A programming framework for autonomic applications," *IEEE Transactions on Systems, Man, and Cybernetics, Part C (Applications and Reviews)*, vol. 36, no. 3, pp. 341–352, May 2006, ISSN: 1094-6977.
[19] J. Zhang and B. H. C. Cheng, "Model-based development of dynamically adaptive software," in *Proceedings of the 28th International Conference on Software Engineering*, ser. ICSE '06, Shanghai, China: ACM, 2006, pp. 371–380.
[20] H. Gomaa, K. Hashimoto, M. Kim, S. Malek, and D. A. Menascé, "Software adaptation patterns for service-oriented architectures," in *Proceedings of the 2010 ACM Symposium on Applied Computing*, ser. SAC '10, Sierre, Switzerland: ACM, 2010, pp. 462–469.
[21] P. Kang, M. Heffner, J. Mukherjee, N. Ramakrishnan, S. Varadarajan, C. Ribbens, and D. K. Tafti, "The adaptive code kitchen: Flexible tools for dynamic application composition," in *2007 IEEE International Parallel and Distributed Processing Symposium*, Mar. 2007, pp. 1–8.
[22] E. Gamma, R. Helm, R. Johnson, and J. Vlissides, *Design Patterns: Elements of Reusable Object-oriented Software*. Boston, MA, USA: Addison-Wesley Longman Publishing Co., Inc., 1995.
[23] H. Gomaa and M. Hussein, "Software reconfiguration patterns for dynamic evolution of software architectures," in *Software Architecture, 2004. WICSA 2004. Proceedings. Fourth Working IEEE/IFIP Conference on*, Jun. 2004, pp. 79–88.
[24] M. Bezold and W. Minker, *Adaptive multimodal interactive systems*. Springer Science & Business Media, 2011.

Goal-Compliance Framework for Self-Adaptive Workflows

Budoor Allehyani, Stephan Reiff-Marganiec

Department of Informatics
University of Leicester
Leicester, UK
Email: {baaa2,srm13}@le.ac.uk

Abstract—**Workflow adaptation involves two major research topics: flexibility and correctness. The former is related to the ability to react to change and adapt workflow structure, while the latter is related to managing this flexibility and ensuring syntactical, semantical as well as behavioural consistencies. Current approaches range from providing flexible workflows to flexible and consistent workflows. They mostly focus on syntactical consistency and generic properties (such as deadlock-freedom), but rarely consider semantic aspects. However, not providing semantic guarantees neglects the importance of preserving the original goal. The primary focus of this research is to ensure goal compliance during workflow reconfiguration. Thus, we analyse the impact of workflow automatic adaptation on the goal in question. As a result, we define goal-compliance constraints and develop a goal-compliance framework, which automatically and dynamically adapts workflow instances through Event-Condition-Action policies. Furthermore, it validates the adaptation against the goal-compliance rules and constraints through model checking and ontology-based approach.**

Keywords–BPMN; Reconfiguration; Goal-Compliance; Model Checking; Ontology; Runtime Verification.

I. Introduction

The Business Process Model and Notation (BPMN) [1] is an efficient language for modelling business processes. However, it is insufficient for analysis and verification purposes. This is due to the fact that BPMN lacks in techniques and tools that support process analysis. However, there exist some successful approaches that map BPMN semantics to several formal languages, such as Petri nets [2] and Communicating Sequential Processes (CSP) [3], which are formal and tool supported. As the business domain is well-known for its dynamicity and complexity, processes should be self-adaptable and self-manageable. Gorton [4] provides self-adaptive workflows (WF) using (Event-Condition-Action(s)) policies to change WF specifications at runtime and on an instance level. We build upon his work aiming at self-management workflows, whic correctly and safely react to change. We aim to make WF systems as flexible as possible without sacrificing their functionality. The main focus of this research is on guaranteeing goal compliance in self-adaptive workflows. The goal model is considered as the main reference for the WF functionality in its entire lifetime from design to development. Therefore, any changes or updates applied to a WF must satisfy the original goal. The novel contributions we present in this paper are: (1) the goal-compliance framework for runtime reconfiguration and verification and (2) the mechanisms to preserving business goal. This research is basically motivated by the following research questions: 1) How can we write specifications that are precise enough to exclude bad implementations (undesired behavior) while at the same time being flexible enough to cope with the kind of changes we wish to allow? 2) How can we detect consistency with a high level specification?

The remainder of this paper is structured as follows: a brief background about the main concepts used throughout this paper is in Section II. Section III provides an overview about the goal-compliance framework, Section IV gives more details about the development of the verification mechanisms used for goal-compliance check. We include an initial evaluation for our framework in Section V. Section VI discusses some related approaches and we conclude the paper in section VII.

II. Background

We briefly introduce the main concepts used in this paper: BPMN, goal specification, domain knowledge. The BPMN process model can be defined through a BPMN diagram, which illustrates what activities are to be executed and in what order. Thus, business process functionality is captured by the BPMN process model. An activity is defined by the BPMN specification as a generic term for work a company performs within its business process. It can be atomic or composite and it is of three types: task, subprocess and call activity.
A goal can be defined as "high-level objectives of the business, organization or system; they capture the reasons why a system is needed and guide decisions at various levels within the enterprise" [5].

In Requirements Engineering, there are different techniques and methods used to "formally" model and declare goals. One of the methods is requirement specification, which relates business goals to functional system components. Keep All Objectives Satisfied (KAOS) [6] is a goal modelling method aimed at requirement elicitating and validating. It encompasses five major concepts: goals, assumptions, agents, objects, and operations. In this research, we only consider the goal concept of KAOS and relate it to the BPMN. In KAOS, a goal model consists of the strategic goal and its refinement objectives. The refinement relation is of two types: 1) AND refinement where all related objectives must be achieved and 2) OR refinement where at least one of the related objectives is achieved.

Domain knowledge is derived according to the goal in question. Ontologies are a common technique for knowledge representation. An ontology is defined as "a formal explicit description of concepts in a domain of discourse (classes (sometimes called concepts)), properties of each concept describing various features and attributes of the concept (slots (sometimes called roles or properties)), and restrictions on slots (facets (sometimes called role restrictions))" [7].

Reconfiguration policies, which are introduced in [4], are used to adapt running BPMN instances and their syntax is defined as follows:

polrule ::= appliesto location [when triggers] [if conditions] do actions
triggers ::= trigger | triggers or triggers
conditions ::= condition | not conditions | conditions or conditions | conditions and conditions
actions ::= action | actions actionop actions actionop ::= and | or | andthen | orelse

III. Goal-Compliance Framework

The presented Goal-compliance framework supports on-the-fly WF adaptation while preserving the WF semantics. Generally speaking, the notable aspects of the framework are:

- Online Workflow Reconfiguration at Instance Level: The framework provides flexibility for WF systems by inserting, deleting and replacing workflow tasks. This flexibility is provided by three important factors for runtime adaptation: change per instance, online adaptation (i.e., change on running instances), automatic adaptation using ECA policies and change management.
- Goal-Compliance Validation Capabilities: A Goal-Compliance check is the key feature of this framework. Before applying any workflow change, the framework has the ability to check the corresponding constraints and decide whether to accept the change or not. Each change variability has its corresponding constraints based on the analysis of its affect on goal satisfaction. Therefore, a goal-task dependency check is related to deleting a task from the running process, while the task-domain conformance check is related to inserting a task to the running process.
- Facilitating Other Semantic Checking: Using the ontology within the framework could also facilitate other types of semantic checks by enhancing/reusing the ontology to add more constraints or define different rules. Furthermore, it could be used for querying the ontology while performing such a semantic verification.

A. Architecture

The runtime framework assumes an adapted process execution engine. For simplicity, we assume here that we have an engine that can execute BPMN processes directly (this allows us to focus on the main aspects rather than worrying about converting these into some executable formats). The engine is able to pause a process instance and also to make changes to instances. Fig. 1 presents the block diagram of the proposed framework.

As the process instance executes it will raise triggers e.g., at the start of a task which are passed to the policy server (a policy enforcement point), which either returns a no change allowing the instance to be processed as it is or a specific change action, e.g., the need to insert a task, which will lead to updating the process structure of the instance. The action that the policy server demands depend on the policies in the repositories and of course the instance data in the process. The policy server retrieves policies from the policy store, checks for the applicability and then considers the actions to be applied. Once it has determined what actions should be applied, the process instance is updated accordingly and would continue executing in its new shape. Through the work presented here an extra phase is added, namely that of checking that the change is appropriate in the sense that it maintains the goal semantics of the original process.

As can be seen from Fig. 1, the proposed framework accepts the original WF specification, the modification details and the domain compliance constraints as inputs. The WF specification is in BPMN file and is in xml format and it is automatically transformed to CSP. The modification details can be in a configuration file that determines the changes to the WF specification through ECA policies.The framework consists of three components namely, Specification Reader, Reconfigurator and Validator. The brief description of each one is provided below.

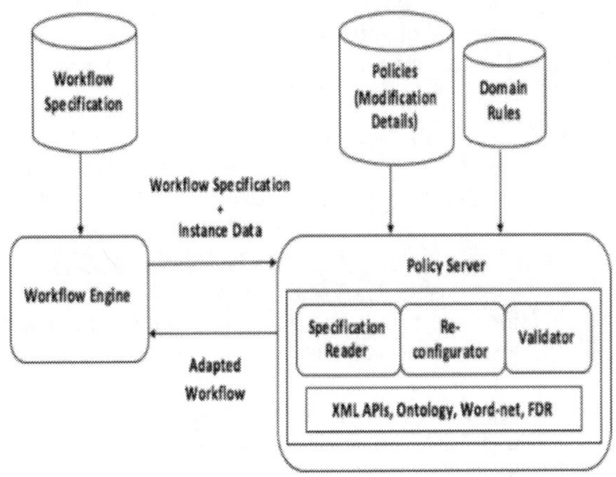

Figure 1. Goal-Compliance Framework Architecture

- Specification Reader: This component is responsible to read the existing WF specification and transform it into an in memory state for fast processing and easy manipulation of the modification. This can be achieved by utilizing some XML interfacing APIs (Application Programming Interface).
- Re-configurator: The re-configurator is responsible to process the actual modification operations e.g., insertion of the new task into existing WF specification. This component is responsible to interact with the Ontology and WordNet tools to carry out the requested modification on the existing WF specification.
- Validator: The validator is responsible to ensure that the modification is according to the given specification and it does not violate any domain compliance rules or constraints. The domain compliance rules are the constraints that help to ensure the preservation of the original goals of the WF. This can be achieved by exploiting the Failure-Divergences Refinement (FDR) and other necessary validation tools.

B. Implementation

The proposed framework is implemented with Java and works in the following sequential order:

1) Read the existing WF specification
2) Read the reconfiguration details
3) Validate the reconfiguration against goal-domain compliance constraints
4) Adapt the WF, if the validation from (3) was successful
5) Produce adapted WF specification for the running instance

The reconfiguration component of the framework supports three processes including insertion, deletion and replacement. The details of each process are included in the following sub sections.

1) Insert: The insert process refers to the facility where the proposed framework allows the modification of existing workflow by allowing the insertion of a new task into the given WF specification. The new inserted tasks can be of any of the following kind of tasks:

- Atomic sequential: This refers to the insertion of a new task in sequential order immediately after a given task. This operation requires the new task name as well as the name of an existing task.
- Atomic parallel: This refers to the insertion of the new task in parallel to an existing task. The operation will insert the parallel gateway to connect the new task and existing task in parallel. The new and existing task names must be provided to perform the operation.
- Composite: The composite task is itself a collection of multiple tasks. The framework allows the insertion of a new composite task. In this operation, the framework will receive multiple task names, which collectively represents the composite task. The framework will then insert those tasks as a composite task in reference to an existing task.

The procedure developed for the insertion of the new task to an existing workflow is the same irrespective of the above mentioned types. The domain-conformance constraint is implemented for insertion verification with ontology support. The short explanation is provided below.

a) In the first step, the framework reads the existing WF specification and then obtains the new task name from the configuration file that contains the modification details. This name is then searched from the available ontology. This search query targets that the task name must match an individual name in the ontology satisfying the constraint that the individual must belong to the same domain as the domain of the WF specification. If the search succeeds, then the Re-configurator will allow the insertion of the new task. Otherwise, it will carry out Step-b. b) In case the given task name is not available in the ontology, then the framework will attempt to explore the possibility to confirm the suitability of the task name through WordNet. The framework assumes that the task name must consist of two words separated by a special character (e.g., _). The first word represents action, while the second word represents object (e.g., Register_Student). The framework interacts with WordNet repository to obtain the synonyms of both words (i.e., action and object). The object part and their synonyms help to identify the corresponding domain of the workflow, whereas the action part hints at the type of the action. For example, "Register" indicates that the task should be of type "Registration" and the "Students" indicates the BPMN domain "UniversityAdmission".
c) Once the synonyms are retrieved, then they are searched in the ontology. The framework will allow the insertion of new task, if any of the synonyms of both parts are found in the ontology. Otherwise, the framework will not allow the insertion of new task.

2) Delete: The delete process of the proposed framework refers to the facility of modifying a given WF specification through allowing the deletion of an existing task. Similarly, to the insert process, the framework allows the deletion of Sequential atomic, Parallel atomic and composite tasks. The goal-task constraint is implemented here with FDR support. The brief description of the main steps is provided below.

a) The framework reads the WF specification file and the configuration file that contains information on the task that is to be deleted. The framework first ensures that the task to be deleted exists in the specification. b) The framework then ensures that the deletion operation does not violate any of the domain compliance rules or any other constraints. If not, then the requested task is deleted from in-memory representation of the WF specification. A modified WF specification must be produced at the end of the process. c) If the deletion of the task violates any of the domain compliance rules or other constraints, then the framework will not allow the deletion of the task.

3) Replace: The replace process of the proposed framework allows the replacement of an existing task with a new one. Within the ontology, all semantically equivalent tasks are defined using the ontology semantical relation "SameIndividualAs" to indicate they hold the same semantic. Therefore, replacing one with another does not affect the process semantic. The brief description is provided below.

a) The framework reads the WF specification file and the configuration file that contains information of the existing task and the new tasks that will be needed to replace. The framework first ensures that the existing task that has to be replaced exists in the specification. b) The framework then searches the ontology to identify whether both of the tasks are the same individuals or not (i.e., they must be semantically equal). If both tasks are the same individual in the ontology, then the framework will allow the replacement.

However, there could be different ways to define semantical relations among task individuals, which might be used to define other constraints for the replace policy.

IV. Goal-Compliance Assurances for Runtime Verification

We individually analyse the impact of the reconfiguration policies on goal satisfaction based on the action indicated within the policy; insert, delete or replace. Therefore, two types of constraints are defined: goal-task dependency and domain-task conformance. The former is defined as a result of deleting BPMN tasks while the latter for inserting or replacing tasks. Model checking is used to validate the goal-task dependency constraint and this is due to its applicability for this type of validation, where a property capturing a certain behaviour must satisfy a model specification. However, inserting new tasks to the BPMN differs from removing existing ones. Therefore, it implies different type of constraints using an ontology-based approach as it encompasses everything about the domain and facilitates this type of verification. If the new task is consistent with the domain, it should satisfy the goal.

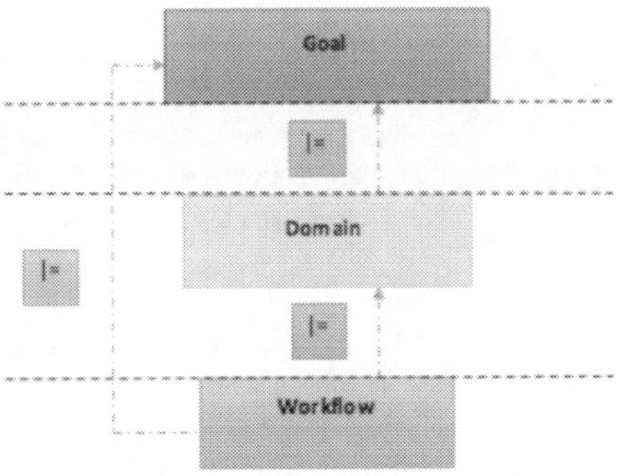

Figure 2. Conformance relationship among workflow, its domain and goal

There exists a satisfaction/conformance relationship between the running process (workflow), the goal in question and its domain, depicted in Fig. 2. Goal specification is located in the top layer since it is considered the main reference for workflow designing as well as development. The middle layer is domain knowledge, which represents concepts of a specified domain and their relationship/semantical relations. The WF specification is localised at the bottom layer. The original as well as the adapted WF specification must satisfy the domain and the goal in question. If the WF satisfies the domain rules, this will lead to goal satisfaction. In the following subsections, we are going to discuss the goal-compliance constraints and their implementation in details.

1) Goal-Task dependency: We define goal-compliance properties based on original goal specification in order to keep it consistent during workflow reconfiguration. As goal and process models are dependent, we establish a link of satisfaction based on the dependency between goals in goal model and tasks in process model called goal-task dependency link. Note that the establishment of this task was inspired from [8] but we consider goal satisfaction at a high level of abstraction. KAOS is used to model the goal formally allowing for specification in LTL (Linear Temporal Logic) with variant patterns [8]: (1) Achieve goals, (2) Cease goals, (3) Maintain goals, (4) Avoid goals. The first and third patterns help to verify the availability of certain desired behaviour.

The establishment of the goal-task dependency link allows us to indicate property specifications, which in turn guarantee goal achievement. Hence, the constraint formulae are written as WF $\models$ P, where P is property specification. CSP is candidate as a process and property specification language. The process model we have is expressed as BPMN diagram and this BPMN is transformed to CSP using Wong's tool [3]. Goal specification is expressed in LTL patterns and they are converted to CSP specifications using Wong's property specification patterns [9]. The above constraint formulae then can be automatically checked using the FDR tool [10] through refinement assertions.

The following represents the steps we follow in order to implement the verification of goal-task dependency constraint:

1) Define the goal for a given domain
2) Identify goal-related tasks based on goal-task dependency link
3) Define property specifications using the result from (1). Property specifications should state the availability of all goal-related tasks and must be consistent with goal specification
4) Convert property specifications from (3) into CSP specifications
5) Check the refinement relation (satisfaction function "P [=R WF"), which indicates that the process specification satisfies the property under Refusal refinement (R).

There are three types of goal-task relationships:

1) One task is contributing to achieve a single objective
2) Groups of tasks are contributing to achieve a single objective and this could be:
    a) OR-grouped tasks
    b) AND-grouped tasks

Those variants are classified according to the refinement relation among their corresponding objectives in KAOS goal specification. CSP refinement notion together with the hiding operator make it possible to model check self-adaptive workflows in a sufficient way. In particular, it facilitates to check the availability of certain events (tasks). So, in property specification we identify the functional behaviour that is related to a goal specification. Then, this property specification is tested through refinement assertion with hiding particular events. Based on the type of the property, the hiding is provided. For properties that are of type (1), we need to hide all process alphabets from WF specification in the right hand side excluding the event that the property holds in the left hand side. This allows the model checker to check for a certain behaviour. In case of properties of type (2), when property specification states at least one of the events is available, then the removed tasks by policy should be hidden from WF specification.

For example, suppose a BPMN process consists of sequenced tasks A, B and C. A OR B are contributing to achieve an objective O_1. C is contributing to achieve O_2. The CSP property specification that captures the availability of A OR B is defined as follows:

P= let Spec0= A $\rightarrow$ Spec2 Spec1= B $\rightarrow$ Spec2 Spec2= C $\rightarrow$ $SKIP$ within Spec0 $\sqcap$ Spec1

Now, suppose a policy wants to delete task A from process specification. The framework is going to verify this by checking the refinement relation between P and WF as follows:

assert P $\sqsubseteq_R$ WF $\setminus$ (A) where $\setminus$ indicates "hide" and it means hide A from WF specification because it is the targeted task by the policy. In this case, the refinement relation holds because B is still running in the process. If A and B are going to be removed, the assertion will fail.

2) Domain-Task Conformance: All desirable actions or functionalities that any organization wishes to achieve are determined basically through goal specification. Those functionalities in predefined order are captured by WF systems. The insert function is used to add extra functionality to the workflow. It can insert a new workflow item (activity or operator) at any position. As a result, it might have a significant impact on achieving the original goal if left uncontrolled. We

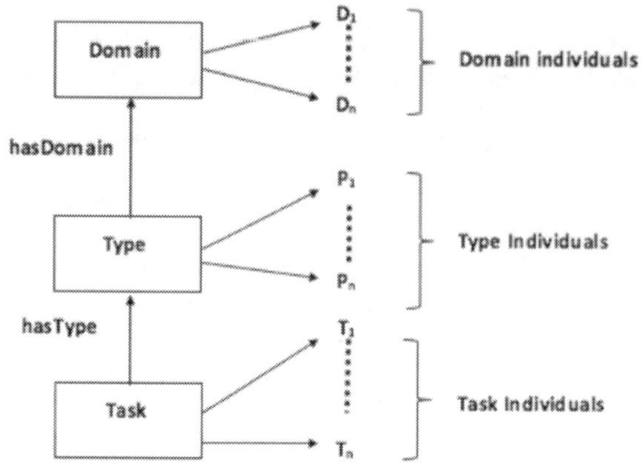

Figure 3. Ontology Structure

focus on the semantical impact in which the functionality being added deviates from the goal or is inconsistent with the knowledge in a given domain. Semantical impact is conceived as undesirable actions that might causes unexpected outcome, which in turn might affect business outcome. Hence, the satisfaction between a workflow and its domain will lead to goal satisfaction. As a result, we develop an ontology for verifying the consistency of adapted BPMNs.

The ontology is consistent with the goal in question. We assume it encompasses everything about the BPMN domain in terms of BPMN tasks, their classification and relationships. The classification allows to group tasks based on their semantic in order to be able to verify consistency. For example, for verification purposes, we classify BPMN tasks according to the work they are designed for, (e.g., the tasks "Notify_ Cancellation" and "Notify_ Timeout" are classified as Notification tasks). However, they could be classified according to different criteria for other types of checking.

Although BPMNs are domain specific, i.e., domains differ in their goals and the purpose they are designed for, we develop a generalized semantic constraint. For example, Flight-Booking is a different domain than Pizza-Delivery as the concepts used within the processes as well as their outcomes are different. The domain is captured in an ontology following the structure Domain-Type-Task. It is defined in the Web Ontology Language (OWL) using Protégé [11].

The ontology combines three classes: Domain class includes different domains, Type class includes type classifications of domain tasks and Task class encompasses all BPMN tasks related to specific domains. Individuals of the three classes are linked using OWL object properties. Basically, we have two object properties: hasType linking tasks with types and hasDomain linking types with domains, see Fig. 3. In this work, BPMN tasks are considered to be the domain concepts as they are the main artifacts in process execution since they are designed to perform work within the process. We use domain knowledge to reason about goal satisfaction. This is due to the fact that goal specification holds the desirable actions but is abstracted from any detail about the process it is designed for. For this reason, we use the domain knowledge to prove consistency with the goal as it holds more details about the executed process and adheres to the goal.

V. Related Work

The correctness of self- adaptive workflow systems has been an active research area in recent years. Correctness is a broad concept and it varies according to adaptation level. Adaptation could be at process, infrastructure, domain or resource level [12]. Generally speaking, process correctness can be divided into three major criteria; syntactic, semantic and behaviour. Each of these can further be divided into several criteria, for example syntactic correctness covers properties like reachability and inheritance. Current approaches focus on syntactic and behaviour correctness. However, semantic assurances, such as data flow correctness, task compatibility, rule compliance are also important aspects to ensure safe adaptation. In the literature, three semantic constraints are defined for workflow validation.

(1) Task-task dependency [13], which is developed to ensure compatibility among tasks in terms of order correctness among running tasks.

(2) Mutual exclusion and Coexistence constraints [14], which express the incompatibility between two tasks to avoid running them together and vice versa.

They are implemented over semantic conformance-oriented ontology for verifying workflow correctness at design time. [15] developed dependency models in order to manage process model variants not instance variants. Satisfying goal is another semantic criteria that must be addressed for self-adaptive systems. Koliadis and Ghose [8] developed GoalBPMN for studying and analysing the effect of changing goal specification in respect with its BPMN. BDI agent technology was used to develop agile goal-oriented business processes [16]. This approach handeled both modeling as well as adapting processes but they assume changing at goal level and restructure the process model accordingly.

In this work, we provide assuarances on goal-compliance (adapted process model is compliance to its original requirements) considering instance variants for running workflows at a high-level of abstraction.

VI. Conclusion and Outlook

A. Conclusion

In this paper, we presented a goal-compliance framework, the motivating approach behind it and its implementation. Basically, our approach focuses on providing assurances that the goal of self-adaptive workflows is still satisfied. As a result, we introduced two major compliance constraints: goal-task dependency and domain-task conformance constraints. The goal satisfaction is considered at a very high-level of abstraction neglecting the implementation details following the fact that workflows are designed to capture business goal. This allows to prevent errors and inconsistency at the abstract level, which in turn will reduce the effort, error and cost at data level.

B. Outlook

The Goal-Compliance framework performs runtime verification in a feasible as well as straightforward fashion. We run ana evaluation process based on the following criteria: 1) framework performance, 2) framework adequacy and 3) ontology accuracy. The performance is to measure time taken to read a BPMN, change its structure as required by policies and verify its compliance to the constraints. The main objective to measure the time is because the framework supposed to do its work at runtime and ensuring that its performance is reliable in practice. This point is planned as a future work and JProfiler [17] was chosen for this purpose.

However, we measure the ime taken by FDR to perform the verification related to the delete policy. FDR showed that the average time to calculate a simple assertion (e.g., the availability of the task "Confirm_Booking" to achieve the objective "FlightBooked" in the Travel domain) is 0.81s. Note that some objectives are achieved by the contribution of more than one task and the property is defined based on the refinement relations between their corresponding objectives in goal specification. For example, the tasks "Quote_Flight" OR "Quote_Hotel" OR "Quote_Car" are contributing to achieve the objective "TravelPlanGenerated". For these types of properties, the average time taken is 0.2s.

The framework adequacy is concerned with the workflow patterns [18] as they are widely accepted and capture most of the WF behaviours. Case by case analysis shows that 33 out of 43 of those patterns are supported within our framework. The unsupported patterns are those that are not implemented by BPMN.

The proposed ontology can be generalised to represent any BPMN domain. It is based on an assumption that it encompasses all tasks (designed and un-designed) that belong to a specific domain. However, predicting all tasks related to instance variants is impossible at modelling time. As a result, WordNet was integrated within the framework for synonyms search. We analysed the proposed ontology taking its accuracy into consideration. The accuracy is classified as a correctness metric and it includes precision, recall and coverage as the main measures [19]. We conducted a number of experiments on different BPMN(s) from different domains. In general, the number of verified tasks, which matched with Task individuals in the ontology, was 33 out of 39. Six tasks were not found in the ontology directly, but 4 were matched through synonyms finding with WordNet, making a total of 37 matches. However, two tasks failed to meet the domain-conformance constraints and as a result were rejected.

Based on theses results, the precision of the D-T-T ontology is 94.8% and the recall is 100%. The results show that this is a very promising approach, as long as the structure of the task name is 'well formed' in a verb-noun form (action followed by object: Send_Mail or Place_Order). The approach will extend to more complex task names, but more parsing and intelligence in the matching with the ontology is required.

REFERENCES

[1] "Object management group business process model and notation," URL: http://www.bpmn.org [accessed: 2016-10-25].

[2] P. C.A., Kommunikation mit Automaten. PhD thesis, Institut fur instrumentelle Mathematik, 1962.

[3] P. Wong, Formalisations and Applications of Business Process Modelling Notation. PhD thesis, University of Oxford, 2011.

[4] S. Gorton, Policy-driven Reconfiguration of Service-targeted Business Processes. PhD thesis, University of Leicester, 2011.

[5] A. Antón, "Goal-based requirements analysis," in Requirements Engineering, 1996., Proceedings of the Second International Conference on. IEEE, 1996, pp. 136–144.

[6] A. Lapouchnian, "Goal-oriented requirements engineering: An overview of the current research," University of Toronto, 2005, p. 32.

[7] N. Noy and D. McGuinness, "Ontology development 101: A guide to creating your first ontology," URL: http://protege.stanford.edu/publications/ontology_development/ontology101-noy-mcguinness.html [accessed: 2016-09-14].

[8] G. Koliadis and A. Ghose, "Relating business process models to goal-oriented requirements models in kaos," in Advances in Knowledge Acquisition and Management. Springer, 2006, pp. 25–39.

[9] P. Wong and J. Gibbons, "Property specifications for workflow modelling," in Integrated Formal Methods. Springer, 2009, pp. 56–71.

[10] "Fdr3 released, oxford university computing laboratory," URL: http://www.cs.ox.ac.uk/projects/concurrency-tools/ [accessed: 2016-10-12].

[11] "Protege," URL: http://protege.stanford.edu [accessed: 2016-08-22].

[12] Y. Han, A. Sheth, and C. Bussler, "A taxonomy of adaptive workflow management," in Workshop of the 1998 ACM Conference on Computer Supported Cooperative Work, 1998.

[13] L. T. Ly, S. Rinderle, and P. Dadam, "Semantic correctness in adaptive process management systems," in International Conference on Business Process Management. Springer, 2006, pp. 193–208.

[14] T.-H.-H. N. Tuan Anh Pham and N. L. Thanh, "Ontology-based workflow validation," in Computing Communication Technologies - Research, Innovation, and Vision for the Future (RIVF), 2015 IEEE RIVF International Conference on, Jan 2015, pp. 41–46.

[15] C. Sell, M. Winkler, T. Springer, and A. Schill, "Two dependency modeling approaches for business process adaptation," in International Conference on Knowledge Science, Engineering and Management. Springer, 2009, pp. 418–429.

[16] B. Burmeister, M. Arnold, F. Copaciu, and G. Rimassa, "Bdi-agents for agile goal-oriented business processes," in Proceedings of the 7th international joint conference on Autonomous agents and multiagent systems: industrial track. International Foundation for Autonomous Agents and Multiagent Systems, 2008, pp. 37–44.

[17] "ej technologies," URL: https://www.ej-technologies.com/products/jprofiler/overview.html [accessed: 2016-09-20].

[18] "Workflow patterns," URL: http://www.workflowpatterns.com [accessed: 2016-09-22].

[19] H. Hlomani and D. Stacey, "Approaches, methods, metrics, measures, and subjectivity in ontology evaluation: A survey," Semantic Web Journal, 2014, pp. 1–5.

Pure Embedding of Evolving Objects

Max Leuthäuser

Software Technology Group
TU Dresden
Email: max.leuthaeuser@tu-dresden.de

Abstract—**Scripting languages are extraordinarily popular due to their very flexible object model. Dynamic extensions (i.e., adding, removing and manipulating behavior and state) allow for the evolution and adaption of objects to context changes at runtime. Introducing this flexibility into a statically typed, object-oriented language would improve programmability and separation of concerns beyond the level of what one could usually gain with inheritance, mixins, traits or manually adapted design-patterns. They often lead to object-schizophrenia or the need for hand-crafted, additional management code. Although there were already attempts bringing flexible objects into statically typed languages with the benefits of an explicitly crafted core calculus or type system, they need their own compiler and tooling which limits the usability, e.g., when dealing with existing legacy code. This work presents an embedding of dynamically evolving objects via a lightweight library approach, which is *pure* in the sense, that there is no need for a specific compiler or tooling. It is written in Scala, which is both a modern object-oriented and functional programming language. Our approach is promising to solve practical problems arising in the area of dynamical extensibility and adaption like role-based programming.**

Keywords–Scala; evolving objects; object-oriented programming; dispatch.

I. INTRODUCTION

Scripting languages like Python, JavaScript, Ruby, Perl or Lua offer very flexible object semantics to the developer. On the one hand side, programmers can rely on classical object-oriented features, such as inheritance, encapsulation and polymorphism, and on the other, they are able to add and remove members (e.g., attributes and functions) from existing objects or merge them at any given point in their life-cycle [1].

This is usually not available in statically typed object-oriented languages. Imagine you have a client that wants to execute some behavior at a (core-) object of interest but that desired behavior is not available (Fig. 1). Using inheritance, mixins, traits or design-patterns is not desirable. The first three techniques will result in a very static system design and exponentially many classes, while the use of patterns often leads to object-schizophrenia [2] and the need of additional management code. Adding and removing members from existing objects at runtime are indeed very useful operations for todays software-systems, that have a very high demand for adaptivity and need to cope with complexity and change [3].

Is bridging the gap between statically-typed, object-oriented languages and evolving objects at runtime via pure embedding possible without too much effort? To answer that, the main contributions of this paper are:

- An introduction and summarizing technological overview on *SCROLL* [4], a lightweight library that allows for pure embedding of evolving objects in a modern, statically typed object-oriented language (Scala [5]), utilizing only those features that are available through its standard compiler. This library itself is small (∼1400 lines of code), allows for easy integration of legacy code and a high separation of concerns. It is limited on the side of type-safety as one might expect. Nevertheless, having a statically-typed host language for evolving objects supports the developer with the best of both worlds: static typing leads to an earlier detection of programming mistakes through static code analysis, better documentation in form of type-signatures, compiler-optimization, runtime-efficiency and an improved design-time development experience, while the latter supports easy prototyping, change to unknown requirements or unpredictable data and application integration. In summary: *"Static typing where possible, dynamic typing when needed!"* [6].
- An abstraction of that library into a more general implementation pattern by requiring only three fairly basic techniques to the host language.
- An example application showing that dynamically evolving objects are useful in the domain of role-based programming.

Scala was chosen as host language for *SCROLL* not only because of its combination of object-oriented and functional programming features, but as well due to its scalability and interoperability with the Java virtual machine providing easy integration of legacy code and the use of already established tools. *SCROLL* in particular takes advantage of Scala's features such as higher order functions, general operator notations, flexible syntax, implicits, compiler rewrites and implicit definitions of parameters.

The remainder of the paper is structured as follows. First, we will introduce in Sec. II the way evolving objects can be implemented with *SCROLL*. Additionally, the most important application programming interface- (API-) calls are explained. Following that, the actual implementation is described and will be abstracted into a more general implementation pattern by laying out its required three basic techniques (Sec. III). The abstraction from roles to evolving objects is demonstrated in Sec. IV and shows how role-based programming can be handled as well. Finally, the *SCROLL* approach is compared to more naive solutions using various design-patterns (Sec. V) and other coeval approaches from the related work (Sec. VI).

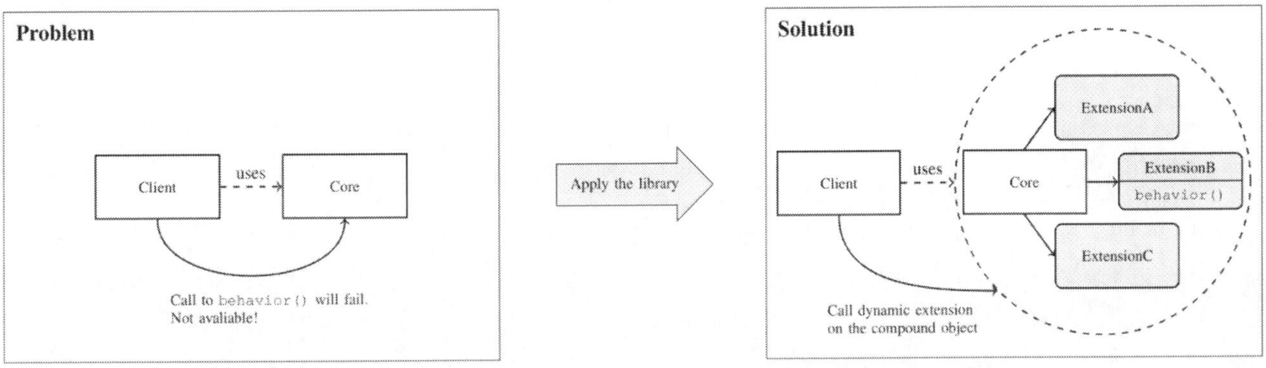

Figure 1. *Problem*: Imagine you have a client that wants to execute some behavior at a (core-) object of interest but that desired behavior is not available (see *left box*). *Solution*: Applying the library allows for dynamically adding new behavior at runtime while wrapping all the extension parts (`ExtensionA`, `ExtensionB` and `ExtensionC`) of the augmented object (`Core`) into one logical *compound object* (see *right box*).

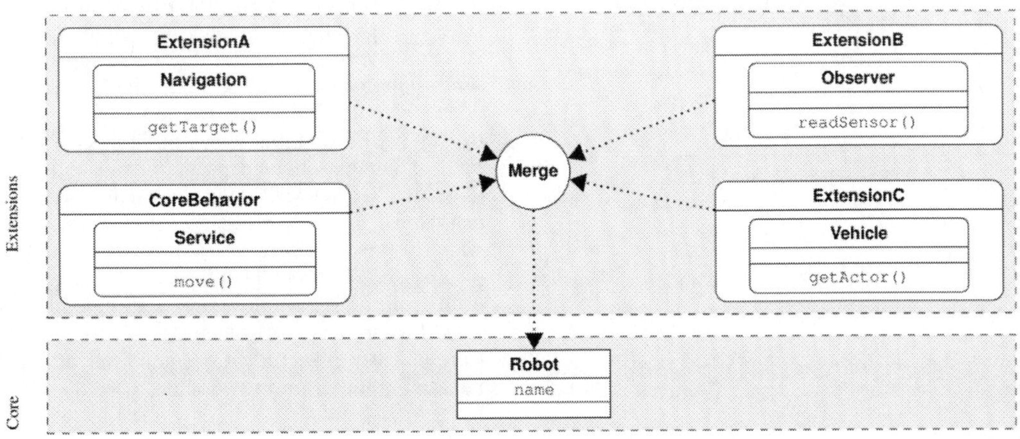

Figure 2. The class `Robot` is constructed (dotted arrows) from different extensions and acquires the contained behavior.

II. EVOLVING OBJECTS IN *SCROLL*

This section provides a brief introduction into the way one can use evolving objects as provided by *SCROLL* by example (see Fig. 2 and 3). A standard Scala case class (`Robot`) should be augmented with new behavior encapsulated in three different extensions (`ExtensionA`, `ExtensionB` and `ExtensionC`). Each of them provides a new aspect of the robot via functions (like finding a target to move to or observing sensor values) attached to case classes. This allows for a high degree of separation of concerns with multiple hierarchically nested components. The core behavior (with case class `Service`) aggregates all of the provided functionality without having to worry about its actual location. There are several calls to *SCROLL* in the example. Those shall be explained in the following:

- `+-Operator` (e.g., at line 6 in Fig. 3): In Scala, method calls can be written as infix operators. `+this` is equivalent to `this.+()`. Because extensions should be merged into any given object, we cannot assume that this object actually provides this +-operator. Thus, Scala's implicit conversion [7] is used to wrap the core object into an equivalent *compound object* exposing the required programming interface. In summary, by calling the +-operator the developer is able to forward arbitrary calls to some extension he assumes should be available on the core object without worrying about their actual location. The function-lookup resolution technique is explained in more depth in Sec. III.
- `play` (e.g., at line 32 in Fig. 3): This method attaches the selected behavior to the core object. The name stems from role-based programming, where roles can be seen as some kind of dynamic extension (Sec. IV). There, playing a role is equivalent to acquiring its behavior and state.
- `Compartment` (e.g., at line 3 in Fig. 3): A compartment is an objectified collaboration with a limited number of participating roles and a fixed scope [8] and stems from role-based programming as well. It was introduced to clearly distinguish from the heavily overloaded term *context*. While a context (e.g., a cold and rainy day in London) is prescriptive, without its own identity, intrinsic behavior or existential parts and with an indefinite lifetime - a compartment (e.g., a first-class train car) is descriptive. Its instances carry identity, have behavior, state, a defined lifetime and contain roles as its parts. Mixing in the `Compartment` trait exposes *SCROLL*'s basic programming interface to the current class. Contained classes or case classes can be seen as containers for new behavior and state that should be attached later on. From the developer's point of view, one could rewrite the introductory sentence to "a compartment is an objectified collaboration with dynamic behavior and state and a fixed scope".

- `merge` (e.g., at line 33 in Fig. 3): The relationship between a core object and all of its extensions is stored compartment-specific (as explained in Sec. III-C). So, executing behavior spanning over multiple extensions like in `CoreBehavior` requires a merging of all the participating extensions (i.e. compartments) with their specific storage.

When running the example code, the console output as shown in Fig. 3 will be generated. There are several slightly more advanced examples available online [9].

```
1  case class Robot(name: String)
2
3  object CoreBehavior extends Compartment {
4    case class Service() {
5      def move() {
6        val name: String = +this name()
7        val target: String = +this getTarget()
8        val sensorValue: Int = +this readSensor()
9        val actor: String = +this getActor()
10       info(s"I am $name and moving to the $target
           ↪ with my $actor w.r.t. sensor value of
           ↪ $sensorValue.")
11     }
12   }
13 }
14
15 object ExtensionA extends Compartment {
16   case class Navigation() {
17     def getTarget = "kitchen"
18   }
19 }
20
21 object ExtensionB extends Compartment {
22   case class Observer() {
23     def readSensor = 100
24   }
25 }
26
27 object ExtensionC extends Compartment {
28   case class Vehicle() {
29     def getActor = "wheels"
30   }
31 }

32 val myRobot = Robot("Pete") play Service() play
     ↪ Navigation() play Observer() play
     ↪ Vehicle()
33 CoreBehavior merge ExtensionA merge ExtensionB
     ↪ merge ExtensionC
34 myRobot move()

35 I am Pete and moving to the kitchen with my
     ↪ wheels w.r.t. sensor value of 100.
```

Figure 3. The robot is constructed from multiple extensions dynamically at runtime. Running the example generates the console output shown above.

III. Implementation

This section explains the basic technologies used by *SCROLL* for the pure embedding of evolving objects. Together, these form an implementation pattern that is useful for adapting this library approach to other host languages.

A. Implicit Conversions

We want to be able to mix in extensions to any given object of any type in Scala. Implicit conversions [7] provide a lightweight way to expose *SCROLL*'s programming interface for adding, removing and transferring behavior or state to any object. Listing 1 gives a brief excerpt.

```
implicit class Player[T](val wrapped: T) {
  /* Applies lifting to Player */
  def unary_+ : Player[T] = this

  def play(role: Any): Player[T] = /* ... */
  def drop(role: Any): Player[T] = /* ... */
  def transfer(role: Any) = new {
    def to(player: Any) { /* ... */ }
  }

  /* ... */
  override def equals(o: Any) = /* ... */
}
```

Listing 1. The generic `implicit` class `Player`.

Scala's implicit conversion is used to wrap the core object into an equivalent *compound object* exposing the required API in a type-safe manner. Furthermore, the issue of *object-schizophrenia* needs to be addressed with a clear notion of object identity. This term has not been introduced explicitly by any publication, but appeared in a set of web-pages in the field of context-oriented programming and can be described like this: "*Object Schizophrenia results when the state and/or behavior of what is intended to appear as a single object are actually broken into several objects (each of which has its own object identity).*" [10]. It can be seen as another instance of the *split object problem* [11]. Here, the identity of an object should be the same independent of which extension is attached. Consequently, object identity should reflect this properly. Four kinds of comparison are possible:

1) `core == core + extension`
2) `core + extension == core`
3) `core + extension == core + extension`
4) `core + extensionA == core + extensionB`

To implement this, we modify the identity-related method of the compound object represented by `Player` as shown in the above code-listing. In fact, `==` and the `equals`-method are equivalent in Scala. That is, the expressions `x == y` and `x.equals(y)` give the same result. We define the `equals`-method in such way that it maps to the implementation of the core object, and, in case the right-hand operator of `==` is an evolving object as well, compare with its core object. This solves the problem for expressions 2 to 4, but unfortunately does not for expression 1, since we cannot modify the `equals`-method of arbitrary objects using a library approach. If the comparison of a plain core object is required apply the `+`-`Operator` (see Sec. II) to it. This will trigger the dynamic conversion using the implicit class `Player` and applies the desired comparison.

B. Dynamic Trait

Behavior and state from extensions that is not natively available to the core object needs to be addressed somehow. Scala's `Dynamic` trait [12] is used to implement that behavior. Once the proper extension is identified and selected (see Sec. III-C and III-D) the actual invocation should take place. To do so, calls to extension-specific functionality, that would normally fail during type-checking phase, are rewritten according to the rules by the compiler itself [13] as shown in Listing 2:

```
foo.method("blah")
  ⇝ foo.applyDynamic("method")("blah")

foo.method(x = "blah")
  ⇝ foo.applyDynamicNamed("method")(("x",
      ↪ "blah"))
foo.method(x = 1, 2)
  ⇝ foo.applyDynamicNamed("method")(("x", 1),
      ↪ ("", 2))

foo.field
  ⇝ foo.selectDynamic("field")
foo.variable = 10
  ⇝ foo.updateDynamic("variable")(10)
```

Listing 2. Compiler rewrite rules from the `Dynamic` trait [13].

That is exactly the point where type safety is lost. The actual set of dynamic extensions that are bound to the core object is not statically known, hence static type-safety is not available. As an example, the method call to the robots `name` attribute from Fig. 3 (line 6) is translated as shown in Listing 3.

```
+this.name
  ⇝ this.unary_+().name
  ⇝ new Player[Robot](this).name
  ⇝ new Player[Robot](this).selectDynamic("name")
```

Listing 3. Rewriting for dynamical access to the `Robot` attribute `name`.

SCROLL hooks into those rewritten methods and triggers the actual invocation and error handling. We refrain from using runtime exceptions or similar exception-based error handling in case of not being able to find the functionality the developer is querying for. Instead, Scala's `Either` container type is used by the library. It has two sub types, `Left` and `Right`. If an `Either[A,B]` object contains an instance of `A`, then the `Either` is a `Left`. Otherwise, it contains an instance of `B` and it is a `Right`. Although, there is nothing in the semantics of this type that would specify one or the other sub type to represent an error or a success, by convention it is used to carry the error case as `Left` (e.g., `DynamicBehaviorNotFound`), whereas the `Right` contains the success value (i.e., the result of executing the dynamic behavior). Together with a sealed type hierarchy with data types using case classes that represent errors, very readable messages compared to actual stack-traces from standard Java exceptions are generated.

C. Graph-based Backend

In *SCROLL*, a graph is used for storing the relations between core objects and its extension instances. That allows for easy querying of extension-specific behavior that was attached to the core object. Furthermore, there are many graph libraries implementing various aspects like caching and distribution. In general, a (labeled) graph H is a 4-tuple (V, E, Lab, L_Σ) with:

- V is a finite set of vertices (nodes) with $|V| \geq 0$,
- E is the set of edges, where E is a relation $E \subseteq V \times V$,
- L_Σ is the set of labels and
- $Lab : V \cup E \rightarrow L_\Sigma$ is the labeling function, which assigns a label to each node in V and edge in E.

For *SCROLL* this can be adapted to:

- V is the set of objects (core and all extension instances),
- E is the set of relations between core objects and its extension instances,
- L_Σ is the set of type names for all objects in V and
- $Lab : V \rightarrow L_\Sigma$ assigns each object in V its type.

JGraphT [14] was chosen as underlying graph library providing already the necessary graph-theory objects like predefined edge- and node-types, as well as simple algorithms for traversing the graph. *SCROLL* abstracts from that making it easy to plug-in any other convenient library, e.g., for easy scaling or distribution of the graph if required. Another implementation making use of Google's Guava framework [15] for caching is available, too. That speeds up querying the core for the actual behavior hidden in some extension if asked by the client. Additionally, with Kiama's pure embedding of attribute-grammars in Scala [16], a third backend is provided. Querying and updating the graph is implemented as (cached-) attributes and rewrites respectively.

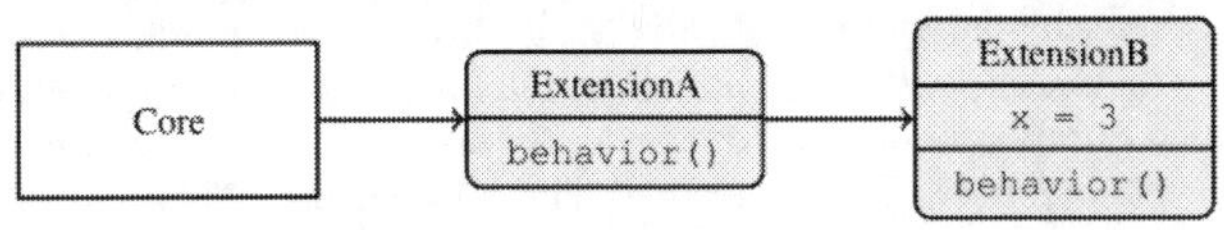


```
implicit val dispatchDescription =
  From(_.isInstanceOf[Core]).
  To(anything).
  Through(anything).
  Bypassing(_ match {
    case ExtensionA() => true
    case ExtensionB(x) if x == 3 => false
    case _ => true // default case
  })
```

Figure 4. An example for the need of customizable dynamic dispatch.

D. Customizable Dynamic Dispatch

Dispatching in adaptive systems is context-dependent. Selecting the appropriate extension that should be selected for answering a call to the required behavior may be ambiguous. The developer should be able to key out the desired selection. *SCROLL* supports this with function composition and Scala's pattern matching making use of an explicit dispatch description which is passed down to the actual method invocation as implicit argument. The given selection functions are applied while traversing the graph-based storage holding the relations between core objects and its extension instances. See Fig. 4 for an example. We construct a new dispatch description using four factory methods provided by the API and pass our selection functions into them. We are only interested in our core object (`_.isInstanceOf[Core]`) so we are using this for the `From`-selector. Now, lets assume we do not care for the types of extensions that are actually around so we pass `anything` to the `To`-selector, which will always evaluate to `true`, so every extension instance will be considered while traversing the graph. Same goes for `Through` on intermediate nodes. Finally, for the `Bypassing`-selector we want to define that an instance of `ExtensionB` with the state `x = 3` should be selected, hence never bypassed. With an explicit dispatch description, the developer defines a sub-graph of the underlying graph as follows: let $H = (V, E, Lab, L_\Sigma)$ and $H' = (V', E', Lab', L_\Sigma{}')$ be those storage graphs. Then H' is a sub-graph generated for dispatching out of H with $H' \subseteq H$, if $V' \subseteq V$, $E' \subseteq E$, $Lab' \subseteq Lab : V' \cup E' \to L_\Sigma{}'$ and $L_\Sigma{}' \subseteq L_\Sigma$.

E. The SCROLL *Implementation Pattern*

So far, we have shown how arbitrary objects can be augmented dynamically with new functionality or state grouped together in extension. Moreover, obstacles arising from object-schizophrenia can be solved with a compound object enabled by dynamic conversions and an adapted notion of object identity (i.e., the identity of an object should be the same independent of which extension is attached). Using Scala's `Dynamic` trait together with a graph-based backend allows for easy querying for behavior that is not natively available at the core object. How to transfer and adapt this? An implementation pattern is a reusable and adaptable solution to a certain problem and shows best practice for developers while offering insights to relationships and interactions between its components.

As introduced in the previous subsections, *SCROLL* requires the concept of a *marker trait* (1) for triggering compiler rewrites handing over calls to the library for finding behavior that is not natively available at the core object. For assembling a compound object from the core plus all its extension *implicit conversions* (2) are needed. The storage of the relationships between each individual core object and its extensions can be done easily with any *graph-based backend* (3), or alternatively with tables or maps. If one is able to find or emulate these three techniques in the desired statically-typed, object-oriented language it is easy to provide an alternative implementation of *SCROLL*.

IV. Separation of Concerns

The main goal of having extensions to dynamically evolve objects is the separation of different entity concerns while being able to plug them altogether at runtime if a context-dependent change to the system occurs. This not only increases adaptability of the overall infrastructure, it improves separation of concerns as well. That pretty much resembles the paradigm and main goal of role-based programming. Although, the concept of roles has been around for decades, starting in the field of databases [17], the research landscape on it is very diverse and fragmented.

Over time researchers have proposed several implementation approaches targeting the contextual nature of roles and their representation at runtime. Unfortunately, until today there is no common definition of what a role actually is. Most of the resulting languages are reinventing the wheel over and over again, implementing different role features for their specific research area [8]. We argue that evolving objects (core objects with addable or removable extension) are the generalization of role-playing objects as a novel reuse and adaptability unit in dynamic collaborations.

The following main features of roles extracted from the literature [8], [18] can be fulfilled by evolving objects as implemented by *SCROLL* while other coeval approaches will fail to do so (this is explained in more depth in Sec. VI).

- **Roles have properties and behaviors.** An extension adds new functionality or state to its core.
- **Objects may acquire and abandon roles dynamically.** Adding and removing new behavior is the main idea of evolving objects. In particular, a role can be transferred from one object to another.
- **Objects may play the same role (type) several times.** With the grouping of extension in compartments as first-class citizens representing contextualized collaborations, one can easily allow for attaching multiple instances of the same extension type in different contexts to one core object.

As a brief example for applying *SCROLL* for role-based programming, see Fig. 5 and 6. We implement a manual transport (class `ManualTransport`) of a `Person` with a `Car` to a certain `Location` by augmenting these core classes with being a `NormalCar` and a `Driver` respectively. For the autonomous transport (class `AutonomousTransport`), it is the `SmartCar` and `Passenger` with different behavior for driving or using the brakes. `Target` and `Source` roles added to locations are used in the actual transportation by the method `travel()` in `TransportationRole`. That role will augment a specific transportation (either the manual or the autonomous one) and alters its behavior. All important API-calls (like the `+-Operator` or `play`) are explained in Sec. II. Note, that the query-function `one[SomeType]()` (e.g., on line 18 in Fig. 5, right side) allows for querying exactly one instance of the given type that should be contained in the current instance of a `Compartment`.

In summary, with respect to the effects on separation of concerns, both role-playing objects and dynamically evolving objects as generalization provide a handy abstraction of context-dependent dynamic behavior and state.

V. Comparison with Manual Implementations and Patterns

The following section demonstrates the advantages of the proposed library approach for pure embedding of evolving objects by comparing it to simple, manually instantiated implementations and design patterns widely used when people try to cope with the required dynamics [19]. For a summary, see Table I.

The most basic solution would be to use one **Single Type** for your core object and all extensions. If they do not differentiate in behavior and you do not plan for future changes, that would be a valid solution without any over-engineering. On the downside, that leads to one single complex type, that may be hard to maintain later on. If extensions introduce many different features, one may think about implementing them as **Separate Types**. That removes coupling and unnecessary tangling of relationships between them. Sadly, it introduces the duplication of features and a loss of integrity with shared state and behavior. Using **Subtypes** for every extension and putting the common things into the supertype for each extension may overcome this issue while being conceptually simple. On the downside the resulting inheritance hierarchy may be hard to adapt with multiple or changing extensions as each of them requires the interface of the supertype to be changed as well.

```
class Person(val name: String)
class Car(val licenseID: String)
class Location(val name: String)

class Transportation() extends Compartment {
  object AutonomousTransport extends Compartment
      ↪ {
    class SmartCar() {
      def drive() {
        info("I am driving autonomously!")
      }
    }
    class Passenger() {
      def brake() {
        info(s"I can't reach the brake. I am
            ↪ ${+this name} and just a
            ↪ passenger!")
      }
    }
  }

  object ManualTransport extends Compartment {
    class NormalCar() {
      def drive() {
        info(s"I am driving with a driver called
            ↪ ${+one[Driver]() name}.")
      }
    }
    class Driver() {
      def brake() {
        info(s"I am ${+this name} and I am hitting
            ↪ the brakes now!")
      }
    }
  }

  class TransportationRole(source: Source,
      ↪ target: Target) {
    def travel() {
      val kindOfTransport = this player match {
          case ManualTransport => "manual"
          case AutonomousTransport => "autonomous"
      }
      info(s"Doing a $kindOfTransport
          ↪ transportation with the car
          ↪ ${one[Car]().licenseID} from
          ↪ ${+source name} to ${+target
          ↪ name}.")
    }
  }

  class Target()
  class Source()
}
```

```
new Transportation {
  val peter = new Person("Peter")
  val harry = new Person("Harry")
  val googleCar = new Car("A-B-C-001")
  val toyota = new Car("A-B-C-002")

  new Location("Munich") play new Source()
  new Location("Berlin") play new Source()
  new Location("Dresden") play new Target()

  harry play new ManualTransport.Driver()
  toyota play new ManualTransport.NormalCar()

  +toyota drive()
  ManualTransport play
    new TransportationRole(
      one[Source]("name" ==# "Berlin"),
      one[Target]()
    ) travel()

  peter play new AutonomousTransport.Passenger()
  googleCar play new
    . ↪ AutonomousTransport.SmartCar()

  +googleCar drive()
  AutonomousTransport play
    new TransportationRole(
      one[Source]("name" ==# "Munich"),
      one[Target]()
    ) travel()

  +peter brake()
  +harry brake()
}
```

Figure 5. The SmartCar example (*instance code*, top) and the corresponding *model code* (left).

```
I am driving with a driver called Harry.
Doing a manual transportation with the car A-B-C
    ↪ -002 from Berlin to Dresden.
I am driving autonomously!
Doing a autonomous transportation with the car A-
    ↪ B-C-001 from Munich to Dresden.
I can't reach the brake. I am Peter and just a
    ↪ passenger!
I am Harry and I am hitting the brakes now!
```

Figure 6. Running the example generates the *console output* shown above.

The classification of domain objects inheritance introduces is static. An alternative to that, would be to use the **Role-Object-Pattern** [20]. The core object now has a multi-valued association to its extensions as separate types with a common supertype. This is a very direct implementation without the need of changing some interface when introducing new extensions. It can become complicated when dealing with constraints between those extensions and again, with shared state. Additionally, object-schizophrenia needs to be targeted explicitly which applies to extensions when trying to implement them with the Role-Object-Pattern. One has to deal with method call dispatch, encapsulation and object comparison manually [21]. We continue with **Multiple Inheritance or Traits**. Although these concepts are semantically fine to implement extensions, they will lead to a very static system again with an exponential blowup in the number of required classes for every new context one needs to add. Additionally, parallel object hierarchies may occur where cross-tree constraints are very hard to maintain. **Delegation** on the other hand mimics the inheritance mechanism on object level. This requires (the generation of) a lot of management code and leads to object-schizophrenia, too. Finally, **Delegation-Layers** define layers that group behavior for sets of objects and for sets of classes. Sadly, it implies fixed hierarchies and thus a system design that is too static.

Table I. COMPARISON OF APPROACHES FOR ESTABLISHING DYNAMIC OBJECTS AT RUNTIME (SOLELY BASED ON [19]). ■ INDICATES THAT THERE IS A PROBLEM IN THE GIVEN CATEGORY. PLEASE NOTE, THAT THIS COMPARISON ONLY CONSIDERS APPROACHES THAT DO NOT RELY ON CUSTOM COMPILERS, GENERATORS OR OTHER TOOLING.

	Single complex type	Shared State / Behavior	Scalability	Interface	Change	Constraints	Object Schizophrenia	Exponential blowup	Static Design	Parallel Hierarchies	Management Code
Single Type	■		■	■	■				■		
Separate Type		■	■			■					■
Subtype With Internal Flag	■	■	■	■	■			■	■		■
Subtype With Hidden Delegation	■	■	■	■	■			■	■		■
Subtype With State Object		■	■	■	■			■	■		■
Role Object Pattern		■				■	■				■
Multiple Inheritance / Traits			■		■			■	■	■	
Delegation / Delegation Layers		■			■		■				■

VI. Related Work

This section summarizes and compares how different runtime environments or technical spaces could be used to realize evolving objects.

A. Evolving objects with other statically-typed, object-oriented languages

First, *SCROLL* requires the concept of a marker trait, i.e., a mixin to an object for triggering compiler rewrites handing over calls to the library for finding behavior that is not natively available at the core object (trait `Dynamic`, as explained in Sec. III-B). *Second*, a technical solution for assembling a compound object from the core plus all its extension bypassing object-schizophrenia [2] is needed. *Third* requirement is the storage of the relationships between each individual core object and its extensions, which should be easy with any graph-based backend, or alternatively with simple tables or maps. If one is able to find or emulate these three techniques in the desired statically-typed, object-oriented language it is easy to provide an alternative implementation of *SCROLL*. In conclusion, this proposed *implementation pattern* (requiring the before-mentioned three basic technologies) is applicable to many host languages. With the *ExpandoObject* [22] C# can be considered as the most promising option to provide such an implementation of *SCROLL* in another language. The ExpandoObject represents an object that allows for dynamically adding and removing its members at runtime. However, this works at another level of granularity compared to *SCROLL*. Only single members, like a function or an attribute, can be attached or removed at a single point in time. With *SCROLL* you are allowed to group them together (e.g., into classes, case classes or objects) and add or remove all contained members at once. Better separation of concerns is achieved that way.

B. Evolving objects with Aspect- / Subject-oriented programming languages

Aspect-oriented programming allows to implement cross-cutting concerns via join-points and pointcuts. Often the composition is done statically although there exist a few dynamic approaches. **ObjectTeams/Java** (OT/J) [23] uses dynamic aspect weaving at bytecode-level for adding behavior. Subject-oriented programming utilizes different class hierarchies from different perspectives. On the downside there is no real composition language and the set of composition operators is fixed. Furthermore, no real control flow on the composition itself exists.

C. Evolving objects with role-based programming languages

Although dynamically evolving objects are the more general concept compared to role-playing objects as outlined in Sec. IV, we consider them to be useful for a technical realization as well. Interestingly, most of the existing role-based programming languages are extensions to Java. They are either compiled to Java source code [24], [25], [26], [27] or to bytecode [23] directly.

Chameleon [24] provides roles through *constituent methods* allowing to overwrite methods of their players, which work like advices in aspect-oriented programming. As a major drawback of Chameleon its roles extend the player to gain access to it, which is conceptually wrong [18] and limits the flexibility of roles. **Rava** [25] overcomes this by employing the *Role-Object-Pattern* [20] extended with the *Mediator-Pattern* [28]. They use special keywords to steer the generation of management code. Due to the use of the Role-Object Pattern and generation to plain Java, this solution suffers from object-schizophrenia [29]. **JavaStage** [27] solves this problem, by only supporting static roles. They are directly compiled into the players as inner classes. To avoid name clashes, a customizable method renaming strategy is applied. Its main advantages are the capability to specify a list of required methods instead of a specific player class. This approach limits itself to static roles as well, unable to represent their relational and context-dependent nature. **Rumer** [30] offers first-class relationships and modular verification over distributed state. Furthermore, it provides several intra-relationship constraints usable to restrict these relationships. Roles are the named places of a relationship with attributes and methods but without inheritance. Roles are only accessible within a relationship and not from their player. **ScalaRoles** [31] is probably the closest relative to *SCROLL*. It is implemented as Scala library as well and utilizes dynamic proxies (from the Java API) to implement roles. The practical implementation using Scala's traits as roles reveals the problem that the order of role binding influences the resulting type, e.g., a person playing the father role first and then the student role is another type than the same person playing those roles the other way around. The most sophisticated and mature approach so far is **ObjectTeams/Java** (OT/J) [23]. Like Chameleon above, OT/J allows to override methods of a player by aspect weaving. It introduces *Teams* to represent compartments whose inner classes automatically become roles. Notably, OT/J supports both the inheritance of roles and teams whereas the latter leads to family polymorphism [32]. On the downside, it does neither support multiple unrelated player types for a role type nor first class relationships and only a limited form of constraints. This is similar to **powerJava** [33], which also introduces compartments, denoted *Institutions*, whose inner classes represent roles. However, powerJava features the distinction between role interface and role implementation where the former is callable from outside a specific institution and the latter is the institution-specific implementation of the same interface. Both Rava and powerJava are the only research prototypes providing a working compiler. Sadly, the project has been abandoned [34]. A more recent approach towards context-oriented programming is **NextEJ** [35] as the successor of EpsilonJ [36]. It provides *Contexts* as first class citizens which do not only group roles but also represent an activation scope at runtime. These *context activation scopes* can be nested and act as a barrier where all roles are instantiated and bound automatically. So far, they only published their type-system of the core calculus and no compiler.

In summary, it is necessary to investigate how well the implementation with SCROLL for binding roles as technical realization for evolving objects blends into contemporary approaches. We use an already published classification scheme from the literature [8], [18]. A compact overview is given in Table II. Most of the role features in question are supported.

Table II. COMPARISON OF COEVAL APPROACHES FOR ROLES AT RUNTIME BASED ON 26 CLASSIFYING FEATURES EXTRACTED FROM THE LITERATURE [8], [18]. IT DIFFERENTIATES BETWEEN FULLY (■), PARTLY (⊞) AND NOT SUPPORTED (□) FEATURES.

Feature [8]	**Chameleon** [24]	**OT/J** [23]	**Rava** [25]	**powerJava** [26]	**Rumer** [30]	**ScalaRoles** [37]	**NextEJ** [35]	**JavaStage** [27]	**SCROLL**
1.	■	■	■	■	■	■	■	■	■
2.	□	⊞	□	⊞	■	□	⊞	□	□
3.	■	■	■	■	■	■	■	■	■
4.	■	■	□	■	■	■	■	□	■
5.	■	■	■	⊞	■	■	■	■	■
6.	□	■	□	■	■	□	□	■	■
7.	■	□	■	■	⊞	■	■	■	■
8.	□	■	□	■	□	■	■	■	■
9.	■	□	□	■	□	■	■	□	■
10.	■	■	■	■	■	■	■	■	■
11.	■	■	■	■	■	■	■	■	■
12.	■	■	■	■	■	■	■	■	■
13.	□	■	■	■	□	■	□	■	■
14.	⊞	⊞	□	□	■	■	⊞	□	■
15.	■	■	■	■	□	■	■	■	■
16.	□	□	□	□	■	□	□	□	□
17.	□	□	□	□	□	□	□	□	□
18.	□	■	□	□	⊞	⊞	⊞	□	■
19.	□	■	□	⊞	⊞	□	■	□	□
20.	□	■	□	■	■	■	■	□	■
21.	□	□	□	■	□	⊞	■	□	■
22.	□	■	□	□	■	□	□	□	■
23.	□	■	□	□	□	□	□	□	■
24.	□	■	□	⊞	■	■	■	□	■
25.	□	■	□	□	□	■	□	□	■
26.	□	■	□	⊞	■	■	■	□	■

VII. Future Work

Several developments are currently work in progress or targeted for investigation in the near future. Because the actual set of dynamic extensions that are bound to a core object can not be statically determined, static type-safety is lost at a certain point as already mentioned in Sec. III-B. The *SCROLLCompilerPlugin* [38] is a plugin for the standard Scala compiler and runs right after its typing phase. It allows for validating the source code (i.e., traversing the syntax tree) and generates meaningful warnings and errors, e.g., if the developer is requesting behavior from a dynamic extension that was never bound. In interdisciplinary collaborations, we aim for other use-cases for applying the concept of dynamically evolving objects. They should help the domain expert to cope with its specific implementation concerns. Specifically in systems biology, and more generally in scientific computing (e.g., with a Next-Generation Parallel Particle-Mesh Language [39]) using this concept looks promising. The separation of concerns achieved this way greatly improves the quality of code written in these field of research. With respect to the required performance, methods for translating the specific binding and behavior-lookup for dynamic objects to a native and fast performing technological platform need to be developed. Another promising direction is the investigation of the `invokedynamic` bytecode keyword introduced with Java 7 to provide an alternative to *SCROLL*. An appropriate implementation and comparison of those two approaches in terms of runtime-efficiency and improvement design-time development experience is currently targeted.

VIII. Conclusions

In summary, this work presents an attempt to bridge the gap between statically-typed, object-oriented languages and evolving objects at runtime by introducing *SCROLL* as a lightweight library that allows for pure embedding of dynamically evolving objects in a modern, statically typed object-oriented language. Arbitrary objects can be augmented with extensions allowing for adding and removing behavior and state at runtime. They are combined to one logical compound object through the library solving object-schizophrenia. The library allows for easy integration of existing (Java Virtual Machine based) legacy code and a high separation of concerns, e.g., when applied to roles in contexts. Ultimately, following the rules of the proposed implementation pattern as the core idea of *SCROLL* one could easily implement a very similar library in another host language.

Acknowledgment

This work is funded by the German Research Foundation (DFG) within the Research Training Group "Role-based Software Infrastructures for continuous-context-sensitive Systems" (GRK 1907) and in the Collaborative Research Center 912 "Highly Adaptive Energy-Efficient Computing". Special thanks go to Sebastian Götz, Ulrike Schöbel and Anthony Sloane for improving this paper.

References

[1] P. H. Menon, Z. Palmer, A. Rozenshteyn, and S. Smith, "Types for flexible objects," Technical report, The Johns Hopkins University, Tech. Rep., 2013.

[2] U. Aßmann, Invasive Software Composition. Springer-Verlag, 2003.

[3] J. F. Furrer, "Zukunftsfähige Softwaresysteme," Informatik-Spektrum, 2015, pp. 1–9. [Online]. Available: http://dx.doi.org/10.1007/s00287-015-0909-6

[4] M. Leuthäuser, "SCROLL," https://github.com/max-leuthaeuser/scroll, 2016, [last viewed 01.12.2016, 09.00].

[5] EPFL, "Scala Website," http://www.scala-lang.org/, 2016, [last viewed 01.12.2016, 09.00].

[6] E. Meijer and A. Peter Drayton, "Static typing where possible," Dynamic Typing When Needed: The End of the Cold War Between Programming Languages, 2004.

[7] M. Odersky, L. Spoon, and B. Venners, "Programming in scala: a comprehensive stepby-step guide," Artima Inc, August, 2008.

[8] T. Kühn, M. Leuthäuser, S. Götz, C. Seidl, and U. Aßmann, "A metamodel family for role-based modeling and programming languages," in Software Language Engineering, ser. Lecture Notes in Computer Science, B. Combemale, D. Pearce, O. Barais, and J. Vinju, Eds. Springer International Publishing, 2014, vol. 8706, pp. 141–160. [Online]. Available: http://dx.doi.org/10.1007/978-3-319-11245-9_8

[9] M. Leuthäuser, "SCROLL Examples," https://github.com/max-leuthaeuser/SCROLL/tree/master/examples/src/main/scala/scroll/examples, 2016, [last viewed 01.12.2016, 09.00].

[10] B. Harrison, "Subject-oriented Programming vs. Design Patterns," http://www.research.ibm.com/sop, 1997, [archived as of May 1997].

[11] C. Dony, J. Malenfant, and P. Cointe, "Prototype-based languages: From a new taxonomy to constructive proposals and their validation," in Conference Proceedings on Object-oriented Programming Systems, Languages, and Applications, ser. OOPSLA '92. New York, NY, USA: ACM, 1992, pp. 201–217. [Online]. Available: http://doi.acm.org/10.1145/141936.141954

[12] EPFL, "Scala Dynamic Trait SIP," http://docs.scala-lang.org/sips/completed/type-dynamic.html, 2016, [last viewed 01.12.2016, 09.00].

[13] EPFL, "Scala Dynamic Trait ScalaDoc," https://github.com/scala/scala/blob/2.12.x/src/library/scala/Dynamic.scala, 2016, [last viewed 01.12.2016, 09.00].

[14] B. Naveh and Contributors, "jGraphT," http://jgrapht.org/, 2016, [last viewed 01.12.2016, 09.00].

[15] Google, "Guava," https://github.com/google/guava, 2016, [last viewed 01.12.2016, 09.00].

[16] A. M. Sloane, L. C. Kats, and E. Visser, "A pure embedding of attribute grammars," Science of Computer Programming, vol. 78, no. 10, 2013, pp. 1752–1769.

[17] C. W. Bachman, "The programmer as navigator," Commun. ACM, vol. 16, no. 11, 1973, pp. 635–658.

[18] F. Steimann, "On the representation of roles in object-oriented and conceptual modelling," Data & Knowledge Engineering, vol. 35, no. 1, 2000, pp. 83–106.

[19] M. Fowler, "Dealing with roles," in Proceedings of PLoP, vol. 97, 1997.

[20] D. Bäumer, D. Riehle, W. Siberski, and M. Wulf, "The role object pattern," in Washington University Dept. of Computer Science, 1997.

[21] S. Herrmann, "Demystifying object schizophrenia," in Proceedings of the 4th Workshop on MechAnisms for SPEcialization, Generalization and inHerItance. ACM, 2010, p. 2.

[22] Microsoft, "Expando Object," https://msdn.microsoft.com/en-us/magazine/ff796227.aspx, 2016, [last viewed 01.12.2016, 09.00].

[23] S. Herrmann, "Programming with roles in ObjectTeams/Java." AAAI Fall Symposium, Tech. Rep., 2005.

[24] K. B. Graversen and K. Østerbye, "Implementation of a role language for object-specific dynamic separation of concerns," in AOSD03 Workshop on Software-engineering Properties of Languages for Aspect Technologies, 2003.

[25] C. He, Z. Nie, B. Li, L. Cao, and K. He, "Rava: Designing a java extension with dynamic object roles," in Engineering of Computer Based Systems, 2006. ECBS 2006. 13th Annual IEEE International Symposium and Workshop on. IEEE, 2006, pp. 7–pp.

[26] M. Baldoni, G. Boella, and L. van der Torre, "Roles as a coordination construct: Introducing powerjava," Electr. Notes Theor. Comput. Sci, vol. 150, no. 1, 2006, pp. 9–29.

[27] F. S. Barbosa and A. Aguiar, "Modeling and programming with roles: introducing javastage," Instituto Politécnico de Castelo Branco, Tech. Rep., 2012.

[28] E. Gamma, R. Helm, R. Johnson, and J. Vlissides, Design patterns: elements of reusable object-oriented software. Pearson Education, 1994.

[29] S. Herrmann, "Demystifying object schizophrenia," in Proceedings of the 4th Workshop on MechAnisms for SPEcialization, Generalization and inHerItance, ser. MASPEGHI '10. New York, NY, USA: ACM, 2010, pp. 2:1–2:5.

[30] S. Balzer, T. Gross, and P. Eugster, "A relational model of object collaborations and its use in reasoning about relationships," in ECOOP, ser. Lecture Notes in Computer Science, E. Ernst, Ed., vol. 4609. Springer, 2007, pp. 323–346.

[31] M. Pradel and M. Odersky, "Scala roles: Reusable object collaborations in a library," in Software and Data Technologies. Springer Berlin Heidelberg, 2009, pp. 23–36.

[32] S. Herrmann, C. Hundt, and K. Mehner, "Translation polymorphism in object teams," TU Berlin, Tech. Rep., 2004.

[33] E. Arnaudo, M. Baldoni, G. Boella, V. Genovese, and R. Grenna, "An implementation of roles as affordances: powerJava," Aug. 31 2009.

[34] G. Wielenga, "On powerjava: "roles" instead of "objects"," https://blogs.oracle.com/geertjan/entry/on_powerjava_roles_instead_of, jan 2013, [Online; accessed 28-May-2014].

[35] T. Kamina and T. Tamai, "Towards safe and flexible object adaptation," in International Workshop on Context-Oriented Programming. ACM, 2009, p. 4.

[36] T. T. S. Monpratarnchai, "The design and implementation of a role model based language, EpsilonJ," in Proceedings of the 5th International Conference on Electrical Engineering/Electronics, Computer, Telecommunications and Information Technology (ECTI-CON 2008), 2008.

[37] M. Pradel and M. Odersky, "Scala Roles - A lightweight approach towards reusable collaborations," in International Conference on Software and Data Technologies (ICSOFT '08), 2008.

[38] M. Leuthäuser, "SCROLLCompilerPlugin," https://github.com/max-leuthaeuser/SCROLLCompilerPlugin, 2016, [last viewed 01.12.2016, 09.00].

[39] S. Karol, P. Incardona, Y. Afshar, I. F. Sbalzarini, and J. Castrillon, "Towards a next-generation parallel particle-mesh," in Proceedings of the 3rd Workshop on Domain-Specific Language Design and Implementation (DSLDI 2015), T. van der Storm and S. Erdweg, Eds., 2015, vol. abs/1508.03536, pp. 7–8. [Online]. Available: http://arxiv.org/abs/1508.03536

A Component Framework for Adapting to Elastic Resources in Clouds

Ichiro Satoh
National Institute of Informatics
2-1-2 Hitotsubashi, Chiyoda-ku, Tokyo 101-8430, Japan
ichiro@nii.ac.jp

Abstract—**The notion of *elasticity*, which enables capabilities and resources to be dynamically provisioned and released, is an adaptive mechanism for managing resources in cloud computing. However, most existing applications for cloud computing cannot support *elastic* capabilities and resources. To solve this problem, this paper proposes an approach for adapting distributed applications in response to elastic changes in their resource availability. The approach can divide a component into more than one components and merge more than one components whose program codes are common into a component by using user defined functions for dividing and merging the data stored at key-value stores. It was constructed as a middleware system for general-purpose software components with the two functions. This paper presents the basic ideas, design, and implementation of the approach evaluates the proposed approach.**

Keywords: Cloud computing, Elasticity, Software deployment

I. Introduction

Cloud computing has recently emerged as a compelling paradigm for managing and delivering services over the Internet. The notion of *elasticity*, which enables capabilities and resources to be dynamically provisioned and released, is an adaptive mechanism for managing resources in cloud computing as a material property with the capability of returning to its original state after a deformation. For example, the NIST definition of cloud computing [10] states that capabilities can be elastically provisioned and released, in some cases automatically, to scale rapidly outward and inward in accordance with demand. To the consumer, the capabilities available for provisioning often appear to be unlimited and can be appropriated in any quantity at any time.

In a cloud computing platform, services are delivered with transparency not considering the physical implementation within the platform. However, the conventional design and development of applications for cloud computing are not able to adapt themselves to elastically provisioning and deprovisioning resources in cloud computing. Furthermore, it is difficult to deprive parts of the computational resources that such applications have already used. There have been a few attempts to solve this problem. For example, Mesos [4] is a platform for sharing commodity clusters between distributed data processing frameworks such as Hadoop and Spark. These frameworks themselves are elastic in the sense that they have the ability to scale their resources up or down, i.e., they can start using resources as soon as applications want to acquire the resources or release the resources as soon as the applications do not need them.

This paper assumes that applications are running on dynamic distributed systems, including cloud computing platforms, in the sense that computational resources available from the applications may be dynamically changed due to elasticity. We propose a framework for enabling distributed applications to be adapted to changes in their available resources on elastic distributed systems as much as possible. The key ideas behind the framework are the duplication and migration of running software components and the integration of multiple same components into single components by using the notion of the MapReduce processing [2]. To adapt distributed applications, which consist of software components, to elasticity in cloud computing, the framework divides applications into some of the components and deploys the components at servers, which are provisioned, and merges the components running at servers, which are deprovisioned, into other components running at other available servers. We construct a middleware system for adapting general-purpose software components to changes at elastic resources in cloud computing.

This paper consists of the following sections. In Section II, we surveys related work. Section III present the basic ideas of the approach presented in this paper. Section IV describes the design and implementation of the system. We show the systems' evaluation in Section V and give some concluding remarks Section VI.

II. Related Work

Before presenting our framework, we discuss existing dynamic resource managements in cloud computing, including elastic resource allocation. Cloud computing platforms allow for novel ways of efficient execution and management of complex distributed systems, such as elastic resource provisioning and global distribution of application components. Resource allocation management has been studied for several decades in various contexts in distributed systems, including cloud computing. We focus here on only the most relevant work in the context of large-scale server clusters and cloud computing in distributed systems. Several recent studies have analyzed cluster traces from Yahoo!, Google, and Facebook and illustrate the challenges of scale and heterogeneity inherent in these modern data centers and workloads. Mesos [4] splits the resource management and placement functions between a central resource manager and multiple data processing frameworks such as Hadoop and Spark by using an offer-based mechanism. Resource allocation is performed in a central kernel and master-slave architecture with a two-level scheduling system. With Mesos, reclaim of resources is handled for unallocated capacity that is given to a framework. The Google Borg system [11] is an example of a monolithic scheduler that supports both batch jobs and long-running services. It provides a single RPC interface to support both types of workload. Each Borg cluster consists of multiple cells, and it scales by distributing the master functions among multiple processes and using multi-threading. YARN [13] is a Hadoop-centric cluster manager. Each application has a manager that negotiates for the resources it needs with a central resource manager. These systems assume the execution of particular applications, e.g., Hadoop and Spark, or can assign resources to their applications before the applications start. In contrast, our framework enables running applications to adapt themselves to changes in their available resources.

Several academic and commercial projects have explored attempts to create auto-scaling applications. Most of them have used static mechanisms in the sense that they are based on models to be defined and tuned at design time. The variety of available resources with different characteristics and costs, variability and unpredictability of workload conditions, and different effects of various configurations of resource allocations make the problem extremely hard if not impossible to solve algorithmically at design time.

Reconfiguration of software systems at runtime to achieve specific goals has been studied by several researchers. For example, Jaeger et al. [6] introduced the notion of self-organization to an object request broker and a publish / subscribe system. Lymberopoulos et al. [9] proposed a specification for adaptations based on their policy specification, *Ponder* [1], but it was aimed at specifying management and security policies rather than application-specific processing and did not support the mobility of components. Lupu and Sloman [8] described typical conflicts between multiple adaptations based on the Ponder language. Garlan et al. [3] presented a framework called Rainbow that provided a language for specifying self-adaptation. The framework supported adaptive connections between operators of components that might be running on different computers. They intended to adapt coordinations between existing software components to changes in distributed systems, instead of increasing or decreasing the number of components.

Most existing attempts have been aimed at provisioning of resources, e.g., the work of Sharman at al. [12]. Therefore, there have been a few attempts to adapt applications to deprovisioned resources. Nevertheless, they explicitly or implicitly assume that their target applications are initially constructed on the basis of master-slave and redundant architectures. Several academic and commercial systems tried introducing *live-migration* of virtual machines (VMs) into their systems, but they could not merge between applications, because they were running on different VMs. Jung et al.[7] have focused on controllers that take into account the costs of system adaptation actions considering both the applications (e.g., the horizontal scaling) and the infrastructure (e.g., the live migration of virtual machines and virtual machine CPU allocation) concerns. Thus, they differ from most cloud providers, which maintain a separation of concerns, hiding infrastructure-level control decisions from cloud clients.

III. Basic Approach

To use *elastic* resources provided in cloud computing platforms, applications need to adapt themselves to changes in their available resources due to elasticity. To solve this problem, we will propose a framework to adapt applications to the provisioning and deprovisioning of servers, which may be running on physical or virtual machines, and software containers, such as Docker, by providing an additional layer of abstraction and automation of virtualization. Our framework assumes that each application consists of one or more software components that may be running on different computers. It has four requirements.

- *Supports elasticity:* Elasticity allows applications to use more resources when needed and fall back afterwards. Therefore, applications need to be adapted to dynamically increasing and decreasing their available resources.
- *Self-adaptation:* Distributed systems essentially lack a global view due to communication latency between computers. Software components, which may be running on different computers, need to coordinate themselves to support their applications with partial knowledge about other computers.
- *Non-centralized management:* There is no central entity to control and coordinate computers. Our adaptation should be managed without any centralized management so that we can avoid any single points of failures and performance bottlenecks to ensure reliability and scalability.
- *Separation of concerns:* All software components should be defined independently of our adaptation mechanism as much as possible. This will enable developers to concentrate on their own application-specific processing.

There are various applications running on a variety of distributed systems. Therefore, the framework should be implemented as a practical middleware system to support general-purpose applications. We also assume that, before the existence of deprovisioning servers, the target cloud computing platform can notify servers about the deprovisioning after a certain time. Existing commercial or non-commercial cloud computing platform can be classified into three types: Infrastructure as a Service (IaaS), Platform as a Service (PaaS), and Software as a Service (SaaS). The framework is intended to be used in the second and third, but as much as possible it does not distinguish between the two.

To adapt applications to changes in their available resources due to elasticity, the framework adapts the applications to dynamically provisioning and de-provisioning resources (Fig. 1).

- *Dynamically provisioning resources* When provisioning servers, if a particular component is busy and the servers can satisfy the requirement of that component, the framework divides the component into two components and deploys one of them at the servers, where the divided components have the same programs but their internal data can be replicated or divided in accordance with application-specific data divisions.
- *Dynamically deprovisioning resources* When deprovisioning servers, components running on the servers are relocated to other servers that can satisfy the requirements of the components. If other components whose programs are the same as the former components co-exist on the latter servers, the framework instructs the deployed components to be merged to the original components.

The first and second adaptations need to deploy components at different computers. Our framework introduces mobile agent technology. When migrating and duplicating components, their internal states stored in their heap areas are transmitted to their destinations and are replicated at their clones.

The framework provides another data store for dividing and merging components. To do this, it introduces two notions: *key-value store* (KVS) and *reduce* functions of the *MapReduce* processing. The KVS offers a range of simple functions for manipulation of unstructured data objects, called *values*, each of which is identified by a unique *key*. Such a KVS is implemented as an array of *key* and *value* pairs. Our framework provides KVSs for components so that each component can maintain its internal state in its KVS. Our KVSs are used to pass the internal data of components to other components and to merge the internal data of components into their unified data. The framework also provides a mechanism to divide and merge components with their internal states stored at KVSs by using *MapReduce* processing. *MapReduce* is a most typical modern computing models for processing large data sets in distributed systems. It was originally studied by Google [2] and inspired by the *map* and *reduce* functions commonly used in parallel list processing (LISP) and functional programming paradigms.

- *Component division* Each duplicated component can inherit partial or all data stored in its original component in accordance with user-defined *partitioning* functions, where each function map of each item of data in its original component's KVS is stored in either the original component's KVS or the duplicated component's KVS without any redundancy.
- *Component fusion* When unifying two components that generated from the same programs into a single component, the data stored in the KVSs of the two components are merged by using user-defined *reduce* functions. These functions are similar to the *reduce* functions of MapReduce processing. Each of our *reduce* functions processes two values of the same keys and then maps the results to the entries of the keys. Figure 1 shows two examples of *reduce* functions. The first concatenates values in the same keys of the KVSs of the two components, and the second sums the values in the same keys of their KVSs.

IV. Design and Implementation

This section presents the design and implementation of our framework. It consists of two parts: component runtime system and components. The former is responsible for executing, duplicating, and migrating components. The later is autonomous programmable entities like software agents. The current implementation is built on our original mobile agent platform as existing mobile agent platforms are not optimized for data processing.

A. Adaptation for elastic resources

When provisioning servers, the framework can divide a component into two components whose data can be divided before deploying one of them at the servers. When deprovisioning servers, the framework can merge components that are running on the servers into other components.

1) Dividing component: When dividing a component into two, the framework has two approaches for sharing between the states of the original and clone components.

- *Sharing data in heap space* Each runtime system makes one or more copies of components. The runtime system can store the states of each agent in heap space in addition to the codes of the agent in a bit-stream formed in Java's JAR file format, which can support digital signatures for authentication. The current system basically uses the Java object serialization package for marshalling agents. The package does not support the capturing of stack frames of threads. Instead, when an agent is duplicated, the runtime system issues events to it to invoke their specified methods, which should be executed before it is duplicated, and it then suspends their active threads.
- *Sharing data in KVS* When dividing a component into two components, the KVS inside the former is

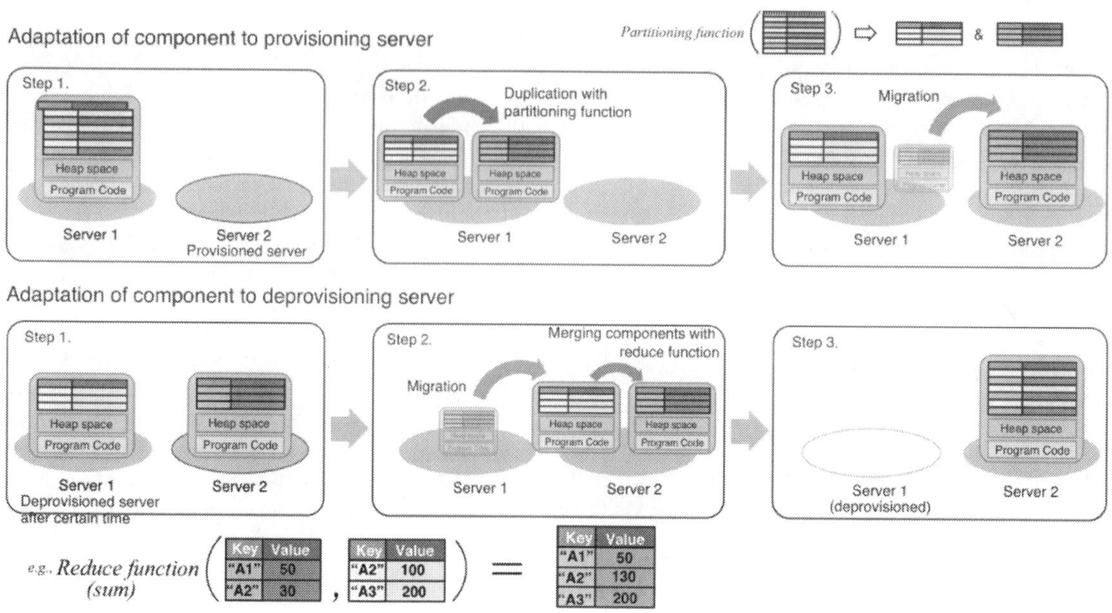

Figure 1. Adaptation to (de)provisioning servers

divided into two KVSs in accordance with user-defined partitioning functions in addition to built-in functions, and the divided KVSs are maintained inside the latter. Partitioning functions are responsible for dividing the intermediate key space and assigning intermediate key-value pairs to the original and duplicated components. In other words, the partition functions specify the components to which an intermediate key-value pair must be copied. KVSs are constructed as in-memory storage to exchange data between components. It provides tree-structured KVSs inside components. In the current implementation, each KVS in each data processing agent is implemented as a hash table whose keys, given as pairs of arbitrary string values, and values are byte array data, and it is carried with its agent between nodes,

where a default partitioning function is provided that uses hashing. This tends to result in fairly well-balanced partitions. The simplest partitioning functions involve computing the hash value of the key and then taking the mod of that value using the number of the original and duplicated components.

2) Merging components: The framework provides a mechanism to merge the data stored in the KVSs of different components instead of the data stored inside their heap spaces. Like the *reduce* of MapReduce processing, the framework enables us to define a *reduce* function that merges all intermediate values associated with the same intermediate key. When merging two components, the framework can discard the states of their heap spaces or keep the state of the heap space of one of them. Instead, the data stored in the KVSs of different components can be shared. A *reduce* function is applied to all values associated with the same intermediate key to generate output key-value pairs. The framework can merge more than two components at the same computers because components can migrate to the computers that execute co-components that the former wants to merge to.

V. Evaluation

Although the current implementation was not constructed for performance, we evaluated the performance of our current implementation. We evaluated the performance of our framework with CoreOS, which is a lightweight operating system based on Linux with JDK version 1.8 with Docker, which is software-based environment that automates the deployment of applications inside software containers by providing an additional layer of abstraction and automation of operating-system-level virtualization on Linux, on Amazon EC2. For each dimension of the adaptation process with respect to a specific resource type, elasticity captures the following core aspects of the adaptation:

- *Adaptation latency at provisioning servers* The response time of scaling up is defined as the time it takes to switch from provisioning of servers by the underlying system, e.g., cloud computing platform.
- *Adaptation latency at deprovisioning servers* The response time of scaling down is defined as the time it takes to switch from deprovisioning of servers by the underlying system, e.g., cloud computing platform.

The latency at scaling up or down does not correspond directly to the technical resource provisioning or deprovisioning time. Table I shows the basic performance. The component was simple and consisted of basic callback methods. The cost included that of invoking two callback methods. The cost of component migration included that of opening TCP transmission, marshaling the agents, migrating the agents from their source computers to their destination computers, unmarshalling the components, and verifying security.

Table I
BASIC OPERATION PERFORMANCE

	Latency (ms)
Duplicating component	10
Merging component	8
Migrating component between two servers	32

Figure 2 shows the latency of the number of divided and merged components at provisioning and deprovisioning servers. The experiment provided only one server to run our target component, which was a simple HTTP server (its size was about 100 KB). It added one server every ten seconds until there were eight servers and then removed one server every ten seconds after 80 seconds had passed. The number of components was measured as the average of the numbers in ten experiments. Although elasticity is always considered with respect to one or more resource types, the experiment presented in this paper focuses on cloud computing platforms for executing components, e.g., servers. There are two metrics in an adaptation to elastic resources, *scalability* and *efficiency*, where scalability is the ability of the system to sustain increasing workloads by making use of additional resources, and efficiency expresses the amount of resources consumed for processing a given amount of work.

- $\overline{A}$ is the average time to switch from an underprovisioned state to an optimal or overprovisioned state and corresponds to the average latency of scaling up or scaling down.
- $\overline{U}$ is the average amount of underprovisioned resources during an underprovisioned period. $\sum \overline{U}$ is the accumulated amount of underprovisioned resources and corresponds to the blue areas in Fig. 2.
- $\overline{D}$ is the average amount of overprovisioned resources during an overprovisioned period. $\sum \overline{D}$ is the accumulated amount of underprovisioned resources and corresponds to the red areas in Fig. 2.

The precision of scaling up or down is defined as the absolute deviation of the current amount of allocated resources from the actual resource provisioning or deprovisioning. We define the average precision of scaling up P_u and that of scaling down P_d. The efficiency of scaling up or down is defined as the absolute deviation of the accumulated amount of underprovisioned or overprovisioned resources from the accumulated amount of provisioned or deprovisioned resources, specified as E_U or E_D.

$$P_u = \frac{\sum \overline{U}}{T_u} \quad P_d = \frac{\sum \overline{D}}{T_d} \quad E_u = \frac{\sum \overline{U}}{R_u} \quad E_d = \frac{\sum \overline{D}}{R_d}$$

where T_u and T_d are the total durations of the evaluation periods and R_u and R_d are the accumulated amounts of provisioned resources when scaling up and scaling down phases, respectively. Table II shows the precision and efficiency of our framework.

Table II
BASIC OPERATION EFFICIENCY

	Rate
P_u (Precision of scaling up)	99.2 %
P_d (Precision of scaling down)	99.1 %
E_u (Efficiency of scaling up)	99.6 %
E_d (Efficiency of scaling down)	99.4 %

In the experiment the target component is a simple HTTP server, since web applications have very dynamic workloads generated by variable numbers of users, and they face sudden peaks in the case of unexpected events. Therefore, dynamic resource allocation is necessary not only to avoid application performance degradation but also to avoid underutilized resources. The experimental results showed that our framework could follow the elastically provisioning and deprovisioning of resources quickly, and the number of the components followed the number of elastic provisioning and deprovisioning of resources exactly. The framework was scalable because its adaptation latency was independent of the number of servers.

VI. CONCLUSION

This paper presented a mechanism for adapting application-level software to changes in available resources in cloud computing platforms. The mechanism was constructed as a framework that enabled distributed applications to adapt themselves to changes in their available resources in distributed systems, in particular cloud computing platforms. It was useful for adapting applications to elasticity in cloud computing. The key ideas behind the framework are *dynamic deployment of components* and *dividing and merging components*. The former enabled components to relocate themselves at new servers when provisioning the servers and at remaining servers when de-provisioning the servers, and the latter enables the states of components to be divided, and passed to other components, and merged with other components in accordance with user-defined functions. We believe that our framework is useful because it enables applications to be operated with elastic capabilities and resources in cloud computing.

REFERENCES

[1] N. Damianou, N. Dulay, E. Lupu, and M. Sloman: The Ponder Policy Specification Language, in Proceedings of Workshop on Policies for Distributed Systems and Networks (POLICY'95), pp.18–39, Springer-Verlag, 1995.

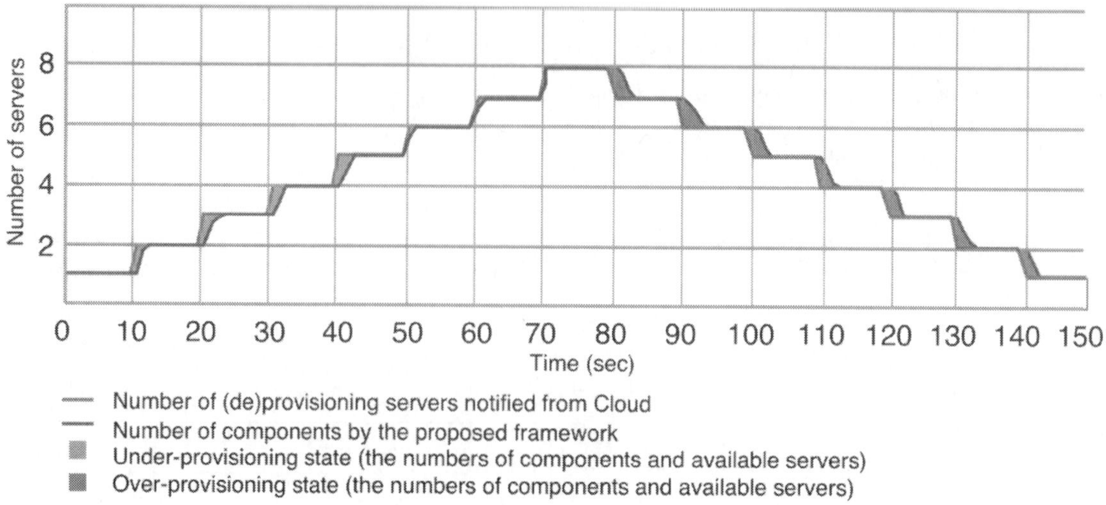

Figure 2. Number of components at (de)provisioning servers

[2] J. Dean and S. Ghemawat: MapReduce: simplified data processing on large clusters, in Proceedings of the 6th conference on Symposium on Opearting Systems Design and Implementation (OSDI'04), 2004.

[3] D. Garlan, S.W. Cheng, A.C.Huang, B. R. Schmerl, P. Steenkiste: Rainbow: Architecture-Based Self-Adaptation with Reusable Infrastructure, IEEE Computer Vol.37, No.10, pp.46-54, 2004.

[4] B. Hindman, A. Konwinski, M. Zaharia, A. Ghodsi, A. Joseph, R. Katz, S. Shenker, and I. Stoica. Mesos: a platform for fine-grained resource sharing in the data center In Proceedings of USENIX Symposium on Networked Systems Design and Implementation (NSDI), 2011.

[5] C. Inzinger, at al., Decisions, Models, and Monitoring–A Lifecycle Model for the Evolution of Service-Based Systems, In Proceedings of Enterprise Distributed Object Computing Conference (EDOC), pp.185-194, IEEE Computer Society, 2013.

[6] M. A. Jaeger, H. Parzyjegla, G. Muhl, K. Herrmann: Self-organizing broker topologies for publish/subscribe systems, in Proceedings of ACM symposium on Applied Computing (SAC'2007), pp.543-550, ACM, 2007.

[7] G. Jung, et. al.: A Cost-Sensitive Adaptation Engine for Server Consolidation of Multitier Applications, In Proceedings of Middleware'2009, LNCS, Vol.5896, pp.163183, Springer, 2009.

[8] E. Lupu and M. Sloman: Conflicts in Policy-Based Distributed Systems Management, IEEE Transaction on Software Engineering, Vol.25, No.6, pp.852-869, 1999.

[9] L. Lymberopoulos, E. Lupu, M. Sloman: An Adaptive Policy Based Management Framework for Differentiated Services Networks, in Proceedings of 3rd International Workshop on Policies for Distributed Systems and Networks (POLICY 2002), pp.147-158, IEEE Computer Society, 2002.

[10] P. Mell, T. Grance: The NIST Definition of Cloud Computing, Technical report of U.S. National Institute of Standards and Technology (NIST), Special Publication 800-145, 2011.

[11] A. Verma, L. Pedrosa, M. Korupolu, D. Oppenheimer, E. Tune, and J. Wilkes: Large-scale cluster management at Google with Borg, EuroSys15, ACM 2015.

[12] U. Sharma, P. Shenoy, S. Sahu, A. Shaikh: A cost-aware elasticity provisioning system for the cloud In Proceedings of International Conference on Distributed Computing Systems (ICDCS'2011), pp.559570, IEEE Computer Society, 2011.

[13] V. K. Vavilapalli, el. al.,: Apache Hadoop YARN: Yet Another Resource Negotiator, In Proceedings of Symposium on Cloud Computing (SoCC'2013), ACM, 2013.

[14] World Wide Web Consortium (W3C): Composite Capability/Preference Profiles (CC/PP), http://www.w3.org/TR/NOTE-CCPP, 1999.

A Component Model for Limited Resource Handling in Adaptive Systems

Karina Rehfeldt, Mirco Schindler, Benjamin Fischer and Andreas Rausch

Technische Universitt Clausthal
Clausthal-Zellerfeld, Germany
email: {karina.rehfeldt, mirco.schindler, benjamin.fischer, andreas.rausch}@tu-clausthal.de

Abstract—**Dynamic adaptive systems are systems that change their behavior at run time, based on system, user, environment and context information and needs. System configuration in terms of structure and behavior of open, self-organized systems cannot completely be predicted beforehand: New components may join, others may leave the system, or the behavior of individual components of the system may change over time. These components may compete for limited resources. Especially in Internet of Things (IoT) applications where service consumers directly interact with service providers, the necessity for a fair and lightweight resource access method arises. Therefore, we have elaborated a method which allocates provided services to applications based on a fair and distributed process. Our approach has been implemented on top of our component model called Dynamic Adaptive System Infrastructure (DAiSI).**

Keywords–dynamic adaptive systems; decentralized configuration; resource allocation.

I. Introduction

Software-based systems pervade our daily life at work as well as at home. Public administration or enterprise organizations can scarcely be managed without software-based systems. We come across devices executing software in nearly every household. The continuous increase in size and functionality of software systems has made some of them among the most complex man-made systems ever devised [1].

In the last two decades, the trend towards 'everything, every time, everywhere' has been dramatically increased through a) smaller mobile devices with higher computation and communication capabilities, b) ubiquitous availability of the Internet (almost all devices are connected with the Internet and thereby connected with each other), and c) devices equipped with more and more connected, intelligent and sophisticated sensors and actuators. These trends also pushed research subjects like Internet of Things (IoT) and applications for smart devices, like smart City, smart home or applications in financial and health technology.

Nowadays, these devices are increasingly used within an organically grown, heterogeneous, and dynamic IT environment. Users expect them not only to provide their primary services but also to collaborate autonomously with each other and thus to provide real added additional value. The challenge is therefore to provide software systems that are correct, stable and robust in the presence of increasing challenges such as change and complexity [2]. Especially in the Internet of Things Domain small autonomous devices are expected to interact and collaborate on their own. Nevertheless, the provided services should be stable and reliable.

In open IoT Systems new sensors, actuators and services may enter the system environment at any time and others may leave the system. Hence, it is essential that our systems are able to adapt to maintain the satisfaction of the user expectations and environmental changes in terms of an evolutionary change.

Dynamic change, in contrast to evolutionary change, occurs while the system is operational. Dynamic change requires that the system adapts at run time. Therefore, we must plan for automated management of adaptation. The systems themselves must be capable of determining what system change is required and initiate and manage the change process wherever needed. This is the aim of self-managed systems.

Providing dynamic adaptive systems is a great challenge in software engineering [2]. In order to provide dynamic adaptive systems, the activities of classical development approaches have to be partially or completely moved from development time to run time. For instance, devices and software components can be attached to a dynamic adaptive system at any time. Consequently, devices and software components can be removed from the dynamic adaptive system or they can fail as the result of a defect. Hence, for dynamic adaptive systems, system integration takes place during run time. In our research group, we have for more than ten years developed a framework for dynamic adaptive (and distributed) systems, called Dynamic Adaptive System Infrastructure (DAiSI).

DAiSI is a service-oriented and component based platform to implement dynamic adaptive systems. Components can be integrated into or removed from a dynamic adaptive system at run-time without causing a complete application to fail. To meet this requirement, each component can react to changes in its environment and adapt its behavior accordingly.

At first, it was only possible for components to ask for a special service based on a domain interface they referred to. In [3], we extended the DAiSI component model by the concept of interface roles which takes runtime information in account for the composition and connection of services. With interface roles a domain interface can be enriched. It allows specifying the role of the interface on the basis of runtime information, like the value of a specific parameter.

In DAiSI, the components connect on local optimization views. Each and every component tries to achieve their best local configuration but the resulting overall system configuration might not meet any global optimization goals or fails to meet context requirements. Therefore, we have elaborated an approach to specify context requirements. We introduced the concept of service application specification and component templates in [4]. A service application specification consists of a set of component templates. A template is a placeholder for a set of component with specific properties. The template can be described without knowing individual components. During run time, DAiSI matches existing components to templates autonomously. With this approach an application is build which meets context requirements.

The development of DAiSI was always motivated through running application examples and demonstrators. As DAiSI has been developed for more than ten years, we have demonstrated the application of our approach and our infrastructure in a couple of different research demonstrators and industrial prototypes and products [5] or [6].

Nowadays, IoT-Applications are an emerging field. IoT is different to classic monolithic software systems. Instead of one big application multiple applications for various users are needed. In the EU project BIG IoT [7], an architecture for interoperable IoT-Systems is introduced. The general idea is to use a central marketplace where service and data providers register their service offerings and service consumers are able to search for their required services and data. But to keep the system scalable, the marketplace only takes care of establishing the connection between consumer and provider. If the consumer directly interacts with providers the necessity to control resource access arises. Since there is no central instance to take care of resource management a distributed method is needed. But also, the method to allocate provider resources for consumers should be fair and lightweight.

The goal of this paper is to introduce such a method on top of the DAiSI component model. The rest of this paper is structured as follows: In Section II, we give an overview of relevant related work. Section III gives a short overview of the DAiSI component model with a few hints for further reading. Our extension for limited resource handling is introduced in Section IV, before the paper is wrapped up by a short conclusion in Section V.

II. Related Work

In the field of large-scale systems component-based development is a solid and state-of-the-art approach [8], [9], [10].

In many cases the used framework influences the architectural structure of a system or the other way around a framework is chosen cause of the underlying architecture and its concepts. One example for component based development are middlewares, which not only defines services and establish an infrastructure, but also specifies a component model on top [11]. The CORBA Component Model (CCM) [12] from CORBA [13], a component based middleware, describes different types of communication as synchronous or asynchronous calls by the port type. These ports are characterized in the interface description of the component.

Another example is the middleware DREAM [14], which defines atomic and composed components, so the interconnection between components could be hierarchical. The connection of components takes place at runtime, but it allows only asynchronous communication. The component model of the middleware RUNES [15] allows the dynamic adding and termination of components at runtime, too as CORBA and DREAM. Furthermore it supports the implementation of a separate algorithm, which realize the arrangement of components.

One of the first frameworks, which supports dynamic adaptive reconfiguration was CONIC. A CONIC application was maintained by a centralized configuration manager [16]. Besides it provides a description technique to adapt and modify the structure of the integrated modules of an application. Another framework, building on the knowledge gained through the research in CONIC, was a framework for Reconfigurable and Extensible Parallel and Distributed Systems (REX) [17]. This frameworks defines its own interface description language to specify the interconnection. Components were considered as types, allowing multiple instances of any component to be present at run-time. The framework allowed the dynamic change of the number of running instances and their wiring [18]. Both, the CONIC and REX framework allowed the dynamic adaptation of distributed applications, but only through explicit reconfiguration programs for every possible reconfiguration.

R-OSGi [19] takes advantage of the features developed for centralized module management in the OSGi platform, like dynamic module loading and unloading. It introduces a way to transparently use remote OSGi modules in an application while still preserving good performance. Issues like network disruptions or unresponsive components are mapped to events of unloaded modules and thus can be handled gracefully a strength compared to many other platforms. However, R-OSGi does not provide means to specify application architecture specific requirements. As long as modules are compatible with each other they will be linked. The module developer has to ensure the application architecture at the implementation level. Opposed to that, our approach proposes a high level description of application architectures through application templates that can be specified even after the required components have been developed.

There are many service-oriented approaches and service-orientated Architectures (SOA) [20], which are capable to handle a dynamic behavior. Unknown components can be integrated into it. However, they have the uncomfortable characteristic that the system itself does not care for the dynamic adaptive behavior. The component needs to register and integrate itself. Also, it has to monitor itself whether the used services are still available and adapt its behavior accordingly, if that is no longer the case. But components can be developed independently and reused [21].

In the context of IoT, Stankovic highlighted in [22] eight research topics and challenges. One of them are "Architecture and Dependencies", he mentioned that the sharing of components across simultaneously running applications can result in many systems-of-systems interface problems. The main reason for this is the interaction with actors. A simple example is described in [22] also, imagine a Smart Home system controlling windows, shades and thermostats. If the sensors and actuators are shared between applications, than it could lead to conflicts when these applications have there own assumptions and strategies to modify the room temperature. As shown in [23] this problem occurs always if a resource like an actuator is limited or applications are competing for these resources. This leads to specific infrastructures like DepSys [24] a sensor and actuator infrastructure for smart homes that provides comprehensive strategies to specify, detect, and resolve conflicts.

Anders and Lehner presented a decentralized graph-based approach for agent networks to solve resource allocation problems [25]. Their approach works for structures where you can easily derive such a network like in smart grid systems.

But we are looking at systems where the agents are changing at runtime and where no clear network for resource exchange can be determined.

Therefore we are using a market-based approach like the ones introduced in [26]. Market-based approaches are generally useful because of their simplicity but effectiveness to achieve a sustainable solution by using little information like price and offer and simple interaction like trading. As presented in the next sections our approach builds up on distributed component models and handles the conflicts of limited resources in a general and generic way.

III. DAiSI Component Model

In this section, we want to shortly introduce the existing DAiSi component model. We build our extension on top of the existing component model in section IV. We will use a common example throughout the whole paper which we will introduce next.

Imagine a biathlon training center. The training center consists of a skiing track and a shooting range with several shooting lanes. Biathlon teams are able to train under their trainer's watch. The training center provides a training overview system for each trainer where he can see the current training data of his athletes. For that purpose, each athlete is equipped with at least a pulse sensor. Moreover, a device which measures the currently used skiing technique is attached to the athlete's gear.

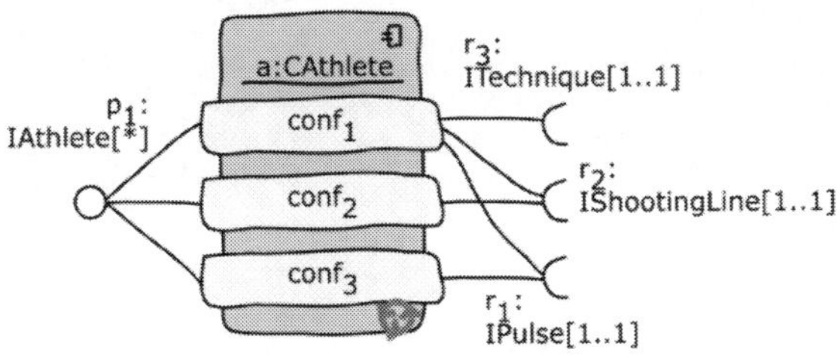

Figure 1. A DAiSI component representing an athlete.

The DAiSI component model is best explained with an example. In Fig. 1, a DAiSI component representing a biathlon athlete is shown. The actual component is the blue rectangle in the background. A DAiSI component consists of different configurations, each of them including one or more provided and required services. The athlete has three different configurations depicted by yellow boxes. Configurations in DAiSI are ordered manually by the designer. The top-most configuration is the best one and therefore the one a component strives to achieve. In Fig. 1, each configuration offers the service IAthlete depicted with a full-circle based on the UML lollipop notation. Accordingly, a required service is depicted by a semicircle. The best configuration in our example requires three different services: ITechnique, a service provided by the skiing technique measuring device; IPulse, a service provided by the pulse device and IShootingLine which is the shooting line evaluating the shooting performance of an athlete.

Fig. 2 shows the DAiSI component model. The different aspects are covered in various papers which were published throughout the years. Therefore, we will stick to a general introduction here and refer to the detailed papers. The orange parts are the extensions introduced in this paper.

The domain architecture of a DAiSI application defines domain interfaces. On the basis of these domain interfaces is decided whether required and provided services can be connected. In [3], the domain interfaces are extended by interface roles. As already mentioned in the introduction interface roles allow the specification of additional constraints for the compatibility of interfaces that use run-time information, bound services and the internal state of a component.

Applications are used to specify context requirements. They narrow down the possible structure of a application configuration. Blueprints for components, so called Templates specify (needed and offered) RequiredTemplateInterfaces and ProvidedTemplateInterfaces which refer to DomainInterfaces and thus form a structure which can be filled with actual services and components by the infrastructure. A more detailed discussion about templates and applications can be found in [4].

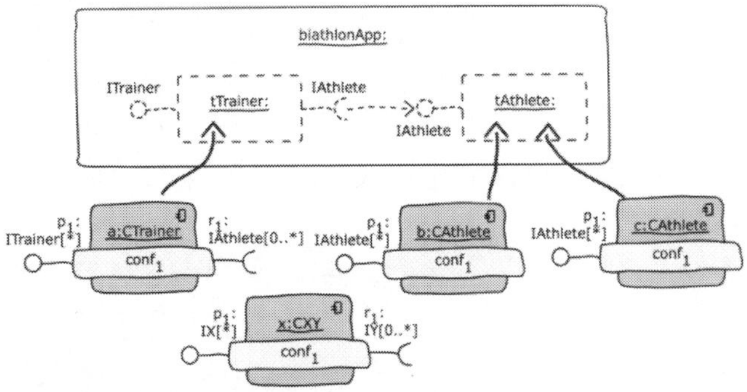

Figure 3. Example for an application with two different component templates.

Fig. 3 shows an example for the usage of templates and applications. biathlonApp specifies an application consisting of two component templates. The first component template tTrainer can be filled with components providing a service referring to the domain interface ITrainer and requiring a service referring to IAthlete. Following this, the second template tAthlete is compatible with components provding an IAthlete service.

With the interface roles and template extension we are now able to describe an application. But in the case of IoT-Domains with many different applications competing for limited resources we have to be able to describe the dependencies between different application instances. In the next section, we will show application scenarios in our biathlon training center introducing our mechanisms and structures for distributed limited resource handling.

IV. Limited Resource Handling on Top of DAiSI

Recall our biathlon example. We have different biathlon teams training in a training center with a limited amount of shooting lanes. Driven by scenarios on top of this example, we will introduce our extensions to the DAiSI component model which were introduced to handle limited resources. The mapping of components to templates and the creation of applications will then no longer be done simply on interface matching criterias but also with regards to resource assignments.

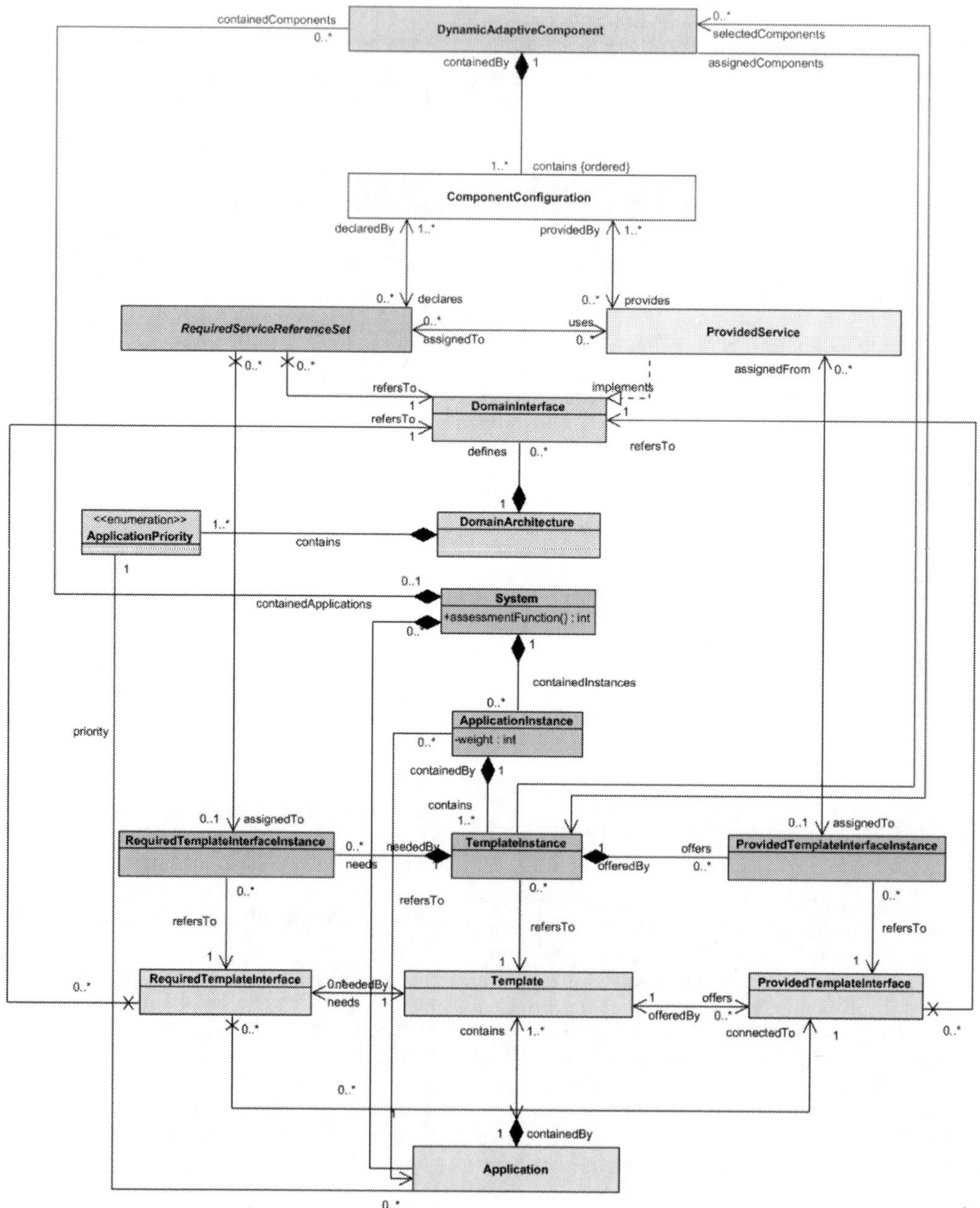

Figure 2. DAiSI component model with Application Instances.

The configuration mechanism of DAiSI which is lengthly introduced in [27], is extended by an agent-based mechanism to broker the association of resources. We will not introduce the technical algorithm here but the component model extension.

A. The Need for Application Instances

Two kind of teams are training in our training center: amateur teams and professional teams. They differ in their configuration and usage of training devices.

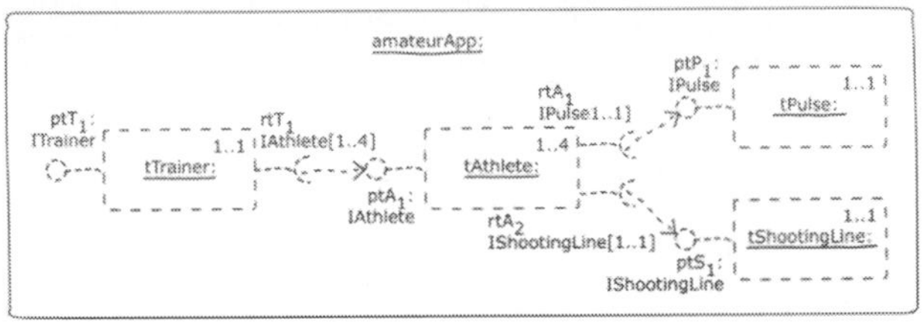

Figure 4. Application for amateur team.

Fig. 4 shows the application and templates for an amateur team. One trainer is training with up to 4 athletes. Each athlete has a pulse measuring device and can use a shooting line. On the other hand, Fig. 5 shows the professional team application. A professional athlete will always use a technique device also.

With the help of our component model until now, we can specify these two application types. But in the training center more than one amateur or professional team might be training. Therefore, the need to introduce an instance level arises. Application and template instances are the first extension made to the DAiSI component model.

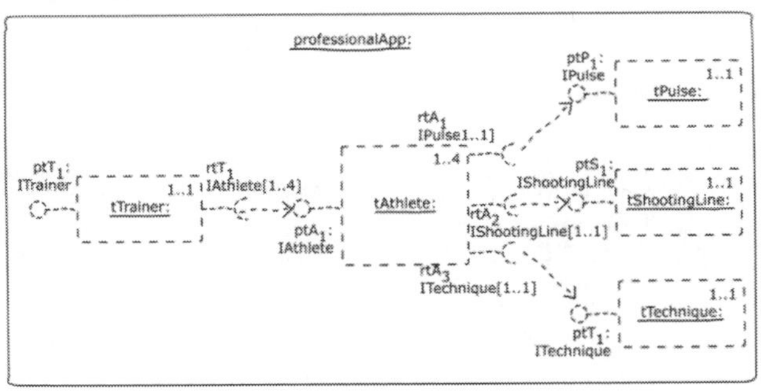

Figure 5. Application for professional team.

The orange parts in Fig. 2 are the extensions made to the component model for limited resource handling. To be able to model a system based on instances, we introduce application instances and template instances. They represent the instance level of our component model. Consequently, the components and provided/required services are no longer bound to the template types but to template instances.

Another new structure is the system. A system is a set of various application instances. It describes the overall configuration of a set of components in these application instances. Each of these application instances may use resources and may even share a resource if the resource allows.

With the help of this extension, we can now describe a system consisting of two amateur team application instances and one professional team application instance.

B. Application Priority

In our example, we have a clearly limited resource: the shooting lanes. Each shooting lane can only be used by one athlete at a time. So the shooting lanes directly influence how many athletes can train on the track. We assume that it is acceptable for a training amateur team to share the shooting lanes. But the professional athletes must have exclusive usage of a shooting lane to train under competitive conditions.

Also, the training of professional athletes is more important, so they should always be preferred to amateur teams. To be able to describe this in our component model, we use ApplicationPriority. ApplicationPriorities are priority classifications for application types. A DomainArchitecture (in our case the biathlon training domain) defines a set of ordered priorities. These priorities are considered by the configuration mechanism when it comes to limited resources. To put it simple, an application type with a higher priority will always be preferred to applications with lesser priority when it comes to limited resources.

Applied to our biathlon example it means that professional team application gets a higher priority than amateur team application. When a professional team wants to use the training center, the assignment of resources will always be in their favor. Application priorities act on type level. But we also need a mechanism for priority on instance level, for example when two different amateur team instances are training. This priority should include run time information because the priority of an application instance may change over time. In the next section, we will introduce our concept and motivate it by another example.

C. Weight

Now that we are able to account for priority on type level, we introduce our concept for priority on instance level. Every ApplicationInstance has a weight. The weight is an indicator for the configuration mechanism how valuable an application instance is for the overall system. During the assignment of resources the weights are used to decide which application ultimately gets the resource.

In our biathlon training center, a training schedule exists. It defines training times for teams. We assign each team instance a weight based on the training schedule. Thereby, we want to make sure that each team may train on their assigned training time but if there are still available shooting lanes in the center, additional teams may train. To be able to achieve that, we assign a team exactly on their training schedule the weight 1. The more the current time differs from their assigned training time, the lower the team's weight gets until it reaches 0. So for instance, until half an hour before their training schedule a team gets the weight 0, a quarter to their training schedule they get the weight 0.5 and exactly on their training schedule they get the weight 1.

Going back to our resource assigning mechanism, if two teams are competing for a shooting lane the team with higher weight, thus closer to their training schedule, will get the assignment of the shooting lane. But a team with weight

0 is also able to get the shooting lane, if no team with a higher weight is asking for it. In the case of same weights, the assignment has to be done randomly. In the end, we have extended our DAiSI component model by an instance level and priorities on type and instance level. With the help of these new features we are now able to handle limited resources on top of DAiSI. It exists a proof-of-concept implementation which will be published in the PhD-Thesis of Benjamin Fischer.

V. Conclusion

We introduced an enhancement to our DAiSI component model which allows modeling for limited resource handling. Limited resources are especially a problem in systems with competing applications or shared actuators, for instance IoT systems. To be able to model more than one possible application, which is necessary for IoT systems, an instance level was created. The assignment of resources may be decided on application type level on the basis of application priorities. Additionally, weights are used on application instance level to model the significance of an application instance to the overall systems.

Klus et. al [4] presented a configuration algorithm to assign components to applications. The introduced enhancement of the component model in this paper may be used in an extended configuration algorithm which also deals with the assignment of limited resources. A possible implementation is conceived and will be published in the PhD-Thesis of Benjamin Fischer.

References

[1] L. Northrop, P. Feiler, R. P. Gabriel, J. Goodenough, R. Linger, T. Longstaff, R. Kazman, M. Klein, D. Schmidt, K. Sullivan et al., "Ultra-large-scale systems: The software challenge of the future," DTIC Document, Tech. Rep., 2006.

[2] J. Kramer and J. Magee, "A rigorous architectural approach to adaptive software engineering," Journal of Computer Science and Technology, vol. 24, no. 2, 2009, pp. 183–188.

[3] H. Klus, D. Herrling, and A. Rausch, "Interface Roles for Dynamic Adaptive Systems," Proceedings of ADAPTIVE, 2015, pp. 80–84.

[4] H. Klus, A. Rausch, and D. Herrling, "Component Templates and Service Applications Specifications to Control Dynamic Adaptive System Configurations," in AMBIENT 2015, The Fifth International Conference on Ambient Computing, Applications, Services and Technologies, vol. 5. Nice, France: IARIA, Jul. 2015, pp. 42 – 51.

[5] A. Rausch, D. Niebuhr, M. Schindler, and D. Herrling, "Emergency management system," in Proceedings of the International Conference on Pervasive Services 2009 (ICSP 2009), 2009.

[6] C. Deiters, M. Köster, S. Lange, S. Lützel, B. Mokbel, C. Mumme, and D. Niebuhr, "Demsy-a scenario for an integrated demonstrator in a smartcity," NTH Computer Science Report, vol. 1, 2010.

[7] B. I. project. Bigiot - bridging the interoperability gap of the internet of things. [Online]. Available: http://big-iot.eu/ (2016)

[8] C. Szyperski, Component Software: Beyond Object-Oriented Programming (2nd Edition), 2nd ed. Addison-Wesley Professional, 2002. [Online]. Available: http://amazon.com/o/ASIN/0201745720/

[9] A. MacCormack, J. Rusnak, and C. Y. Baldwin, "The impact of component modularity on design evolution: Evidence from the software industry," SSRN Electronic Journal, 2007.

[10] B. Councill and G. T. Heineman, "Definition of a software component and its elements," Component-based software engineering: putting the pieces together, 2001, pp. 5–19.

[11] P. A. Bernstein, "Middleware: a model for distributed system services," Communications of the ACM, vol. 39, no. 2, 1996, pp. 86–98.

[12] N. Wang, D. C. Schmidt, and C. O'Ryan, "Overview of the corba component model: Component-based software engineering," G. T. Heineman and W. T. Councill, Eds. Boston, MA, USA: Addison-Wesley Longman Publishing Co., Inc, 2001, pp. 557–571. [Online]. Available: http://dl.acm.org/citation.cfm?id=379381.379581

[13] Object Management Group - OMG, "Corba component model specification," 2006. [Online]. Available: http://www.omg.org/spec/CCM/4.0/PDF

[14] M. Leclercq, V. Quéma, and J. Stefani, "Dream: a component framework for constructing resource-aware, configurable middleware," IEEE Distributed Systems Online, vol. 6, no. 9, 2005, p. 1.

[15] P. Costa, G. Coulson, C. Mascolo, G. P. Picco, and S. Zachariadis, "The runes middleware: A reconfigurable component-based approach to networked embedded systems," in 2005 IEEE 16th International Symposium on Personal, Indoor and Mobile Radio Communications, vol. 2, 2005, pp. 806–810.

[16] J. Magee, J. Kramer, and M. Sloman, "Constructing distributed systems in conic," IEEE Transactions on Software Engineering, vol. 15, no. 6, 1989, pp. 663–675.

[17] J. Kramer, J. Magee, M. Sloman, and N. Dulay, "Configuring object-based distributed programs in rex," Software Engineering Journal, vol. 7, no. 2, 1992, pp. 139–149.

[18] J. Kramer, "Configuration programming-a framework for the development of distributable systems," in COMPEURO'90: Proceedings of the 1990 IEEE International Conference on Computer Systems and Software Engineering-Systems Engineering Aspects of Complex Computerized Systems. IEEE, 1990, pp. 374–384.

[19] J. S. Rellermeyer, G. Alonso, and T. Roscoe, "R-osgi: distributed applications through software modularization," in Proceedings of the ACM/IFIP/USENIX 2007 International Conference on Middleware. Springer-Verlag New York, Inc., 2007, pp. 1–20.

[20] H. Li and Z. Wu, "Research on distributed architecture based on soa," in 2009 International Conference on Communication Software and Networks, pp. 670–674.

[21] M. Turner, D. Budgen, and P. Brereton, "Turning software into a service," Computer, vol. 36, no. 10, 2003, pp. 38–44.

[22] J. A. Stankovic, "Research directions for the internet of things," IEEE Internet of Things Journal, vol. 1, no. 1, 2014, pp. 3–9.

[23] Y. Yu, L. J. Rittle, V. Bhandari, and J. B. LeBrun, "Supporting concurrent applications in wireless sensor networks," in Proceedings of the 4th International Conference on Embedded Networked Sensor Systems, ser. SenSys '06. New York, NY, USA: ACM, 2006, pp. 139–152. [Online]. Available: http://doi.acm.org/10.1145/1182807.1182822

[24] S. Munir and J. A. Stankovic, "Depsys: Dependency aware integration of cyber-physical systems for smart homes," in 2014 ACM/IEEE International Conference on Cyber-Physical Systems (ICCPS), pp. 127–138.

[25] G. Anders and P. Lehner, "Self-Organized Graph-Based Resource Allocation," in Self-Adaptive and Self-Organizing Systems (SASO), 2016 IEEE 10th International Conference on, Sept 2016.

[26] S. H. Clearwater, Market-based control: A paradigm for distributed resource allocation. World Scientific, 1996.

[27] H. Klus, A. Rausch, and D. Herrling, "DAiSIDynamic Adaptive System Infrastructure: Component Model and Decentralized Configuration Mechanism," International Journal On Advances in Intelligent Systems, vol. 7, no. 3 and 4, 2014, pp. 595 – 608. [Online]. Available: http:sse-world.deindex.phpdownloadfileviewinline370

A Holistic Approach for Managed Evolution of Automotive Software Product Line Architectures

Christoph Knieke, Marco Körner, Andreas Rausch,
Mirco Schindler, Arthur Strasser, and Martin Vogel
TU Clausthal, Department of Computer Science, Software Systems Engineering
Clausthal-Zellerfeld, Germany
Email: {christoph.knieke|marco.koerner|andreas.rausch|
mirco.schindler|arthur.strasser|m.vogel}@tu-clausthal.de

***Abstract*—The automotive industry aspires a high degree of reuse in software development in order to reduce the development costs. The reuse is achieved by a product-wide development for different vehicle variants, as well as by reuse in subsequent products. However, the increasing complexity and degree of variability of automotive software systems hinders the capabilities for reusability and extensibility of these systems to an increasing degree. After several product generations, software erosion is growing steadily, resulting in an increasing effort of reusing software components, and planning of further development. Here, we give a holistic approach for a long-term manageable and plannable software product line architecture for automotive software systems. Furthermore, we consider automotive product development and prototyping based on software product lines, and propose an approach for architecture compliance checking to avoid software erosion. We demonstrate our methodology on a real world case study, a brake servo unit (BSU) software system from automotive software engineering.**

Keywords–Architecture Evolution; Software Product Lines; Software Erosion; Architecture Compliance Checking; Automotive.

I. Introduction

In the development of electronic control unit (ECU) software for vehicles, the reduction of development costs and the increase of quality are essential objectives. A significant measure to achieve these goals is the reuse of software components [1]. The reuse is mainly achieved by a product-wide development for different vehicle variants: Different configurations of driver assistance systems, comfort functions, or powertrains can be variably combined, creating an individual and unique product. Furthermore, for each new vehicle generation, the software of preceding generations of the vehicle is reused or adopted [2].

However, the possibilities for reuse and extensibility of existing functions can not be fully exploited in many cases. Rather, it can be observed that due to the increase in so-called "accidental" complexity [2] (see Section V-B), the reusability and further developability reaches its limits. One reason for this is the lack of a product-line-oriented overall planning, based on the concepts of software product line engineering already established in other domains. A central factor here is the planning based on a product line architecture (PLA), on the specification of which the individual products are derived. The PLA describes the structure of all realizable products. Each product that is developed has an individual product architecture (PA) whose structure should be mapped onto the PLA.

However, an overall specification of a PLA is often missing in the automotive domain [3]: The knowledge of the overall, product independent structure is not explicitly documented, and therefore exists only implicitly in the minds of the participants. Here, we refer to the results shown in a preceding paper [3] to create a PLA as a prerequisite for our approach by applying strategies for architecture recovery and discovery.

However, the application of the software product line development must take into account the special properties, boundary conditions and requirements that exist in the automotive environment [4]. Therefore, a method adapted to the automotive environment is required and is presented in this paper.

An important aspect is the design and planning of further developments of the product line architecture. When designing the product line architecture, the architecture must be based on architecture principles appropriate for the automotive domain, aiming at reusability and further development [2]. Since a wide range of products can be affected by the further development of the product line architecture, changes must be carefully planned: High demands are placed on the reliability of the systems, but the reliability is endangered by extensive adaptations.

In the further development, it must be ensured that the product architecture remains compliant with the product line architecture. However, due to the high time and cost pressure in the automotive sector, it is not possible, for every further development to be controlled via the product line. Rather, some product-specific adjustments have to be made. This can lead (intentionally or unintentionally) to a product architecture that differs in comparison to the product line architecture: the architecture erodes. In the long term, this leads to reduced reusability and extensibility of the software artifacts. Due to the size of the product line architecture, an automated consistency check is necessary, which is an essential part of our approach to counteract architectural erosion.

The major objectives of our approach can be summarized as follows:

- Long-term minimization of architecture erosion.
- High degree of reusability.
- Scalability to manage a huge number of variants in real world automotive systems.

The paper is structured as follows: Section II gives an overview on the related work. In Section III, we propose a methodology for managed evolution of automotive software product line architectures. Section IV introduces parts of the architecture description language, which we will refer to in the following sections. In Section V, we apply our approach on a real world example, a brake servo unit, from automotive software engineering. The results of a corresponding field study are evaluated and discussed in Section VI. Section VII concludes.

II. Related Work

To the best of our knowledge, no continuous overall development cycle for automotive software product line architectures exists. Several aspects of our process are already covered in literature:

A. Reference Architectures

The purpose of the reference architecture is to provide guidance for future developments. In addition, the reference architecture incorporates the vision and strategy for the future. The work in [5] examines current reference architectures and the driving forces behind development of them to come to a collective conclusion on what a reference architecture should truly be. Furthermore, in [5], reference architectures are assumed to be the basis for the instantiation of product line architectures (so-called family architectures, see [5]).

Nakagawa et. al. discuss the differences between reference architectures and product line architectures by highlighting basic questions like definitions, benefits, and motivation for using each one, when and how they should be used, built, and evolved, as well as stakeholders involved and benefited by each one [6]. Furthermore, they define a reference model of reference architectures [7], and propose a methodology to design product line architectures based on reference architectures [8][9].

B. Software Erosion

In [10], de Silva and Balasubramaniam provide a survey of technologies and techniques either to prevent architecture erosion or to detect and restore architectures that have been eroded. However, each approach discussed in [10] refers to architecture erosion for a single PA, whereas architecture erosion in software product lines are out of the scope of the paper. Furthermore, as discussed in [10], none of the available methods singly provides an effective and comprehensive solution for controlling architecture erosion.

Van Gurp and Bosch [11] illustrate how design erosion works by presenting the evolution of the design of a small software system. The paper concludes that even an optimal design strategy for the design phase does not lead to an optimal design. The reason for this are unforeseen requirement changes in later evolution cycles. These changes may cause design decisions taken earlier to be less optimal.

The work in [12] describes an approach to flexible architecture erosion detection for model-driven development approaches. Consistency constraints expressed by architectural aspects called architectural rules are specified as formulas on a common ontology, and models are mapped to instances of that ontology. A knowledge representation and reasoning system is then utilized to check whether these architectural rules are satisfied for a given set of models. Three case studies are presented demonstrating that architecture erosion can be minimized effectively by the approach.

C. Software Product Line Architectures

As discussed in [3] an overall automotive product line architecture is often missing due to software sharing. Thus, architecture recovery and discovery has to be applied by concepts of software product line extraction [3]. The aim of software product line extraction is to identify all the valid points of variation and the associated functional requirements of component diagrams. The work in [13] shows an approach to extract a product line from a user documentation. The Product Line UML-based Software Engineering (PLUS) approach permits variability analysis based on use case scenarios and the specification of variable properties in a feature model [14]. In [15], variability of a system characteristic is described in a feature model as variable features that can be mapped to use cases. In contrast to our approach, these approaches are based on functional requirements whereas our approach is focused on products.

In numerous publications, Bosch et. al. address the field of product line architecture, software architecture erosion, and reuse of software artifacts: The work in [16] proposes a method that brings together two aspects of software architecture: the design of software architecture and software product lines. Deelstra et al. [17] provide a framework of terminology and concepts regarding product derivation. They have identified that companies employ widely different approaches for software product line based development and that these approaches evolve over time. The work in [18] discusses six maturity levels that they have identified for software product line approaches. In [19], a methodical and structured approach of architecture restoration in the specific case of the brake servo unit (BSU) is applied. Software product lines from existing BSU variants are extracted by explicit projection of the architecture variability and decomposition of the original architecture.

The work in [20] gives a systematic survey and analysis of existing approaches supporting multi product lines and a general discussion of capabilities supporting multi product lines in various domains and organizations. They define a multi product line (MPL) as a set of several self-contained but still interdependent product lines that together represent a large-scale or ultra-large-scale system. The different product lines in an MPL can exist independently but typically use shared resources to meet the overall system requirements. According to this definition, a vehicle system is also an MPL assuming that each product line is responsible for a particular subsystem. However, in the following, we only regard classic product lines, since the dependencies between the individual product lines in vehicle systems are very low, unlike MPL.

D. Software Product Line Architecture Evolution

Thiel and Hein [21] propose product lines as an approach to automotive system development because product lines facilitate the reuse of core assets. The approach of Thiel and Hein enables the modeling of product line variability and describes how to manage variability throughout core asset development. Furthermore, they sketch the interaction between the feature and architecture models to utilize variability.

Holdschick [22] addresses the challenges in the evolution of model-based software product lines in the automotive domain. The author argues that a variant model created initially quickly becomes obsolete because of the permanent evolution of software functionalities in the automotive area. Thus, Holdschick proposes a concept how to handle evolution in variant-rich model-based software systems. The approach provides an overview of which changes relevant to variability could occur in the functional model and where the challenges are when reproducing them in the variant model.

Automotive manufacturers have to cope with the erosion of their ECU software. The work in [2] proposes a systematic approach for managed and continuous evolution of dependable automotive software systems. It is described how complexity of automotive software systems can be managed by creating modular and stable architectures based on well-defined requirements. Both architecture and requirements have to be managed in relation. Furthermore, to face the lack of flexibility of existing hieratic automotive software systems development approaches, they are focusing on four driving factors: systems engineering and agile function development, feature and function driven team development, agile management principles, and a seamless tooling infrastructure supporting continuously and iteratively evolving automotive software systems in a flexible manner.

To counteract erosion it is necessary to keep software components modular. But modularity is also a necessary attribute for reuse. Several approaches deal with the topic reuse of software components in the development of automotive products [1][23]. In [1], a framework is proposed, which focuses on modularization and management of a function repository. Another practical experience describes the introduction of a product line for a gasoline system from scratch [23]. However, in both approaches a long-term minimization of erosion is not considered.

A previous version of our approach is described in [3] focusing on the key ideas of the management cycle for product line architecture evolution. Furthermore, an approach for repairing an eroded software consisting of a set of product architectures by applying strategies for recovery and discovery of the product line architecture is proposed.

III. Overall Development Cycle

Our methodology for managed evolution of automotive software product line architectures is depicted in Figure 1. The methodology consists of two levels of development: The cycle on the top of Figure 1 constitutes the development activities for product line development, whereas the second cycle is required for product specific development. Not only both levels of development are executed in parallel but even the activities within a cycle may be performed independently. The circular arrow within the two cycles indicates the dependencies of an activity regarding the artifacts of the previous activity. Nevertheless, individual activities may be performed in parallel, e.g., the planned implementations can be realized from activity `PL-Plan`, while a new PLA is developed in parallel (activity `PL-Design`). The large arrows between the two development levels indicate transitions requiring an external decision-making process, e.g., the decision to start a new product development or prototyping, respectively.

In the following subsections, we will explain the basic activities of our approach in detail by referring to the terms depicted in Figure 1. Table I gives a brief overview on the objectives of each of the 12 activities, including inputs and outputs.

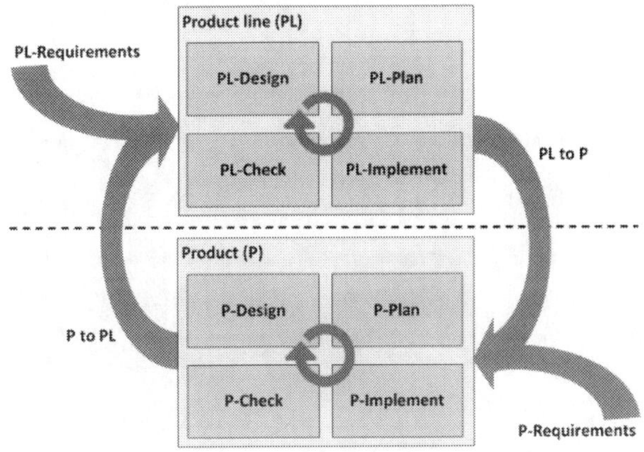

Figure 1. Overall development approach

We distinguish between the terms 'project' and 'product' in the following: A project includes a set of versioned software components, so-called modules. These modules contain variability so that a project can be used for different vehicles. A product on the other hand is a fully executable software status for a certain vehicle based on a project in conjunction with vehicle related parameter settings.

A. *Planning and Evolving Product Line Architectures*

(`PL-Requirements`) Software system and software component requirements from requirements engineering serve as input to the management cycle of the PLA. Errors occurring during the phase of requirements elicitation and specification have turned out to be major reasons for the failure of IT projects [24]. In particular, errors occur in case the requirements are specified erroneous or the requirements have inconsistencies and incompleteness. Errors during the phase of requirements elicitation and specification can be avoided by choosing an appropriate specification language enabling the validation of the requirements. In [25], e.g., activity diagrams are considered for the validation of system requirements by directly executable models including an approach for symbolic execution and thus enabling validation of several products simultaneously.

(`P to PL`) Artifacts of the developed product from the product cycle in Figure 1 serve as further input to the management cycle of the PLA: The product documentation contains architectural adaptations and change proposals, which can be integrated in the PLA. Furthermore, the modified modules in their new implementation are committed to the management cycle of the PLA for integration in product line.

(`PL-Design`) Next, we consider the design of the PLA. Generally, a software system architecture defines the basic organization of a system by structuring different architectural elements and relationships between them. The specification of "good" software system architecture is crucial for the success of the system to be developed. By our definition, a "good" architecture is a modular architecture which is built according to the following: (a) design principles for high cohesion, (b) design principles for abstraction and information hiding, and (c) design principles for loose coupling. In [2], we propose methods and techniques for a good architecture

TABLE I. EXPLANATION OF THE ACTIVITIES IN FIGURE 1.

Activity	*Input*	*Objective*	*Output*
PL-Design	Software system / component requirements and documentation from product development.	Further development of PLA with consideration of design principles. Application of measuring techniques to assess quality of PLA.	New PLA (called "PLA vision").
PL-Plan	PLA vision.	Planning of a set of iterations of further development toward the PLA vision taking all affected projects into account.	Development plan including the planned order of module implementations and the planned related projects.
PL-Implement	Development plan for product line.	Implementation including testing as specified by the development plan for product line development.	Implemented module versions.
PL-Check	Architecture rules and set of implemented modules to be checked.	Minimization of product architecture erosion by architecture conformance checking based on architecture rules.	Check results.
P-Design	Project plan and product specific requirements.	Designing product architecture and performing architecture adaptations taking product specific requirements into account. Compliance checking with PLA to minimize erosion.	Planned product architecture.
P-Plan	Product architecture.	Definition of iterations to be performed on product level toward the planned product architecture.	Development plan for product development.
P-Implement	Development plan for product development.	Product specific implementations including testing as specified by the development plan for product development.	Implemented module versions.
P-Check	Architecture rules and set of implemented modules to be checked.	Architecture conformance checking between PLA and PA.	Check results.
PL to P	Development plan for product line.	Defining a project plan by selecting a project from the the product line.	Project plan.
P to PL	Developed product.	Providing product related information of developed product for integration into product line development.	Product documentation and implementation artifacts of developed products.
PL-Requirements	Requirements.	Specification and validation of software system and software component requirements by requirements engineering.	Software system and software component requirements.
P-Requirements	Requirements in particular from calibration engineers.	Specification of special requirements for a certain vehicle product including vehicle related parameter settings.	Vehicle related requirements.

design. Based on these methods and techniques a new PLA is defined (called PLA vision) taking the new requirements (`PL-Requirements`) and product related information (`P to PL`) into account. To assess the quality of the designed PLA, it is necessary to measure complexity and to describe the results numerically. In particular, we consider properties such as cohesion, coupling, reusability and variability in order to draw conclusions about the quality of the PLA.

(`PL-Plan`) As further development of the PLA will effect a high number of products, the changes have to be planned carefully in order to avoid errors within the corresponding products and to avoid architecture erosion. Thus, the planning phase has to define a set of iterations of further development towards the PLA vision. All allowed changes are planned as a schedule containing the type of change and timestamp. It is planned in which order the implementation of corresponding modules should take place. It should be emphasized that there are many parallel product developments, which must be taken into account when planning. Next, either affected projects and modules are determined or a pilot project is selected.

Some further developments can lead to extensive architectural changes. In this case the effects of the architectural changes on the associated projects have to be closely examined. For this purpose further development projects can be defined as prototype projects for certain iterations of the PLA. These projects are then tested within the product cycle.

B. Automotive Product Development and Prototyping based on Software Product Lines

(`PL-Implement`) The former planning activity has determined the schedule for PLA adaptations and product releases. Thus, on the implementation level, new versions of the software are planned, too. Vehicle functions are modeled using a set of modules, specifying the discrete and continuous behavior of the corresponding function. As required by ISO 26262, each module needs to be tested separately. Established techniques for model-based testing necessitate a requirements specification from which a test model can be derived. In practice, requirements are specified by natural language and on the level of whole vehicle functions instead of modules so that test models on module level can not be derived directly. Therefore, in [26], a systematic model-based, test-driven approach is proposed to design a specification on the level of modules, which is directly testable. The idea of test-driven development is to write a test case first for any new code that is written [27]. Then the implementation is improved to pass the test case. Based on the approach in [26] we use the tool Time Partition Testing (TPT) because it suits particularly well due to the ability to describe continuous behavior [28]. The modules may be developed in ASCET or MATLAB/Simulink.

(`P-Requirements`) Releasing a fully executable software status for a certain vehicle product requires a specification of vehicle related parameter settings. Furthermore, special requirements for a specific product may exist necessitating further development of certain implementation artifacts. Building an executable software status for a certain vehicle product is realized by the cycle at the bottom of Figure 1. In contrast, the product line cycle in Figure 1 includes the development of sets of software artifacts of all planned projects.

(`PL to P`) Automotive software product development and prototyping starts with selecting a product from the product line. Therefore, the project plan is transferred containing module descriptions and descriptions of the logical product architecture integration plan with associated module versions.

(`P-Plan`) The product planning defines the iterations to be performed. An iteration consists of selected product architecture elements and planned implementations. An iteration is part of a sequence of iterations.

(`P-Implement`) An iteration is completed when all

planned elements of an iteration are implemented according to the test-driven approach of [26].

C. Architecture Conformance Checking for Automotive Software Product Line Development

Architecture erodes when the implemented architecture of a software system diverges from its intended architecture. Software architecture erosion can reduce the quality of software systems significantly. Thus, detecting software architecture erosion is an important task during the development and maintenance of automotive software systems. Even in our model-driven approach where implementation artifacts are constructed w.r.t. a given architecture the intended architecture and its realization may diverge. Hence, monitoring architecture conformance is crucial to limit architecture erosion.

Each planned product refers to a set of implementation artifacts, called modules. These modules constitute the product architecture. The aim of `PL-Check` and `P-Check` is the minimization of product architecture erosion. In [12], a method is described to keep the erosion of the software to a minimum: Consistency constraints expressed by architectural aspects called architectural rules are specified as formulas on a common ontology, and models are mapped to instances of that ontology. Based on this approach we are extracting rules from a PLA to minimize the erosion of the product architecture. During the development of implementation artifacts the rules can be accessed via a query mechanism and be used to check the consistency of the product architecture. Those rules can, e.g., contain structural information about the software like allowed communications. In [12], the rules are expressed as logical formulas which can be evaluated automatically to the compliance to the PLA.

(`PL-Check`) After each iteration planned in activity `PL-Plan` all related product architectures have to be checked. As `P-Check` refers to one product only, the check is performed after all related implementation artifacts of the product are developed.

(`P-Design`) The creation of a new product starts with a basically planned product architecture commonly derived from the product line. For the development of the product, new functionalities have to be realized and thus necessary adaptations to the planned product architecture are made. In order to keep the erosion to a minimum we have to ensure the compliance to the architecture design principles of the PLA. Therefore, we check consistency of the planned product architecture by applying architecture rules from the PLA.

However, in the case of prototyping it may be desired that the planned product architecture differs from PLA specifications. Thus, as a consequence, the architecture rules are violated. As pointed out in Section III-A, product related information is returned to the management cycle of the PLA after product delivery. If the development of a product required a differing product architecture w.r.t. the PLA, this could advance the erosion. Necessary changes must be communicated to `PL-Design` and `PL-Plan` s.t. the changes can be evaluated and adopted. As changes to the PLA can have severe influences on all the other architectures the changes are not applied immediately but considered for further development.

IV. Architecture Description Language

Evolution of the logical architecture and module architecture in product line and in product development involves a huge number of architecture elements and their relations. To handle this complexity, model based techniques are used within our methodology.

To develop the logical architecture and the module architecture using model based techniques we defined a description language by a metamodel. For each activity in our approach instances of the metamodel with several *views* are modeled. Each view focuses on different architecture elements. The product line phase deals with architecture elements for several product architectures. To derive product architectures from the product line phase *variant handling* has to be considered. We will describe these concepts of our approach in detail in the following.

EMAB metamodel: The **E**inheitliche **M**odulare **A**rchitektur **B**eschreibung (EMAB) is used to describe the decomposition structure and connection structure of logical architectures and module architectures.

Figure 2 depicts a simplified part of the metamodel that shows the abstract syntax of the two architecture layers DESIGN and IMPLEMENT. The architecture elements of these two layers are used to model product lines and product architectures. In the following, we describe the two layers in detail.

The DESIGN layer contains architecture elements to describe abstract software aspects. `LogicalArchitectureElement` is used to decompose these aspects into groups of corresponding implementation artifacts. Some of those elements may have dependencies with other elements of the logical architecture. In this case `LogicalElementConnection` connects exactly two logical architecture elements as a directed connection between one source and one target element. Each `LogicalArchitectureElement` can be referenced by a number of connections. The connection between two elements semantically allows the communication constrained by the source/target direction.

In the IMPLEMENT layer, code relevant software aspects are described. Thus, `ModuleArchitectureElement` decomposes the software code aspects into groups. For example, a header file and a c-code file of a certain software application are represented by a `ModuleArchitectureElement`. Directed dependencies between

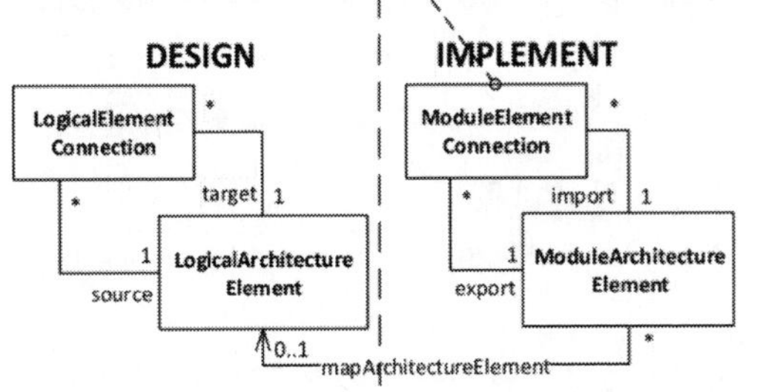

Figure 2. Simplified EMAB metamodel

exactly one export and one import element are connected by the ModuleElementConnection. Each ModuleArchitectureElement can be referenced by a number of connections. The connection between two elements semantically allows the communication constrained by the import/export direction.

LogicalArchitectureElements have to be referred to implementation artifacts for product development. Therefore, the EMAB metamodel determines that the ModuleArchitectureElement can reference at most one LogicalArchitectureElement using the mapArchitectureElement to determine the appropriate module elements of a logical element.

Connections between two LogicalArchitectureElements have to be properly considered at the implementation in the IMPLEMENT layer: Connections between ModuleArchitectureElements have to be conform with the connections specified in the DESIGN layer. To ensure that connections are realized properly, conformance rules are applied. One example OCL rule is shown in Figure 2 that constraints the ModuleElementConnection as context element for the check.

Views: The DESIGN layer focuses on the logical architecture. Figure 3 represents the DESIGN view as block diagram with two instances of logical architecture elements and the connection between them. The roles source and target indicate the direction of the connection.

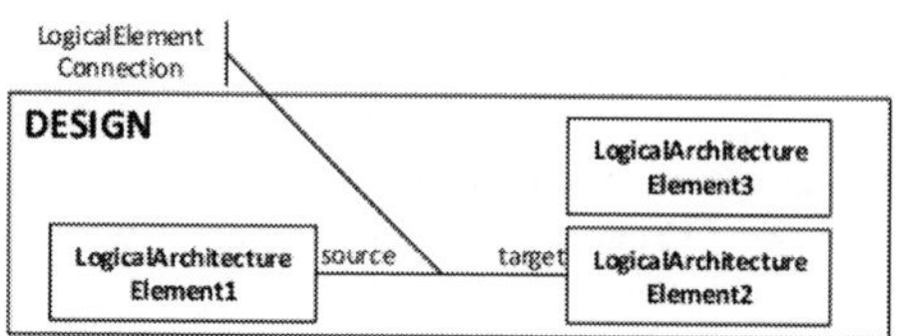

Figure 3. DESIGN view as part of the metamodel instance

The IMPLEMENT view in Figure 4 represents the module architecture instances as blocks and their connection as connection instances. Moreover, each module architecture element is referencing one logical architecture element represented by dashed connections between a module element block and logical element block.

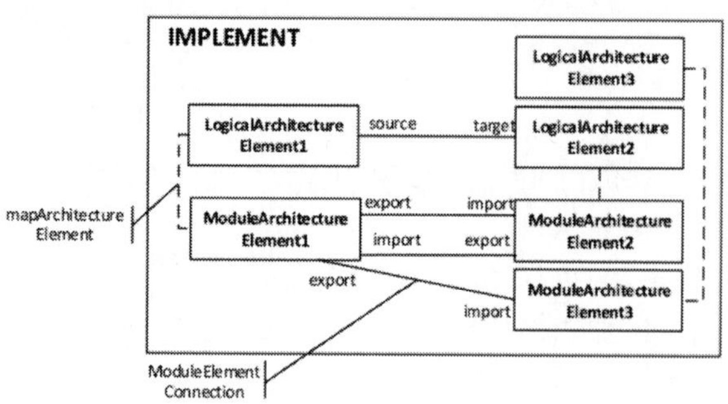

Figure 4. IMPLEMENT view as part of the metamodel instance

Figure 5 shows an example for the CHECK view, checking the conformance rule on connections of the DESIGN layer's logical architecture elements and IMPLEMENT layer's module architecture elements. The check of the OCL rule in the middle of Figure 5 is fulfilled as the specified connection between the two module architectures elements correspond to the connection between the mapped logical architecture elements. However, the further checks of the OCL rule fail: In the first case, the direction from import to export constitutes a violation. And in the next case, as ModuleArchitectureElement3 maps to LogicalArchitectureElement3 no connection is allowed from ModuleArchitectureElement1.

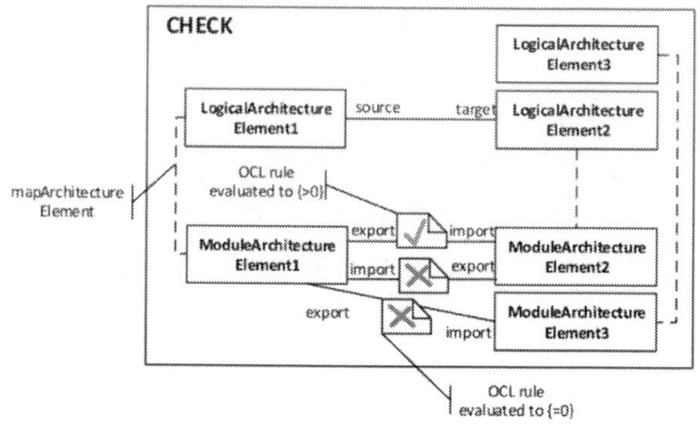

Figure 5. CHECK view as part of the metamodel instance

Variant handling: In product line development, architecture elements of module and logical architectures are realized to be reused in several software products. The architecture models enclose decomposition variants and behavior variants. During product development, the decomposition variants and the behavior variants have to be determined. Therefore, a further part of the EMAB metamodel provides the syntax to describe structure variants, behavior variants and valid selection conditions. Selection conditions are necessary to derive architectures and to derive behavior for product development. The part of the EMAB metamodel dealing with variants is out of the scope of this contribution in order to focus on the methodology.

Version handling: Each architecture element of the product line development and of the product development is kept in a repository. The repository provides a version control capability. A modified or created element is committed with a unique version ID into the repository. Predecessor relations are defined in case of modifications of an existing version. The repository also enables the selection of elements for product line development or product development. The part of the EMAB metamodel dealing with versioning is out of the scope of this contribution in order to focus on the methodology.

V. Real World Example: Brake Servo Unit (BSU)

In this section, we present an example of a software system we developed in cooperation with Volkswagen. The main task of this system is to ensure a sufficient vacuum within the brake booster that is needed to amplify the driver's braking force. At first, we describe the context the system is embedded in and a view onto the system's structure. We show how the system has evolved. After the presentation of the mapping of the evolution onto our approach, we give results and a discussion.

A. System Structure and Context of BSU

In vehicles, a vacuum brake booster (brake servo unit/BSU) is mounted between the brake pedal and the hydraulic brake cylinder. It consists of two chambers separated through a movable diaphragm. If the driver is not braking, the air is evacuated from both chambers. When he pushes on the brake pedal a valve opens and atmospheric pressure air flows into one chamber. Due to the differential air pressure within the BSU the diaphragm starts to move towards the vacuum chamber creating a force. This force is used to amplify the driver's braking force.

The vacuum can be generated using different techniques. The BSU is either attached to the intake manifold using its internal lower pressure or to an electrically or mechanically driven vacuum pump. Using the intake manifold as vacuum generator can be problematic. Special operating modes of other vehicle's subsystems can increase the intake manifold pressure so much that its internal vacuum is not sufficient to evacuate the BSU when needed.

The software system realizes a set of feedback controllers to reduce the disturbances caused by other systems or to switch on the vacuum pump, respectively. Since it makes no sense to use all controllers at the same time it is necessary to coordinate their activation. Besides the controlling of BSU vacuum and the coordination of controllers, the software has to provide valid pressure information all the time. In order to realize that the software selects from several sensors the one that provides the best quality of pressure information. The logical view of the designed architecture is presented in Figure 6.

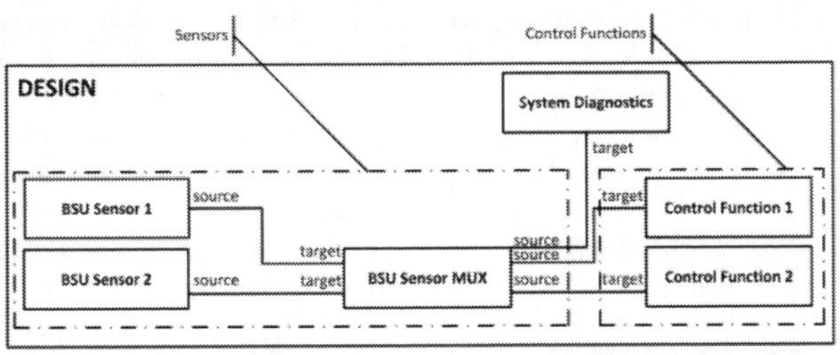

Figure 6. Logical view of the software architecture of BSU

The BSU hardware system is part of a wide range of products within the huge family of cars. Since the diversity of the used hardware components like sensors and actuators that are mounted to the braking system and features that influence the BSU software one important goal of the architecture development was to support variability. The BSU software system is decomposed into two major parts: `sensors` and `control functions`. The decomposition of the sensor component into parts for every sensor type each allows a one to one mapping from features to components. To realize variability in an efficient way, standardized interfaces are used for communication. A coordinating component just has to provide a sufficient amount of ports for the interaction with the sensors and control functions.

The `control functions` component is decomposed using a similar technique. Every control function is realized by a specific component. These components provide standardized interfaces for communication with subsequent vehicle functions, which must follow the BSU commands, e.g., disable the start-stop system (not depicted in Figure 6).

B. Evolution of BSU

As it was customary in the automotive domain, BSU's hardware and software have been implemented by various suppliers in the past. The requirements for the functionalities of the system were the same for all suppliers, but there were differences in the type of implementation by the respective suppliers. During the further development of the system over many years, new requirements had to be continuously implemented. Examples of this are the support of various engine variants such as otto, diesel and electric engines. As the range of functions increased, the essential complexity grew; however, the accidental complexity [29] has increased disproportionately. The growth of accidental complexity results from a "bad" architecture with strong coupling and a low cohesion which have evolved over the time. Despite extensive further development of the system, the original structure of the software was not adequately adapted. Overall, the monolithic structure of the software remained. The software consisted of a single software module, which, however, was internally characterized by increasing accidental complexity. The variability was realized completely by annotations. Thereby, the system's maintainability and expandability has been complicated additionally.

In recent years, many automotive manufacturers have begun to develop software primarily in-house to save costs and to secure important know-how. However, the hardware components are still being developed by the supplier companies in general. Against this background, Volkswagen decided to develop the BSU in-house in the future. Together with our institute, Volkswagen developed its own software for the BSU in 2012 on the basis of the existing system. Configurability, extensibility and comprehensibility were defined as essential quality targets. In addition, new architecture and design concepts have been introduced to meet these quality objectives in the long term and permanently.

After successful introduction of the system into series production, the software system was continuously developed after 2012. In all, the BSU system was reused in more than 140 project versions, some of them with adaptations. There were, for example, the introduction of five additional control functions that were necessary because of changes to the system environment. This includes, in particular, the introduction of new components such as actuators, which were essentially driven by the electrification of the powertrain. In the following sections, we will present our methodology by means of the BSU's further development and discuss the results. However, due to the obligation of secrecy, we can not name real-world functions. Instead, we will abstract from real control functions, actuators, and sensors in the following sections.

C. Application of our Approach to BSU Further Development

In this section, we will outline the evolution of BSU further development, described in the previous section, mapped to the overall development cycle visualized in Figure 1. As mentioned in Section V-B, the development started in 2012 and continues until today. We will pick out the milestones of this evolution process and explain in detail, how our approach supports the management of development. Therefore, we will describe the further development of the BSU chronologically. The architecture of the BSU at this point is equivalent to Figure 6.

The first considerable development activities leading to architectural evolution results from two new control functions. These new control functions are specified as product line requirements (`PL-Requirement`). In the following activity `PL-Design`, the new requirements including all open requirements and feedbacks from the ongoing product development activities submitted by activity `P to PL`, are took into account by the designing of the new PLA (called "PLA vision"). The resulting PLA includes two new components, whereby each component represents one of the new control functions.

After assessing and determining the new PLA vision, the `PL-Plan` activity starts. It was decided to realize the new PLA vision in two iterations, per iteration cycle, one of the new components should be implemented completely. Regarding to the development plan in activity `PL-Implement` the first component was implemented. `PL-Check` activity is triggered after the new component is fully implemented. In this activity, the conformance of the implementation is checked against the planned architecture (PLA vision), as illustrated in Section IV. The outcome of the checks was positive so the next iteration was started.

Parallel to the implementation of the second defined component some concrete products are selected to integrate the new developed control function in real products (activity `PL to P`). It was decided to setup a new pilot product additionally. The pilot got a special requirement by a `P-Requirement` activity. The proving by prototypes or pilots is a common approach in the automotive domain. Due to the specification of the special requirement, which includes a new control function with a coordinating feature, a prototyping approach was used to realize this requirements. This simply means that we have a main control function and a backup control function, if the main function is not available the backup function should be used.

The solution of the `P-Design` activity was a solution which fulfills all requirements. It was decided to add a new component representing the new control function and to establish an additional coordinator component. The coordinator has the responsibility of the controlling of main and backup functions and realizing the coordinating feature.

In the `P-Plan` activity the iterations to be performed had to be defined and scheduled. The outcome was a development plan with two iteration steps. In the first step, the new control function and the coordinator component should be implemented. And in a second step, all existing control functions had to be adapted, because they had to be defeatable to perform as main or backup function.

According to the development plan, the `P-Implement` activity was performed. After each iteration step, a conformance check was done (`P-Check`). In our case study we detected a violation of an architectural rule. Consequently, it was evaluated and discussed, if the solution of the violation results in adapting the implementation or in adapting the architectural rule itself - or in simple words, is there a crummy implementation or an insufficient architecture. In terms of internal classification we cannot go in detail at this point.

After evaluating the product realization all adaptations and changes of architecture and implementation are forwarded to the product line architecture level by a `P to PL` activity. These are inputs for the next `PL-Design` activity, thereby it had to be decided which changes should be integrated into the product line architecture and its implementation or otherwise which had to be declared as a "special" solution. In our case the coordinator concept was established in the product line. The final architecture is visualized in Figure 7 including all newly developed control functions, the coordinator component, and the additional connections between the control functions and the coordinator for the controlling of activation.

In summary, the architecture of the BSU is largely stable after the introduction of the coordinator concept until today.

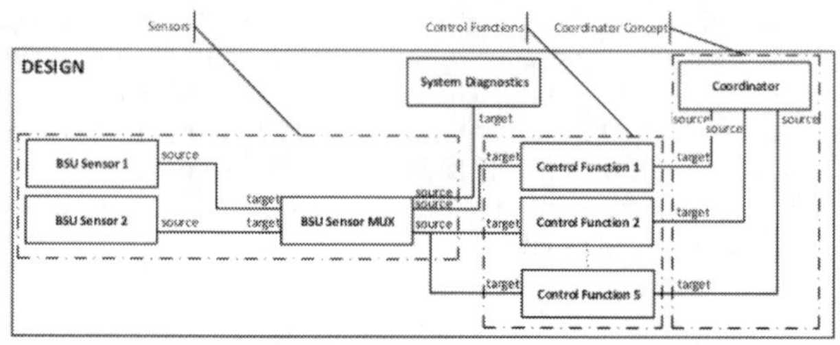

Figure 7. Logical view of the software architecture of BSU including the coordinator concept and the three new Control Functions

Overall we state that our approach can deal with many parallel activities at product line and product level. This becomes apparent by the controlling character of the synchronization points both in the development cycle on product line and product level by activities `PL-Check` and `P-Check` and between the product line and product level by activities `PL to P` and `P to PL`. In this way, it was possible to detect architecture erosion in an early state and to take adequate countermeasures. Furthermore, we can take care of a planned generalization on the one hand and a planned specialization or exceptional case handling on the other hand. This is evidenced by the coordinator concept: A concept which was designed and fully realized and proved by a pilot product and than transferred into the product line architecture and finally fully integrated within the next development iterations in the product line architecture and all products belonging to this architecture.

VI. Evaluation and Discussion

To evaluate our methodology, we present the quantitative analysis for the BSU software development that is realized and maintained in cooperation with our project partner over a period of 5 years. In the following, we focus on the applicability of the product line and product development activities. Two criteria are important to evaluate. First, the amount and kinds of modifications on architecture elements calling this *complexity controlling*. Second, the amount and kinds of design configurations calling this *variant controlling*.

Table II shows the result of the quantitative analysis. The data record for the quantitative analysis refers to the development of the BSU software and the product realizations consisting of the BSU software and further vehicle functions. The record contains the version control graph of the past 5 years of BSU software development, called *repository* in the following. Each node is a version of an architecture element or realized

TABLE II. RESULT OF THE QUANTITATIVE ANALYSIS FOR THE BSU SOFTWARE FOR THE INTERVAL OF 5 YEARS.

	Count	*Number of versions*	*Average number of versions*	*Min. number of versions*	*Max. number of versions*
LAE	15	15	15/15 = 1	1	1
MAE	15	58	58/15 ≈ 4	1	6
Projects	21	146	146/21 ≈ 7	1	12

TABLE III. FURTHER RESULTS OF THE QUANTITATIVE ANALYSIS FOR THE BSU SOFTWARE.

	Number of versions used in projects	*Cumulated number of versions used over all project versions*	*Average degree of reuse of each version*	*Number of used design configurations*
MAE	46	1611	1611/46 ≈ 35	n/a
Projects	n/a	n/a	n/a	14

product. Edges connect two subsequent versions. Table II shows the number of logical architecture element (LAE) versions, of module architecture element (MAE) versions, and of project versions from the record. Modifications were triggered by the realization of BSU software `PL-Requirements` or by the realization of products due to `P-Requirements`.

Table II shows the count of 15 LAE referring to modifications at the DESIGN layer and the count of 15 MAE referring to modifications at the IMPLEMENT layer. The kind of modifications refers to the connection structure and to the architecture element structure of the appropriate MAE. Each LAE is available in exactly one version in the repository. Thereby, the current state of the logical architecture is represented which is unmodified since the beginning of the record. Unfortunately, the data of prior development stages of the BSU software logical architecture is not considered by the record due to data protection reasons. In total, 58 versions for MAE exist. A module element of the module architecture was modified in minimum 1 time, in maximum 6 times, and in average 4 times. Thereby, each version of the MAE is mapped in this case to exactly one version of the appropriate LAE.

Line "Projects" in Table II refers to the product development of the BSU software and shows that 21 projects containing the BSU software exist. A project defines a set of architecture element versions from logical architecture and from module architecture used to realize a product. In the following, we call the set of versions of architecture elements *design configuration*. Each time a project is modified, a new version of that project is committed to be used for subsequently realize the product. The project modifications resulting in a new version commit always refers to changes of the design configuration. In total, the project version number is 146. The average number of versions is 7, the minimum number is 1, and the maximum number is 12.

The data in Table III shows two quantitative aspects. First, the number of BSU software architecture element versions used in projects is 46 and the cumulated number of BSU software architecture element versions used in all project versions is 1611. Hence, the average degree of reuse of each version of MAE is 35. Second, the number of different design configurations of all project version concerning the BSU software is 14. This induces the fact that 14 architecture structure variants of the BSU software architecture (logical and module) are used in projects to realize products in the past 5 years.

Complexity controlling: Complexity in BSU software is induced by modifications on architecture elements of the logical architecture and the module architecture which are triggered to realize the two kinds of requirements described by the record. To handle complexity, each modification must be controlled for violations on architecture elements and on violations referring quality properties.

Our methodology aims to control violations of quality properties in the `Design` activity and of violations of architecture rules in the `Check` activity. The `Design` activity provides the modified DESIGN layer in each iteration and the `Implement` activity provides the modified IMPLEMENT layer in each iteration. The BSU software modifications are applied to realize requirements resulting in a product dependent BSU software or in a new product independent realization of the BSU software. Therefore, `PL-Requirements` corresponding to new features triggers the controlling of BSU software modifications during the product line development activities, using the versions of logical architecture at the DESIGN layer and of versions of module architecture at the IMPLEMENT layer. New project related requirements corresponding to `P-Requirements` triggers the product development activities to control all modifications considering project related versions and architecture related versions corresponding to the appropriate layers and of the EMAB metamodel.

After applying the methodology two important results are observed: First, no violations on architecture quality properties at the DESIGN layer were found. Second, after checking the modifications of the BSU software applying inter alia the rule described by the EMAB metamodel in Section IV, no violations between the layers of the BSU software are found, too. This evaluation result shows that all modifications of BSU software in the past 5 years preserved the architecture conformance of the IMPLEMENT layer to the DESIGN layer. Moreover, the structure of the DESIGN layer is well realized considering the quality properties. Therefore, the DESIGN layer remained unmodified.

Variant controlling: The term variant in the case of BSU software describes a software architecture variant reused to realize a software product. Thereby, each project version refers to exactly one design configuration to define architecture elements for reuse that are contained in the software architecture variant. Modifications of the logical and module architecture can introduce violations on expected derivable structure variants. To handle such violations the control of variants must be applied to the modifications. The control of such architecture rule violations is applied during the `Check` activity of the product line development considering the versions corresponding to the IMPLEMENT layer and to the DESIGN layer. After applying our methodology, no violations are found in the past 5 years of development. This corresponds to the result of complexity evaluation where conformance of the EMAB layers is confirmed.

VII. Conclusion and Future Work

We proposed a holistic approach for a long-term manageable and plannable software product line architecture for automotive software systems. Our approach aims at a long-term minimization of architecture erosion, and thereby guarantee a constant high degree of reusability. Thus, we propose concepts like architecture design principles, architecture quality measurements, architecture compliance checking, and further development scheduling with specific adaptations to the automotive domain. The focus is on scalability, to manage a huge number of variants in real world automotive systems.

We demonstrated our methodology on a real world case study, a brake servo unit (BSU) software system from automotive software engineering. As a result, we could avoid architecture erosion for several years. All further developments have followed the originally planned architectural principles. Moreover, we were surprised at the high number of reuse of the modules: Each module was reused on average in 35 projects. Even the high number of potential variants could be managed with the approach.

As a future work, we aim at realizing a tool-chain which enables the architecture description of the different architectures (PLA, PA, including versioning), the measure and evaluation of quality attributes, as well as the integration of the ArCh-Framework [12]. Appropriate abstraction techniques are crucial to cope with the huge set of adjustable parameters within the ECU software and to manage variability. Thus, we are currently developing a concept including a prototypical tool environment which enables the description and visualization of variability.

References

[1] B. Hardung, T. Kölzow, and A. Krüger, "Reuse of Software in Distributed Embedded Automotive Systems," in Proceedings of the 4th ACM International Conference on Embedded Software, ser. EMSOFT'04. ACM, 2004, pp. 203–210.

[2] A. Rausch et al., "Managed and Continuous Evolution of Dependable Automotive Software Systems," in Proceedings of the 10th Symposium on Automotive Powertrain Control Systems, 2014, pp. 15–51.

[3] B. Cool et al., "From Product Architectures to a Managed Automotive Software Product Line Architecture," in Proceedings of the 31st Annual ACM Symposium on Applied Computing, ser. SAC'16. ACM, 2016, pp. 1350–1353.

[4] A. Pretschner, M. Broy, I. H. Krüger, and T. Stauner, "Software Engineering for Automotive Systems: A Roadmap," in 2007 Future of Software Engineering, ser. FOSE '07. IEEE Computer Society, 2007, pp. 55–71.

[5] R. Cloutier et al., "The Concept of Reference Architectures," Systems Engineering, vol. 13, no. 1, Feb. 2010, pp. 14–27.

[6] E. Y. Nakagawa, P. O. Antonino, and M. Becker, "Reference Architecture and Product Line Architecture: A Subtle but Critical Difference," in Proceedings of the 5th European Conference on Software Architecture, ser. ECSA'11. Berlin, Heidelberg: Springer-Verlag, 2011, pp. 207–211.

[7] E. Y. Nakagawa, F. Oquendo, and M. Becker, "RAModel: A Reference Model for Reference Architectures," in Proc. of the 2012 Joint Working IEEE/IFIP Conference on Software Architecture and European Conference on Software Architecture, ser. WICSA-ECSA '12. IEEE Computer Society, 2012, pp. 297–301.

[8] E. Y. Nakagawa, M. Becker, and J. C. Maldonado, "Towards a Process to Design Product Line Architectures Based on Reference Architectures," in Proceedings of the 17th International Software Product Line Conference, ser. SPLC '13. ACM, 2013, pp. 157–161.

[9] E. Y. Nakagawa, M. Guessi, J. C. Maldonado, D. Feitosa, and F. Oquendo, "Consolidating a Process for the Design, Representation, and Evaluation of Reference Architectures," in Proceedings of the 2014 IEEE/IFIP Conference on Software Architecture, ser. WICSA '14. Washington, DC, USA: IEEE Computer Society, 2014, pp. 143–152.

[10] L. de Silva and D. Balasubramaniam, "Controlling Software Architecture Erosion: A Survey," Journal of Systems and Software, vol. 85, no. 1, Jan. 2012, pp. 132–151.

[11] J. van Gurp and J. Bosch, "Design Erosion: Problems & Causes," Journal of Systems and Software, vol. Volume 61, 2002, pp. 105–119.

[12] S. Herold and A. Rausch, "Complementing model-driven development for the detection of software architecture erosion," in Proceedings of the 5th International Workshop on Modeling in Software Engineering, ser. MiSE '13. IEEE Press, 2013, pp. 24–30.

[13] I. John and J. Dörr, "Elicitation of Requirements from User Documentation," in Proceedings of the 9th International Workshop on Requirements Engineering: Foundation for Software Quality (REFSQ'03), ser. Essener Informatik Beiträge, vol. 8. Essen: Universität Duisburg-Essen, 2003, pp. 3–12.

[14] H. Gomaa, Designing Software Product Lines with UML: From Use Cases to Pattern-Based Software Architectures. Addison-Wesley, 2004.

[15] P. Clements and L. Northrop, Software Product Lines: Practices and Patterns. Addison-Wesley, 2001.

[16] J. Bosch, Design and Use of Software Architectures: Adopting and Evolving a Product-Line Approach. Addison-Wesley, 2000.

[17] S. Deelstra, M. Sinnema, and J. Bosch, "Product derivation in software product families: a case study," Journal of Systems and Software, vol. 74, no. 2, 2005, pp. 173–194.

[18] J. Bosch, "Maturity and Evolution in Software Product Lines: Approaches, Artefacts and Organization," in Proceedings of the Second International Conference on Software Product Lines, ser. SPLC 2. London, UK, UK: Springer-Verlag, 2002, pp. 257–271.

[19] A. Strasser et al., "Mastering Erosion of Software Architecture in Automotive Software Product Lines," in SOFSEM 2014: Theory and Practice of Comp. Sc., ser. LNCS, vol. 8327. Springer, 2014, pp. 491–502.

[20] G. Holl, P. Grünbacher, and R. Rabiser, "A Systematic Review and an Expert Survey on Capabilities Supporting Multi Product Lines," Inf. Softw. Technol., vol. 54, no. 8, Aug. 2012, pp. 828–852.

[21] S. Thiel and A. Hein, "Modeling and Using Product Line Variability in Automotive Systems," IEEE Softw., vol. 19, no. 4, Jul. 2002, pp. 66–72.

[22] H. Holdschick, "Challenges in the Evolution of Model-based Software Product Lines in the Automotive Domain," in Proceedings of the 4th International Workshop on Feature-Oriented Software Development, ser. FOSD '12. ACM, 2012, pp. 70–73.

[23] M. Steger et al., "Introducing PLA at Bosch Gasoline Systems: Experiences and Practices," in Software Product Lines. Springer, 2004, pp. 34–50.

[24] The Standish Group International, Inc., "CHAOS Chronicles 2003 report," West Yarmouth, MA, 2003.

[25] C. Knieke and M. Huhn, "Semantic Foundation and Validation of Live Activity Diagrams," Nordic Journal of Computing, vol. 15, no. 2, 2015, pp. 112–140.

[26] H. Peters et al., "A Test-driven Approach for Model-based Development of Powertrain Functions," in Agile Processes in Software Engineering and Extreme Programming. 15th International Conference on Agile Software Development, XP 2014. Springer-Verlag, 2014, pp. 294–301.

[27] K. Beck, Test Driven Development. By Example. Addison-Wesley Longman, 2002.

[28] E. Lehmann, "Time Partition Testing," Ph.D. dissertation, Fakultät IV – Elektrotechnik und Informatik, TU Berlin, 2004.

[29] F. P. Brooks, Jr., "No Silver Bullet Essence and Accidents of Software Engineering," Computer, vol. 20, no. 4, Apr. 1987, pp. 10–19.

Automotive Software Systems Evolution: Planning and Evolving Product Line Architectures

Axel Grewe, Christoph Knieke, Marco Körner, Andreas Rausch,
Mirco Schindler, Arthur Strasser, and Martin Vogel
TU Clausthal, Department of Computer Science, Software Systems Engineering
Clausthal-Zellerfeld, Germany
Email: {axel.grewe|christoph.knieke|marco.koerner|andreas.rausch|
mirco.schindler|arthur.strasser|m.vogel}@tu-clausthal.de

***Abstract*—Automotive software systems are an essential and innovative part of nowadays connected and automated vehicles. The automotive industry is currently facing the challenge to re-invent the automobile. Consequently, automotive software systems, their software systems architecture, and the way we engineer those kinds of software systems are confronted with the challenge of managing complexity of the desired automotive software systems and the corresponding engineering process. We will present an approach that helps engineers to manage system complexity based on architecture design principles, techniques for architecture quality measurements and processes to iteratively evolve automotive software systems. Based on a running sample, we will demonstrate and illustrate the main assets of the proposed engineering approach.**

Keywords–Architecture Evolution; Software Product Lines; Software Erosion; Architecture Quality Measures; Automotive.

I. INTRODUCTION

Usually many variants of a vehicle exist – different configurations of comfort functions, driver assistance systems, connected car services, or powertrains can be variably combined, creating an individual and unique product. To keep the vehicles cost efficient, modular components with a high reuse rate cross different types of vehicles are required. With respect to innovative and sophisticated functions, coming with the connected car and automated resp. autonomous driving the functional complexity, the technical complexity, and the networked-caused complexity is continuously and dramatically increasing. It is, and will be in future, a great challenge to further manage the resulting complexity.

Here, we propose an approach that helps engineers to manage functional software systems complexity based on modular, well-defined, and linked requirements as well as architectures. The goal is to create solid requirements and adequate architectures with the help of abstract principles, patterns, and describing techniques. In addition, we present a systematic approach for planning of development iterations and prototyping.

A software system architecture defines the basic organization of a system by structuring different architectural elements and relationships between them. The specification of "good" software system architecture is crucial for the success of the system to be developed. By our definition, a "good" architecture is a modular architecture which is built according to the following:

1) Design principles for high cohesion
2) Design principles for abstraction and information hiding
3) Design principles for loose coupling

In the evolutionary development of automotive software systems, the range of functionalities grows steadily. Thus, the "essential" complexity of the architecture increases continuously due to the growth of the number of functions. However, the "accidental" complexity of the architecture of automotive software systems grows disproportionately to the essential complexity as illustrated in Figure 1 [1]. The growth of accidental complexity results from a "bad" architecture with strong coupling and a low cohesion which have evolved over the time. "Bad" architectures increase accidental complexity and costs, hinder reuseability and maintainability, and decrease performance and understandability. The three design principles for a good architecture mentioned above focus on the reduction of accidental complexity and on the changeability of the architecture.

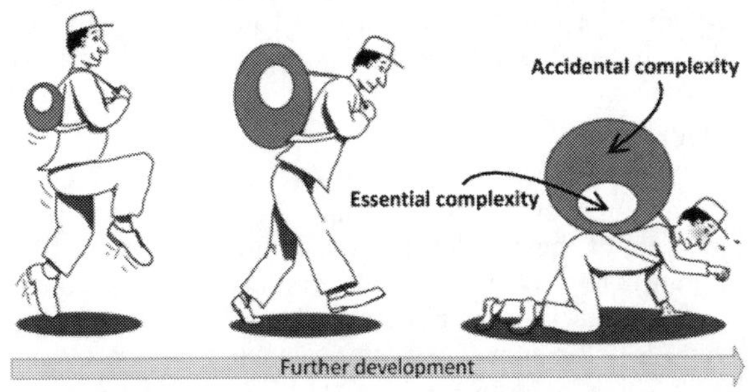

Figure 1. "Essential" vs. "Accidental" complexity

As an approach to manage software systems evolution, we propose three steps:

1) Methods and techniques for a good architecture design (Section IV-A)
2) Understanding of architecture and measuring of architecture quality (Section IV-B)
3) Systematic approach for planning of development iterations and prototyping (Section IV-C)

To make a statement about complexity, it is necessary to measure complexity and describe the results numerical. These numbers allow drawing conclusions from a system. Furthermore, it is necessary to describe complex relationships in a system. For this purpose, meaningful and understandable description techniques are needed. Such techniques allow complexity to be manageable. Finally, a systematic approach for planning of development iterations and prototyping is required.

The paper is structured as follows: Section III gives an overview on the related work. This paper refers to an overall development cycle for managed evolution of automotive software product line architectures that is proposed in Section II. In addition, Section II gives some formal definitions and introduces a real world example, a longitudinal dynamics torque coordination software, from automotive software engineering. Based on this example, we propose our methodology for planning and evolving automotive product line architectures in Section IV. Section V concludes.

II. Basics

A. Overall Development Cycle

Our methodology for managed evolution of automotive software product line architectures is depicted in Figure 2 (see [2]). The methodology consists of two development cycles which are executed concurrently: One cycle constitutes the development activities for product line development, whereas the second cycle is required for product specific development. Each cycle addresses the design of the logical architecture, the planning of development iterations and product releases, the implementation of software components, and architecture conformance checking.

We distinguish between the terms 'project' and 'product' in the following: A project includes a set of versioned software components, so-called modules. These modules contain variability so that a project can be used for different vehicles. A product on the other hand is a fully executable software status for a certain vehicle based on a project in conjunction with vehicle related parameter settings.

In the following subsections, we will explain the basic activities of our approach in detail by referring to the terms depicted in Figure 2. Table I gives a brief overview on the objectives of each of the 12 activities, including inputs and outputs:

Software system and software component requirements from requirements engineering (`PL-Requirements`) and artifacts of the developed product from the product cycle in Figure 2 (`P to PL`) serve as input to the management cycle of the product line architecture (PLA). Activities `PL-Design` and `PL-Plan` aim at designing, planning and evolving product line architectures and are explained in detail in this paper (see Section IV).

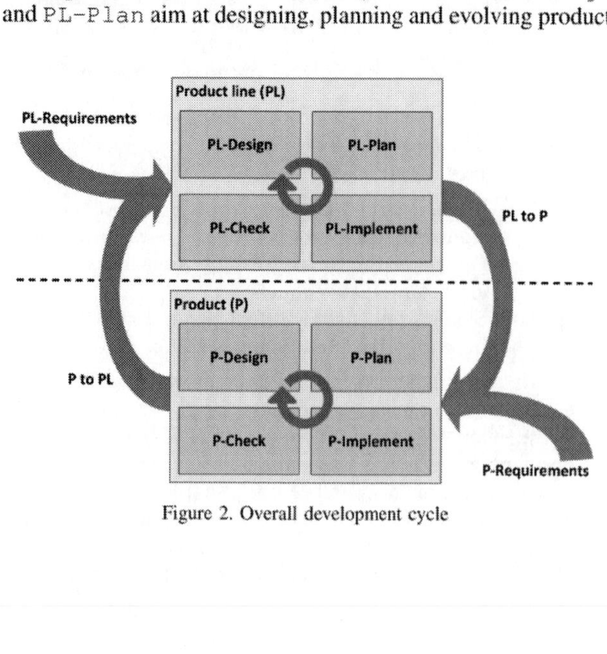

Figure 2. Overall development cycle

The planned implementation artifacts are implemented in `PL-Implement` on product line level whereas in `P-Implement` product specific implementation artifacts are implemented. For the building of a fully executable software status for a certain vehicle project, the project plan is transferred (`PL to P`) containing module descriptions and descriptions of the logical product architecture integration plan with associated module versions. In addition, special requirements for a specific project are regarded (`P-Requirements`). The creation of a new product starts with a basic planned product architecture commonly derived from the product line (`P-Design`). The product planning in `P-Plan` defines the iterations to be performed. An iteration consists of selected product architecture elements and planned implementations. An iteration is part of a sequence of iterations.

Each planned project refers to a set of implementation artifacts, called modules. These modules constitute the product architecture. The aim of `PL-Check` and `P-Check` is the minimization of product architecture erosion by architecture conformance checking for automotive software product line development. Furthermore, we apply architecture conformance checking to check conformance between the planned product architecture and the PLA in `P-Design`.

B. General structure and definitions

The relation between PLA, products, and modules is illustrated in Figure 3. We indicate the development points $t \in \mathbb{N}$ by the timeline at the bottom. Next, we give brief definitions of the terms PLA, product, and module.

PLA: On the top of Figure 3 the different versions of the PLA are illustrated. A PLA consists of logical architecture elements $l \in$ LAE (cf. `A`, `B`, `C` in Figure 3) and directed connections $c \in C$ between these elements. At each development point t exactly one version of the PLA exists. A certain PLA version is denoted by $\text{pla}_x \in PLA$, with $x \in \mathbb{N}$ to distinguish

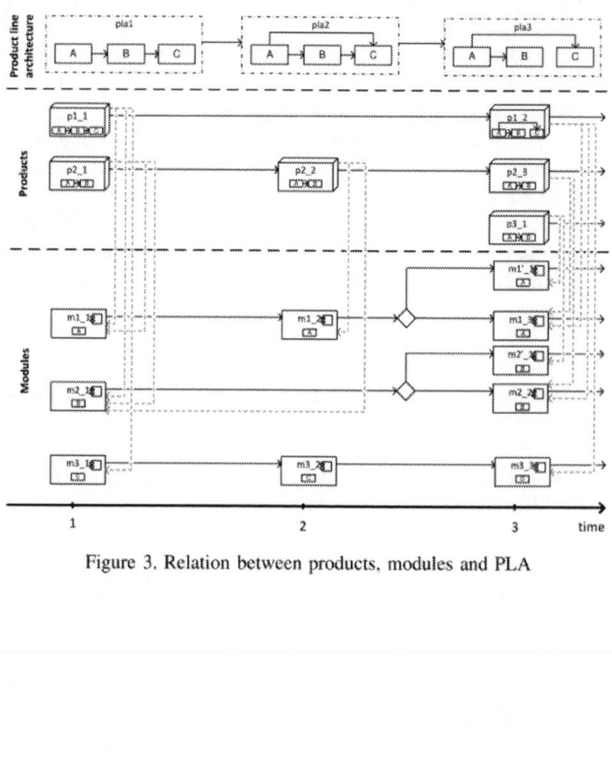

Figure 3. Relation between products, modules and PLA

TABLE I. EXPLANATION OF THE ACTIVITIES IN FIGURE 2.

Activity	*Input*	*Objective*	*Output*
PL-Design	Software system / component requirements and documentation from product development.	Further development of PLA with consideration of design principles. Application of measuring techniques to assess quality of PLA.	New PLA (called "PLA vision").
PL-Plan	PLA vision.	Planning of a set of iterations of further development toward the PLA vision taking all affected projects into account.	Development plan including the planned order of module implementations and the planned related projects.
PL-Implement	Development plan for product line.	Implementation including testing as specified by the development plan for product line development.	Implemented module versions.
PL-Check	Architecture rules and set of implemented modules to be checked.	Minimization of product architecture erosion by architecture conformance checking based on architecture rules.	Check results.
P-Design	Project plan and product specific requirements.	Designing product architecture and performing architecture adaptations taking product specific requirements into account. Compliance checking with PLA to minimize erosion.	Planned product architecture.
P-Plan	Product architecture.	Definition of iterations to be performed on product level toward the planned product architecture.	Development plan for product development.
P-Implement	Development plan for product development.	Product specific implementations including testing as specified by the development plan for product development.	Implemented module versions.
P-Check	Architecture rules and set of implemented modules to be checked.	Architecture conformance checking between PLA and PA.	Check results.
PL to P	Development plan for product line.	Defining a project plan by selecting a project from the the product line.	Project plan.
P to PL	Developed product.	Providing product related information of developed product for integration into product line development.	Product documentation and implementation artifacts of developed products.
PL-Requirements	Requirements.	Specification and validation of software system and software component requirements by requirements engineering.	Software system and software component requirements.
P-Requirements	Requirements in particular from calibration engineers.	Specification of special requirements for a certain vehicle product including vehicle related parameter settings.	Vehicle related requirements.

between PLA versions. The sequence of PLA versions is indicated by the arrows between the PLAs in Figure 3.

Product: A product $p_{i\_j} \in P$ has a product identifier i and a version index j, with $i, j \in \mathbb{N}$. The sequence of versions is indicated by the flow relation between products in Figure 3. We assume a distinct mapping of p_{i_j} to a certain $pla_x \in PLA$. A product p_{i_j} contains a product architecture $pa_{i\_j} \in PA$, where pa_{i_j} is a subgraph of the corresponding pla_x. The set of corresponding modules of a product is indicated by the dashed arrows in Figure 3.

Module: A module $m_{k\_l} \in M$ has a module identifier k and a version index l, with $k, l \in \mathbb{N}$. The sequence of versions is indicated by the flow relation between modules in Figure 3. We assume a distinct mapping of m_{k_l} to a certain $l \in \text{LAE} \cup \{\perp\}$. By $\perp$ we allow m_{k_l} not to be assigned to a logical architecture element, called unbound m_{k_l}. A logical architecture element can be assigned to several modules, but a module can only be assigned to exactly one or no logical architecture element. A module $m_{k\_l} \in M$ can belong to several products $p_{i\_j} \in P$.

As illustrated in Figure 3, we assume a high degree of reuse: The same module version may be included in different products. Branches of the development path are depicted by the diamond symbol. Module $m_{1'\_1}$ indicates a branch of the development path concerning module m_{1_3}.

C. Real World Example: Longitudinal Dynamics Torque Coordination

Our approach for designing the logical architecture described in the next section is based on our experience in the automotive environment. In numerous projects with the focus on software development for engine control units, we have developed architectural principles and concepts for architectural design and tested them on real sample projects. The following example shows frequent problems that arise as a result of strongly increasing accidental complexity. The approaches described in the next section are intended to help avoid the problems presented here by controlling the complexity. This paves the way for long-term maintenance and extensible architectures.

In our example, we consider the control of the braking and acceleration process, which is controlled by the driver via the brake and accelerator pedal, respectively. The implementation of these controls was originally carried out on completely separate developments. In the course of time, however, additional functions have been added: Not only the driver can act here by actuating the throttle or brake pedal. There are a number of additional functions, such as the ESP or ACC, which can act as accelerator and decelerator. In the case of longitudinal dynamics torque coordination (see Figure 4), both acceleration and braking processes must be coordinated with one another since there are interdependent interdependencies.

As a solution to the coordination problems, point-to-point connections between the software components were introduced, which however led to a strong increase in the accidental complexity: The realization of the reciprocal coordination

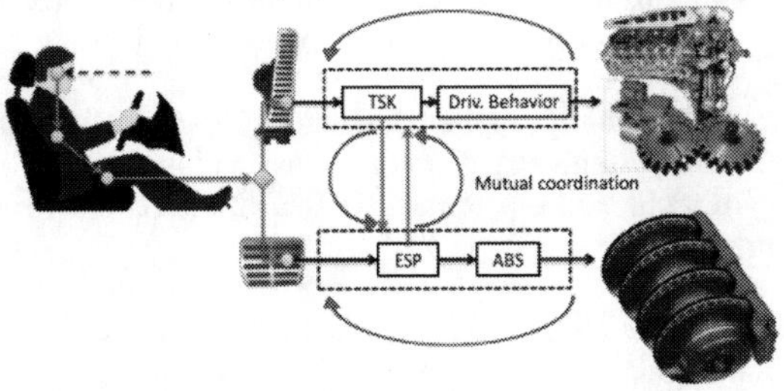

Figure 4. Automotive powertrain example: Mutual coordination

of the requesters was implemented in the example by the addition of a new explicit communication for the solution of coordination problems (see Figure 4, "mutual coordination"). In addition, existing functions had to be replicated in another context for the realization of the explicit communication. As a result, redundancies were created from the heads to the models. In addition, accidental complexity has increased disproportionately because of the wide interfaces and strong coupling within the architecture of the system.

III. Related Work

Next, we give an overview on the related work concerning software product line architecture design, evolution, and measurement of architecture quality. Mostly, we focus on approaches that are related to automotive and embedded software systems.

A. *Software Product Line Architecture Design*

In [3], reference architectures are assumed to be the basis for the instantiation of product line architectures (so-called family architectures). The purpose of the reference architecture is to provide guidance for future developments. In addition, the reference architecture incorporates the vision and strategy for the future. The work in [3] examines current reference architectures and the driving forces behind development of them to come to a collective conclusion on what a reference architecture should truly be. Nakagawa et. al. define a reference model of reference architectures [4], and propose a methodology to design product line architectures based on reference architectures [5].

As discussed in [6] an overall automotive product line architecture is often missing due to software sharing. Thus architecture recovery and discovery has to be applied by concepts of software product line extraction [6]. In [7], a methodical and structured approach of architecture restoration in the specific case of the brake servo unit (BSU) is applied. Software product lines from existing BSU variants are extracted by explicit projection of the architecture variability and decomposition of the original architecture.

The work in [8] proposes a method that brings together two aspects of software architecture: the design of software architecture and software product lines.

Thiel and Hein [9] propose product lines as an approach to automotive system development because product lines facilitate the reuse of core assets. The approach of Thiel and Hein enables the modeling of product line variability and describes how to manage variability throughout core asset development. Furthermore, they sketch the interaction between the feature and architecture models to utilize variability.

Patterns and styles are an important means for software systems architecture specification and are widely covered in literature, see, e.g., [10][11]. However, architecture patterns are not explicitly applied for the development of automotive software systems yet. For automotive industry, we propose the use of architecture patterns as a crucial means to overcome the complexity.

B. *Software Product Line Architecture Evolution*

In order to enable the evolution of software product line architectures, architecture erosion has to be avoided. In [12], de Silva and Balasubramaniam provide a survey of technologies and techniques either to prevent architecture erosion or to detect and restore architectures that have been eroded. However, each approach discussed in [12] refers to architecture erosion for a single product architecture, whereas architecture erosion in software product lines is out of the scope of the paper.

Holdschick [13] addresses the challenges in the evolution of model-based software product lines in the automotive domain. The author argues that a variant model created initially quickly becomes obsolete because of the permanent evolution of software functionalities in the automotive area. Thus, Holdschick proposes a concept how to handle evolution in variant-rich model-based software systems.

The work in [14] proposes a systematic approach for managed and continuous evolution of dependable automotive software systems. They have identified three main challenges to strengthen automotive software systems engineering for the upcoming evolution: Complexity of automotive software systems and engineering processes has still to be manageable, flexibility has still to be provided, and dependability has still to be guaranteed. The work in [14] describes how complexity of automotive software systems can be managed by creating modular and stable architectures based on well-defined requirements.

To counteract erosion it is necessary to keep software components modular. But modularity is also a necessary attribute for reuse. Several approaches deal with the topic reuse of software components in the development of automotive products [15][16]. In [15], a framework is proposed, which focuses on modularization and management of a function repository. Another practical experience describes the introduction of a product line for a gasoline system from scratch [16]. However, in both approaches a long-term minimization of erosion as well as a long-term evolution is not considered.

A previous version of our approach is described in [6] focusing on the key ideas of the management cycle for product line architecture evolution. Furthermore, an approach for repairing an eroded software consisting of a set of product architectures by applying strategies for recovery and discovery of the product line architecture is proposed in [6].

C. *Measurement of Software Product Line Architecture Quality*

To successfully plan and develop PLAs, it is necessary to measure key figures. These key figures are the basis for further developments. In [17], the SystEM-PLA framework is presented, which uses 98 metrics to assess the quality of a PLA. The analysis uses UML metrics to calculate key figures. A procedure is presented in [18] to measure NFA on PLAs. It is important to identify problems with regard to certain quality features as early as possible. The method uses different metrics to measure 3 NFAs: Maintainability, binary, and performance. The procedure results in possibilities to restrict products.

The work in [19] shows how traceability supports the evolution of SPL on feature level. For this purpose, a method is used to merge feature models, build files and source code with each other and to implement a change impact analysis by using metrics. As a result, erosion and problems are recognized at an early stage, and counter-measures can be taken.

In [20], PL are measured with the metric maintainability index (MI). The "Feature Oriented Programming" is used to map an SPL to a graph. The values are transformed into several matrixes. Next, singular value decomposition is applied to the matrixes. The metric maintainability index is then applied at different levels (product, feature, product line). The results show that by using the metric, features could be identified that had to be revised. The number of possible refactorings could be restricted.

In [21], several metrics are presented which are specifically used for measuring PLAs. The metrics are applied to "vADL" to determine the similarity, reusability, variability, and complexity of a PLA. The measured values can be used as a basis for further evolutionary steps.

IV. Planning and Evolving Automotive Product Line Architectures

A. Concepts for Designing Automotive Product Line Architectures

For the specification of software architectures design patterns, architectural patterns or styles are an important and suitable means, also in other engineering disciplines [10]. We subsume these under the term of architecture concepts. An architecture concept is defined as: "*a characterization and description of a common, abstract and realized implementation-, design-, or architecture solution within a given context represented by a set of examples and/or rules.*"

At the architectural level, these are often associated with terms as a client-server system, a pipes and filters design, or a layered architecture. An architectural style defines a vocabulary of components, connector types, and a set of constrains on how they can be combined [10]. To get a better understanding of the wide spectrum of architecture concepts typical samples of concepts are listed in the following:

- *Conventions:* naming, package/folder structure, vocabulary, domain model...
- *Design Patterns:* observer, factory, ...
- *Architectural Patterns:* client-server system, layered architecture, ...
- *Communication:* service-oriented, message based, bus, ...
- *Structures:* tiers, pipes, filters, ...
- *Security:* encryption, SSO, ...
- ...

Architectural concepts can be described in the form of classical patterns, by describing a particular recurring design problem that arises in specific design contexts and presents a well-proven generic scheme for its solution. The solution scheme specifies all constituent components, their responsibilities and relationships, and the way in which they will collaborate [11].

In the same way, we will illustrate some examples that we worked out in our automotive domain projects. Generally, the central issue is the increasing complexity of software systems with their technical and functional dependencies. A mapping of these dependencies to point-to-point connections will result in a huge, complex and difficult to maintain communication network. This leads to a likewise huge effort in the field of maintenance and further development for these software systems - small changes result in high costs.

This problem of a not manageable number of connections emerged in many industrial projects we explore for our field study. In the following we will present architectural concepts, which are addressing this problem in particular. Figures 5 and 6 show different components, whereby the components `Coordinator` and `Support` are atomic components and the components labeled as `Filter` are not atomic components, i.e., they can be decomposable.

1) Architecture Design Principle "Coordinator - PipesAndFilters - Support": The complexity of a component increases artificially with every new product, without integrating new functions. The reason for this phenomenon is due to the fact that each component had to calculate the system state for itself and this for each existing environment and product the component will be used in. In general, components are analyzing system data like sensor values for example and process them to realize their functionality. Thereby, it happens very often that a processing function is implemented several times. Besides data from other components are used, but this export data can change over time, so it can result in error states.

The design principle introduces a classification of data. If it is possible to classify the data, than it is possible to establish the typing of channels, as shown in Figure 5.

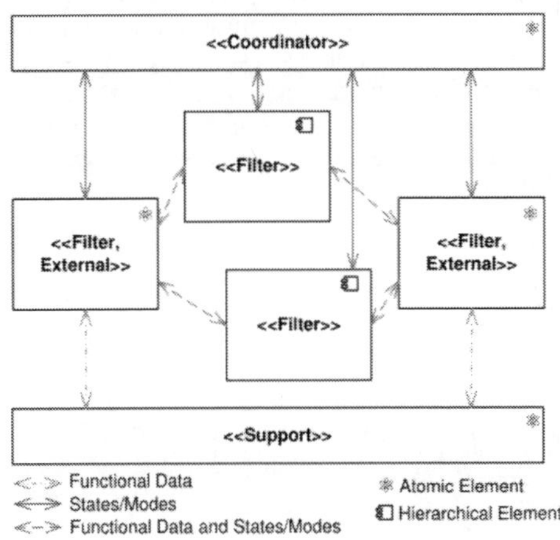

Figure 5. Architecture design principle: External elements

Each component has to declare a port for states and modes to uncouple the calculation of the system state from the component. A `Coordinator` component determines the global state for a set of components and uses the new defined port to coordinate the other components. The coordinator provides only states/modes and no functional data. A component in Figure 5 named as `Filter`, referring to the classical Pipes-and-Filters architecture pattern, can react to a state change automatically. Parameters are manipulated directly with the states/modes without an additional calculation. Components can be directly activated or stopped. The scheduling of the coordinator is independent from the scheduling of the other components, as each `Filter` checks the state/mode first. The functionality of the system is realized by the `Filter` components. For them it is allowed to exchange functional data as well as state and modes. Values which are required for the calculation within different components are provided by a so called `Support` component.

2) Architecture Design Principle "External Elements": Today it is customary that not all components are developed in-house, some functions are implemented by external suppliers. But OEM components have requirements resulting in changes of interfaces, behavior or functionalities of theses external developed functions and components. It is not that easy to identify these external components on architectural level, but this information is essential for an economic development process because changes of external components are very effort and cost intensive.

Figure 5 shows a simple solution to handle external elements: `Filter` components which are developed external are annotated with `Filter, External`, so it is effortless to identify which component is external and which connections are affected.

3) Architecture Design Principle "Hierarchical Communication": Over the time more and more components and functionality are added to a product. Different developers with different programming styles are working on the same product. Components without any reference to each other are organized in the same package or other organizational and structural units. Due to this accidental complexity it is not possible for a developer, system integrator or architect to get a well-founded knowledge of the whole system.

As presented in Figure 6, a `Filter` component can be decomposable, a so called non-atomic component contains a structure which follows the design principle visualized in Figure 5. It includes a `Coordinator` and `Support` component and an arbitrary number of `Filter` components. Whereby the inner `Filter` components have explicit defined responsibilities.

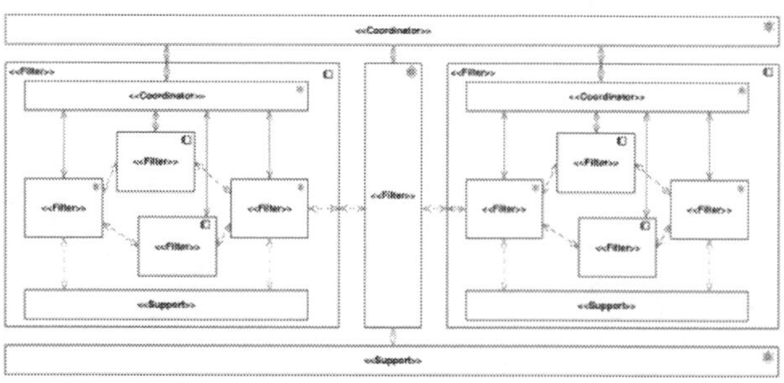

Figure 6. Architecture design principle: Hierarchical communication

By this design principle a repetitive structure on each abstraction level is established, which enables an easy and technical independent orientation in the whole system.

4) Architecture Design Principle "Component Model": Components require knowledge about the behavior or the state/mode of the connected components. This results in a high coupling of components and the processing time increases, too.

As presented in Figure 7, a component consists of two parts with different responsibilities - `Execution control` and `Function algorithms`. Each part has a defined set of interfaces, types of communication channels, and exchange data.

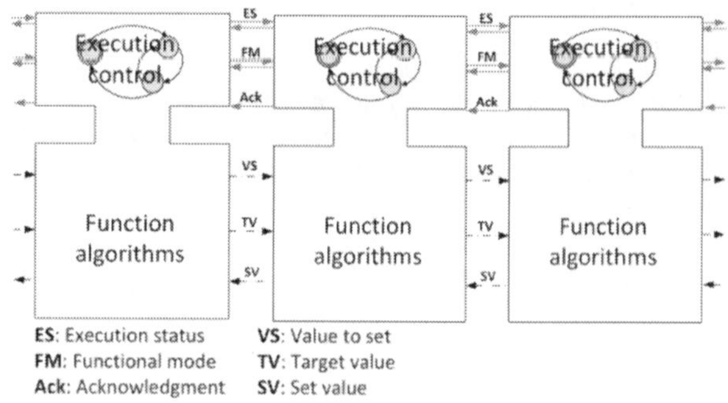

Figure 7. Communication scheme

The communication scheme is divided into two areas: the execution control and the functional algorithms. The execution control includes, on the one hand, the activation of the component, which is represented by the execution status. In addition, in the execution control, the functional mode (components internal mode) of the component is determined. The execution control sends an acknowledgment to the predecessor component when this component is active. The execution control communicates only by states/modes.

The function algorithms are processed when the execution status is set. Component specific values are calculated in the function algorithms. As output, they supply a manipulated variable and a target value. The manipulated variable is the value to set by the actuator. The target value is the value which is to be achieved in the future. The set value of the function algorithms is the value that is set by the controller. The functional algorithms only have functional data as input.

5) Architecture Design Principle "Feedback Channel": The complexity of component-based control systems is increasing continuously, since there are more and more functional dependencies between the individual components. A mapping of these dependencies on point-to-point connections between the components results in a complex, hard-to-maintain communication network.

In component-based control engineering systems, control cascades are generated by connecting several components consecutively. The main data flow in this system is called the effect chain. In more complex systems, there are several effect chains that can partly overlap. In an effect chain, there are functional dependencies between components that are not directly connected one behind the other. To resolve these dependencies, additional point-to-point connections are added, which are technical dependencies between the components. The additional direct point-to-point connections between the components increase the coupling between the components and lead to a deterioration in the fulfillment of non-functional requirements, such as maintainability, understandability and extensibility. For example, the technical dependencies have to be taken into account in a further development. The worst case is a complete graph with cross-links between all components.

As a solution to this problem we introduce *feedback channels* (patent pending): The introduction of feedback channels enables the dissolution of functional dependencies without the introduction of technical point-to-point connections (see Figure 8). The feedback channel is parallel to the effect chain. Thereby, the necessary functional information is passed through the components of the effect chain. The feedback is directed against the effect direction. Components of an effect chain must provide feedback. This creates a technical communication network with which the functional information can be exchanged. Thus, there are only technical dependencies to neighboring components in the effect chain. The maintainability is improved as only technical dependencies on neighboring components in the effect chain have to be considered. Figure 8 shows the architecture design principle *feedback channel.*

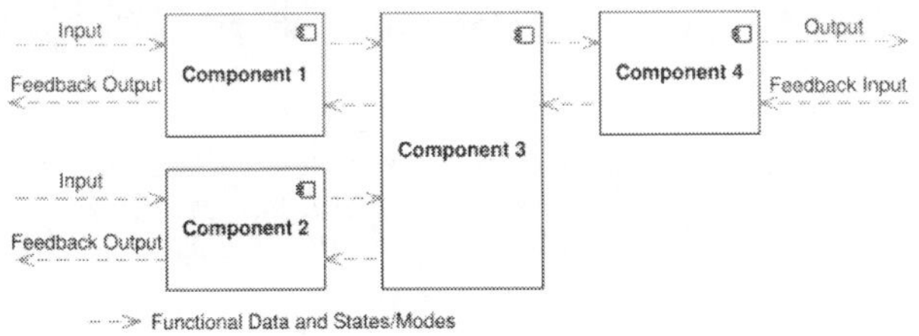

Figure 8. Architecture design principle: Feedback channel

All information / data from the end of the effect chain to the beginning of the effect chain are provided via the feedback. Thus, a component can adapt itself to the current situation in the effect chain without the necessity to create an explicit connection to all components in the effect chain. Furthermore, only the dependency of a component to the adjacent components of an effect chain exists. If the processing order of the components is selected s.t. all inputs are processed first and then the feedback, all components of the effect chain have the information on the current system state available in the next computing cycle. The effect chain to Figure 8 then looks as follows: The four components process their inputs in the effect direction. The components are then processed in the reverse order and the feedback is processed, i.e., from `Component 4` to `Component 1`. Here, components 1 and 2 can be interchanged in their processing.

In summary, the overall system is more maintainable and easier to expand by this architecture design principle. The individual components do not have to be connected to all components in order to know the system state. Through the feedback channel there is an information exchange between all components in the same computing cycle. Controllers can adapt themselves directly if they do not have access to an actuator.

Summary

The presented architectural concepts in this section were developed within different industrial projects in the automotive domain involving different software architects and project members. Nevertheless, there are similarities between the presented concepts, which become explicit by generalization and the representation by a uniform description language. Thereby, the projects focused the same as well as varying problem issues and requirements. With this representation technique it was possible to reuse the concepts in other projects to increase the quality in an early phase of development and to economize effort, because the projects start discussing about architectural concepts.

The architectural concepts presented in this paper are developed iteratively and in some cases the development time took over one year. As a result from our field study we can outline that there are similarities between the architectural evolution of product lines and the abstract and generic development process of concepts which is not surprising. The evolution of an architectural concept looks like the same - reuse and adaptation in other projects, which sometimes results in a new concept. Besides we can observe that the different levels of abstraction we have for architecture descriptions, we can find for concepts, as well. For example, the architecture design principle IV-A4 (Component Model, Figure 7), describes coordinating functionality, status and mode information and functional data connections. All these aspects we can find in the design principle IV-A2 (Coordinator, PipesAndFilters, Support, Figure 5), too. With the difference that the `Component Model` concept is for low level control functions, whereas the other concept deals with components on another abstraction level - to clarify the `Component Model` principle can be applied for a `Filter`, for example.

Architecture concepts like the ones presented before and all other aspects mentioned in the introduction of this section, especially the specification of wording and naming conventions help to build a collective experience of skilled software engineers. They capture existing, well-proven experience in software development and help to promote good design practice [11].

The result of making these concepts explicit on this abstraction level leads to discussions about architectural problems and generic solution schemes. In particular at the product line architecture level the focus is shifted from the more technical driven problems upon the more abstract and software architecture oriented issues. Over time this leads to new architectural concepts, which are documented, evaluated, maybe extracted from existing products, but making them explicit and integrating them at the right places in the further development process.

Another very important aspect dealing with architectural concepts is the monitoring of the concrete realizations of them. In our approach the `Check` activity takes care of it. All the presented concepts can be represented by a logical rule set, as described in [22]. Related to the fact that all elements of the software are subjects to the evolution process, architectural concepts can change or had to be adapted over time. This means that the violation of an architectural rule indicates not always a bad or defective implementation, it can additionally give the impulse to review the associated concept and the context. In our approach the assessment of the rule violation is included in the `Check` activity and if there is an indication for a rule adaptation this will be analyzed and worked out in detail in the next `Design` activity. Overall it leads to a managed evolution.

B. Understanding of Architecture and Measuring of Architecture Quality

Software development is an evolutionary and not a linear process. The costs caused by errors in software in the last years, especially in the automotive industry, are very high (15-20% form earnings before interest and taxes). Thus, it is necessary to understand and evaluate the architecture to support further development. In a vehicle, software will occupy a larger and larger part and the costs caused by errors will be rising. Therefore, it is important to control the quality of the software continuously. Problems/Errors can be detected early so that the quality of the software increases. The quality of the software depends in particular on the quality of the corresponding software architecture. In our approach, we use PLAs for automotive software product line development. PLAs are special types of software architectures. They do not only describe one system, but many products which can be derived from this architecture. Variability of the architecture, reuse of products, and the complexity are important values to assess the quality of this architecture.

Today, metrics mainly focus on code level. The most common metrics are *Lines of Code*, *Halstead*, and *McCabe*. In object-oriented programming (OOP), *MOOD metrics* and *CK metrics* are used. However, these metrics are not suitable for measuring PLAs. For assessing a PLA, the most important value is variability, as the degree of variability increases complexity in PLAs. Further important values are complexity and maintainability of the possible products and the PLA. As products shall be reused for other products, a high reuse-rate of products is an important objective of the PLA. A high reuse-rate also implies a high focus on maintainability of the products.

In our approach, we assess the *modification effort*, *reuse rate* and *cohesion* of a PLA, since we can thus evaluate the properties discussed above. In the following, we give formulas for the calculation of modification effort, reuse rate and cohesion. Here, we refer to the definitions of Section II-B, and the system structure depicted in Figure 3.

1) Modification effort: The modification effort measures the effort caused by the planned changes in the PLA: How many logical architecture elements (LAE), and products are affected by the change? The calculated result value is between 0 (no elements have to be changed) and 1 (all elements have to be changed). Simple changes can have a high impact to products and modules. The value supports the architect to improve understanding the architecture. Maybe there is a better solution to design the new PLA with less modification effort.

The modification effort $\mathcal{E}$ to develop a new PLA version pla_{x+1} for a given PLA pla_x is calculated as follows on the level of PLA and products:

$$\mathcal{E}^{PLA} = \frac{number\ of\ concerned\ LAE}{number\ of\ all\ LAE} \tag{1}$$

$$\mathcal{E}^{P} = \frac{number\ of\ concerned\ products}{number\ of\ all\ products} \tag{2}$$

where $concerned\ LAE/products$ denote the logical architecture elements/products that have to be modified or added/deleted when introducing the new PLA version. In Table II we apply $\mathcal{E}$ on the example in Figure 3.

TABLE II. MODIFICATION EFFORT FOR THE EXAMPLE OF FIGURE 3.

$\mathcal{E}$	$pla_1 \rightarrow pla_2$	$pla_2 \rightarrow pla_3$
$\mathcal{E}^{PLA}$	$\frac{\lvert\{A,C\}\rvert}{\lvert\{A,B,C\}\rvert} = \frac{2}{3}$	$\frac{\lvert\{B,C\}\rvert}{\lvert\{A,B,C\}\rvert} = \frac{2}{3}$
$\mathcal{E}^{P}$	$\frac{\lvert\{p_1,p_2\}\rvert}{\lvert\{p_1,p_2\}\rvert} = \frac{2}{2} = 1$	$\frac{\lvert\{p_1,p_2,p_3\}\rvert}{\lvert\{p_1,p_2,p_3\}\rvert} = \frac{3}{3} = 1$

Consider, e.g., step $pla_1 \rightarrow pla_2$ in Table II: Note that each module is assigned to only one LAE in this example. Hence, modules are not considered in this example. In practice an LAE can be assigned to several modules to realize functionality. In this step the architect adds a connection between the LAE A and LAE C on the PLA. The modification effort for the PLA is $\frac{2}{3}$, because two of three LAE are affected by this change. On product level the modification effort $\mathcal{E}^P$ is 1: p_{1_1} and p_{2_1} contain LAE A and are thus affected. Note that for $\mathcal{E}^P$ we do not specify the version index in the calculation in Table II.

In this example, all products are affected by the modification in both development steps. There is no other way to reduce the modification effort. However, new product versions are not released at each point in time even if the product is concerned by the PLA modification (see product p_1 at $time = 2$ in Figure 3).

2) Reuse rate: To keep the vehicles cost efficient, modular products with a high reuse rate cross different types of vehicles are desired. The aim is to reuse modules in different products. The reuse rate $\mathcal{R}^m$ of a module m in a certain PLA version pla_x is calculated as follows:

$$\mathcal{R}^m = \frac{number\ of\ usage\ of\ m\ in\ all\ products\ of\ pla_x}{number\ of\ all\ products\ of\ pla_x} \tag{3}$$

Average reuse rate $\mathcal{R}^M$:

$$\mathcal{R}^M = \frac{\sum \mathcal{R}^m}{number\ of\ all\ modules} \tag{4}$$

In Table III we apply $\mathcal{R}$ on the example in Figure 3.

TABLE III. REUSE RATE FOR THE EXAMPLE OF FIGURE 3.

$\mathcal{R}$	pla_1	pla_2	pla_3
$\mathcal{R}^{m_1}$	$\frac{2}{2}$	$\frac{1}{1}$	$\frac{2}{3}$
$\mathcal{R}^{m_2}$	$\frac{2}{2}$	$\frac{1}{1}$	$\frac{2}{3}$
$\mathcal{R}^{m_3}$	$\frac{1}{2}$	$\frac{0}{1}$	$\frac{1}{3}$
$\mathcal{R}^{m'_1}$	–	–	$\frac{1}{3}$
$\mathcal{R}^{m'_2}$	–	–	$\frac{1}{3}$
$\mathcal{R}^{M}$	$\frac{5}{2}/3 \approx 0.84$	$\frac{2}{1}/3 \approx 0.67$	$\frac{7}{3}/5 \approx 0.47$

Consider, e.g., pla_1 and $\mathcal{R}^{m1}$ in Table III: Modules m_{1_1} and m_{2_1} are both used in products p_{1_1} and p_{2_1}. Thus, the reuse rate is $\frac{2}{2} = 1$ (100%). In the example the average reuse rate for pla_1 is 0.84 (84%). This value constitutes a high degree of reuse. For pla_3 and $\mathcal{R}^{m1}$ the reuse rate has to take the new product p_{3_1} into account. As m_{1_3} is used in two products and the number of products is three, $\mathcal{R}^{m1} = \frac{2}{3}$ ($\approx$ 67%).

In the example the average reuse rate in pla_3 is 0.47. The comparison between pla_1 and pla_3 shows that the reuse rate has deteriorated. This is to be expected since new products and modules are added. In the next planning phase of a new PLA these new modules should be used in more products to increase the reuse rate.

3) Cohesion: A high cohesion is preferable. The value for cohesion denotes the rate, how many export values of the modules are used inside a product. The higher the value, the better the cohesion of the product. We call export and import values of modules *exports* and *imports* in the following.

The cohesion $\mathcal{A}^p$ of a product p is calculated as follows:

$$\mathcal{A}^p = \frac{number\ of\ all\ exports\ of\ all\ modules\ used\ in\ p}{number\ of\ all\ exports\ of\ all\ modules\ in\ p} \quad (5)$$

The average cohesion $\mathcal{A}^P$ of products of a PLA version is calculated as follows:

$$\mathcal{A}^P = \frac{\sum \mathcal{A}^p}{number\ of\ all\ products} \quad (6)$$

The cohesion of the PLA $\mathcal{A}^{PLA}$ is calculated as follows:

$$\mathcal{A}^{PLA} = \frac{number\ of\ all\ exports\ of\ modules\ used\ in\ all\ products}{number\ of\ all\ exports\ of\ all\ modules\ of\ all\ products} \quad (7)$$

In the following Table IV, we set randomly chosen values for exports and imports at $time = 1$ for the modules. We assume that the architect has access to the whole information of LAE, all products, and all modules at this time.

TABLE IV. EXPORTS AND IMPORTS AT TIME=1 IN FIGURE 3.

Module	*Number of export values*	*Number of import values*
m_{1_1}	3	1
m_{2_1}	4	3
m_{3_1}	2	3

TABLE V. COHESION FOR THE EXAMPLE OF FIGURE 3.

$\mathcal{A}$	pla_1	pla_2	pla_3
$\mathcal{A}^{p_1}$	$\frac{1+1+0}{3+4+2} \approx 0.22$	–	$\frac{2+0+0}{3+4+2} \approx 0.22$
$\mathcal{A}^{p_2}$	$\frac{1+0}{3+4} \approx 0.14$	$\frac{1+0}{3+4} \approx 0.14$	$\frac{1+0}{3+4} \approx 0.14$
$\mathcal{A}^{p_3}$	–	–	$\frac{1+0}{3+4} \approx 0.14$
$\mathcal{A}^P$	≈ 0.18	≈ 0.14	≈ 0.17
$\mathcal{A}^{PLA}$	$\frac{1+1+0+1+0}{3+4+2+3+4} \approx 0.19$	$\frac{1+0}{3+4} \approx 0.14$	$\frac{2+0+0+1+0+1+0}{3+4+2+3+4+3+4} \approx 0.17$

Consider, e.g., pla_1 and $\mathcal{A}^{p_1}$ in Table V: Product p_{1_1} has three modules (m_{1_1}, m_{2_1}, m_{3_1}). In product p_{1_1} LAE A has a connection (export) to B and B has a connection (export) to C. In Table IV all export values are listed. The cohesion is calculated as follows:

$$\frac{\sum used\ exports\ of\ m_{1\_1}, m_{2\_1}, m_{3\_1}}{\sum all\ exports\ of\ m1\_1, m2\_1, m3\_1} = \frac{1+1+0}{3+4+2} \approx 0.22$$

For a whole PLA all used export values of modules in all products are aggregated. The result for pla_2 shows that the change operation concerns all products and a part of the LAE and modules. The expected cohesion in pla_3 is worse compared to pla_1. The quality of the PLA has slightly deteriorated. Modules realize more than one functionality because they are used in more than one project. Therefore, cohesion is competing to the reuse rate. It is planned to evaluate these metrics and determine the intervals of the values for "good" and "bad" with the help of experts in one of our industrial projects.

4) Applying change operations on a PLA: A software architect changes the PLA to fulfill new requirements. The aim is to implement the new requirements with the least possible adaptation on the product/module level.

Figure 9 exemplarily describes the procedure of applying change operations on a PLA. The procedure starts with the current PLA and all products and modules at $time = 1$. To make change operations, the software architect performs the following steps:

1) The architect adds a new change operation to the PLA.
2) The above metrics are performed on the intermediate PLA b. The results are considered as bad by the architect and the changes are rejected.
3) The architect adds a new change operation to the PLA. The above metrics are performed on the intermediate PLA. The results are evaluated as good and the PLA c serves as the basis for the next step.
4) The architect adds a new change operation to the PLA c.
5) The above metrics are performed on the intermediate PLA d. The results are considered as bad by the architect and the changes are rejected.
6) The architect adds a new change operation on the PLA c resulting in PLA e. Again, the metrics are applied. The results are rated as good. As all requirements have been implemented, PLA e is the new PLA vision and serves as input for the planning.

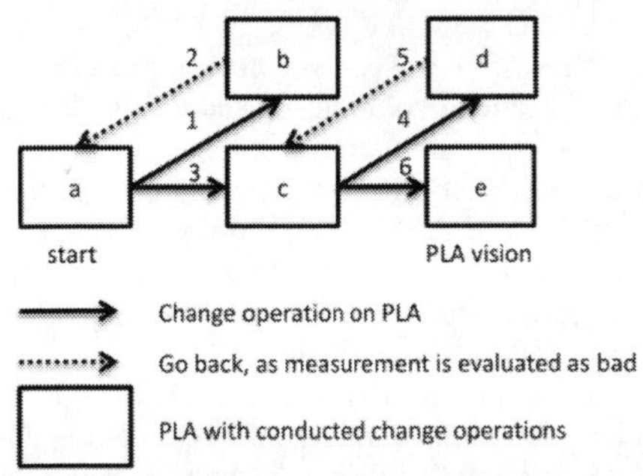

Figure 9. Example: Applying change operations on a PLA

C. Planning of Development Iterations and Prototyping

In our case the planning of the further development involves several activities, e.g., performing planning of each modification of PLA and PA. The problem arises when `PL-Requirements` or `P-Requirements` needs to be realized within certain development time and within certain development costs. Planning solves the problem by defining timed activities considering the effort limitations.

Planning consists of a sequence of iterations. Iterations are defined as a number of architecture elements that must be realized in a time period bounded by t_{start} and t_{end} with $t_{start}, t_{end} \in \mathbb{N}, t_{start} < t_{end}$. Within each time period the activities `Design`, `Plan`, `Implement` and `Check` are ordered. The iteration is completed when all modifications are realized by `Design`, `Implement`, and checked to be conform to architecture rules by `Check`. An example of a sequence of three iterations is shown in Figure 3. In Figure 3, the expected result of modifications on PLA at several time points is defined, which corresponds to `PL-Plan`. Moreover, the expected result of modifications on PA are defined where products, modules and their mapping for three time points is shown in Figure 3.

The effort caused to realize the planned number of architecture elements is estimated by the activities `Design` and `Implement`, to achieve the PLA and PA development within given effort limitations. In case of a deviation between planned and actual estimations the initial plan is modified. Therefore, effort estimations are made by considering the necessary effort of PLA or PA modifications from `Design` and from `Implement`. In the following, details about effort estimations according to PLA and PA modifications are presented to achieve estimation based planning.

The first estimation concept is based on metrics to evaluate the modification effort. For example, modification effort according to connection structure and component structure is estimated by rating cohesion of components. Another estimation concept is to evaluate the effort based on modification realizing a new pattern in the appropriate PLA or PA. Hence, simple connection or component related modifications are lightweight, pattern based structure modifications are heavyweight. Modifications rated as heavyweight often involve a huge number of architecture components and products. Therefore, in such a case our methodology suggests to outsource such heavyweight modifications into a prototype projects. This special case is enclosed by the activity `PL to P` of our methodology.

V. CONCLUSION

We introduced a sophisticated approach for automotive software systems evolution by concepts for planning and evolving product line architectures. To manage functional software systems complexity we proposed an approach based on modular, well-defined, and linked requirements as well as architectures. First, we proposed methods and concepts to create adequate architectures with the help of abstract principles, patterns, and describing techniques. Such techniques allow making complexity manageable. Next, we suggested techniques for understanding of architecture and measuring of architecture quality. With the help of numerical results of these measurements, we can make a statement about complexity, as well as conclusions about a system. Finally, we described how to plan development iterations and prototyping. We demonstrated our concepts by examples especially from the automotive domain.

REFERENCES

[1] F. P. Brooks, Jr., "No silver bullet essence and accidents of software engineering," Computer, vol. 20, no. 4, Apr. 1987, pp. 10–19.

[2] C. Knieke et al., "A Holistic Approach for Managed Evolution of Automotive Software Product Line Architectures," in Special Track: Managed Adaptive Automotive Product Line Development (MAAPL) along with ADAPTIVE 2017, 2016, accepted.

[3] R. Cloutier et al., "The Concept of Reference Architectures," Systems Engineering, vol. 13, no. 1, Feb. 2010, pp. 14–27.

[4] E. Y. Nakagawa, F. Oquendo, and M. Becker, "RAModel: A Reference Model for Reference Architectures," in Proc. of the 2012 Joint Working IEEE/IFIP Conference on Software Architecture and European Conference on Software Architecture, ser. WICSA-ECSA '12. IEEE Computer Society, 2012, pp. 297–301.

[5] E. Y. Nakagawa, M. Becker, and J. C. Maldonado, "Towards a Process to Design Product Line Architectures Based on Reference Architectures," in Proceedings of the 17th International Software Product Line Conference, ser. SPLC '13. ACM, 2013, pp. 157–161.

[6] B. Cool et al., "From Product Architectures to a Managed Automotive Software Product Line Architecture," in Proceedings of the 31st Annual ACM Symposium on Applied Computing, ser. SAC'16. New York, NY, USA: ACM, 2016, pp. 1350–1353.

[7] A. Strasser et al., "Mastering Erosion of Software Architecture in Automotive Software Product Lines," in SOFSEM 2014: Theory and Practice of Comp. Sc., ser. LNCS, vol. 8327. Springer, 2014, pp. 491–502.

[8] J. Bosch, Design and Use of Software Architectures: Adopting and Evolving a Product-Line Approach. Addison-Wesley, 2000.

[9] S. Thiel and A. Hein, "Modeling and Using Product Line Variability in Automotive Systems," IEEE Softw., vol. 19, no. 4, Jul. 2002, pp. 66–72.

[10] M. Shaw and D. Garlan, Software Architecture: Perspectives on an Emerging Discipline. Prentice-Hall, Inc., 1996.

[11] F. Buschmann, R. Meunier, H. Rohnert, P. Sommerlad, and M. Stal, Pattern-Oriented Software Architecture - Volume 1: A System of Patterns. Wiley Publishing, 1996.

[12] L. de Silva and D. Balasubramaniam, "Controlling Software Architecture Erosion: A Survey," Journal of Systems and Software, vol. 85, no. 1, Jan. 2012, pp. 132–151.

[13] H. Holdschick, "Challenges in the Evolution of Model-based Software Product Lines in the Automotive Domain," in Proceedings of the 4th International Workshop on Feature-Oriented Software Development, ser. FOSD '12. ACM, 2012, pp. 70–73.

[14] A. Rausch et al., "Managed and Continuous Evolution of Dependable Automotive Software Systems," in Proceedings of the 10th Symposium on Automotive Powertrain Control Systems, 2014, pp. 15–51.

[15] B. Hardung, T. Kölzow, and A. Krüger, "Reuse of Software in Distributed Embedded Automotive Systems," in Proc. of the 4th ACM intern. conf. on Embedded software. ACM, 2004, pp. 203–210.

[16] M. Steger et al., "Introducing PLA at Bosch Gasoline Systems: Experiences and Practices," in Software Product Lines. Springer, 2004, pp. 34–50.

[17] A. G. Chiquitto, I. M. S. Gimenes, and E. Oliveira, "Symples-cvl: A sysml and cvl based approach for product-line development of embedded systems," in Proceedings of the 2015 IX Brazilian Symposium on Components, Architectures and Reuse Software, ser. SBCARS '15. IEEE Computer Society, 2015, pp. 21–30.

[18] N. Siegmund, M. Rosenmüller, M. Kuhlemann, C. Kästner, and G. Saake, "Measuring non-functional properties in software product line for product derivation," in Proceedings of the 2008 15th Asia-Pacific Software Engineering Conference, ser. APSEC '08. IEEE Computer Society, 2008, pp. 187–194.

[19] L. Passos et al., "Feature-oriented software evolution," in Proceedings of the Seventh International Workshop on Variability Modelling of Software-intensive Systems, ser. VaMoS '13. ACM, 2013, pp. 17:1–17:8.

[20] G. Aldekoa, S. Trujillo, G. S. Mendieta, and O. Díaz, "Quantifying Maintainability in Feature Oriented Product Lines," in Proceedings of the 12th European Conference on Software Maintenance and Reengineering. IEEE, 2008, pp. 243–247.

[21] T. Zhang, L. Deng, J. Wu, Q. Zhou, and C. Ma, "Some Metrics for Accessing Quality of Product Line Architecture," in 2008 International Conference on Computer Science and Software Engineering, vol. 2, 2008, pp. 500–503.

[22] S. Herold, "Architectural Compliance in Component-Based Systems. Foundations, Specification, and Checking of Architectural Rules." Ph.D. dissertation, Technische Universität Clausthal, 2011.

Towards a Formalised Approach for Integrated Function Updates of Mechatronic Systems

Tim Warnecke, Karina Rehfeldt, Andreas Rausch

Technische Universität Clausthal
38678 Clausthal-Zellerfeld, Germany
email: {tim.warnecke, karina.rehfeldt, andreas.rausch}@tu-clausthal.de

David Inkermann, Tobias Huth, Thomas Vietor

Technische Universität Braunschweig
38106 Braunschweig, Germany
email: {d.inkermann, tobias.huth, t.vietor}@tu-braunschweig.de

***Abstract*—Looking at different everyday products, we are facing the situation that they are replaced although their technical life time has not ended. The main reason for this is that customers often replace products like smart phones or household devices, because there are new ones available providing new and additional functions and features. These functions and features are predominately based on software and follow shorter development and innovation cycles. From the resource point of view the mismatch between technical life time and use period of products leads to great disposal. In order to address this challenge, a common concept is to update existing products. To provide substantial new functions, such updates have to concern both hardware and software components. Due to the complexity of dependencies between these components, it is not an easy task to come up with these integral and verified updates. As a first step to tackle this problem, we propose a formalized approach to describe integrated hardware and software upgrades. Based on this formalism, we present our ongoing research and preliminary results in the fields of functions and systems modeling.**

***Index Terms*—Complex Systems; Design for Maintainability; Release Management; Software Product Lines; Software Evolution.**

I. Introduction

In most of modern products like vehicles, household devices or machine tools, functions are realized by a combination of hardware, electronics and software components. These components are the results of development within different domains and are often differing with regard to the time needed for their realization, their innovation cycles and their specific technological advancements. Fast technological developments, for instance in the fields of comfort or communication interfaces, are often driven by software engineering. However, engineering and development of hardware components like a car body or drive train are missing the speed of these advancements. At the same time, implementation of new software often requires specific hardware like sensors or actors. Therefore, common practice is to implement and release new functions only within new released product generations. This leads to the situation that the actual use period of products compared to their technical life span is greatly shortened [1], [2]. Products are shut down or disposed of, although their functionality is still given from the technical point of view [3]. This is caused by the customers buying decisions which are tremendously influenced by features like comfort, assistance or multimedia-based functions. Furthermore, the gap between technical life span and actual use period leads to the disposal of still valuable resources like materials but energy - for instance of the manufacturing process stored within the mechanical components - as well. In order to counteract this trend and increase the ecological sustainability of products, there are several restrictive laws planned. For instance, it is planned to define a minimum service life span for electric components [4]. Another expedient and less restrictive strategy is a so called planned product upgrade of an existing product. Within this paper we follow the second strategy.

A. Challenge of Integrated Product Updates

There is a great body of literature dealing with the adaptability and changeability of products. General approaches referred to as Design for Changeability [5], Design for Flexibility [6] or modularization [7] provide basic strategies to adapt system properties and functions during the life cycle. However, these approaches are focusing on the classical life cycle understanding and do not consider upgrades of existing products. The focus of these approaches is to support the initial design of products.

In the domain of software engineering, product updates are generally possible if the software was designed accordingly. However, when it comes to systems, including both hardware and software like embedded systems, software upgrades are limited by the installed hardware components. Furthermore, software updates are often hindered because new software

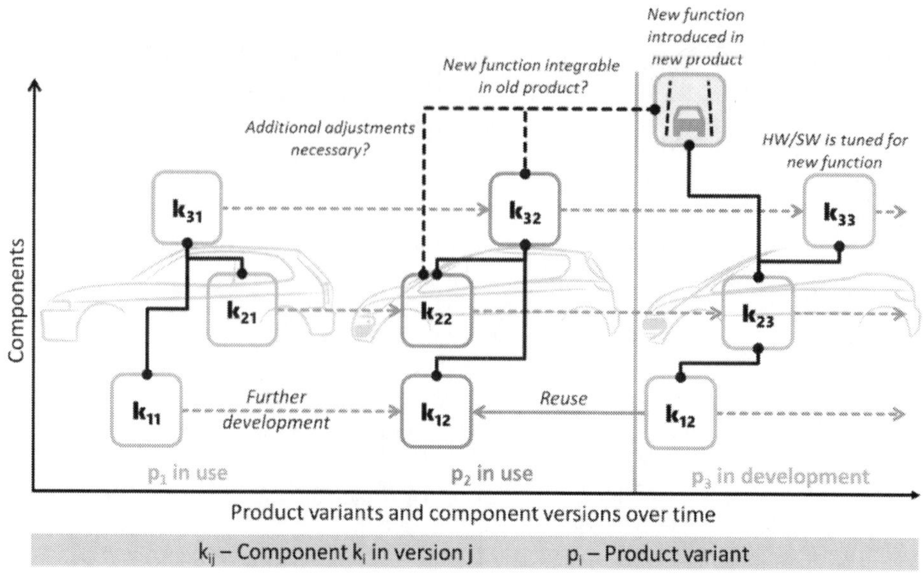

Fig. 1. Illustration of the question whether an existing product variant can be updated with a new function.

is developed with current hardware components in mind and does not consider limitations of older hardware components. Therefore, compatibility with existing hardware components of previous product variants is not guaranteed. This forward-looking development drives progress, but makes the integration of new software functions into existing products even harder. In the domain of hardware engineering, it is even worse, since most of the used hardware components can't be easily changed after the initial handover to the customer. Furthermore, it is hard to identify and define required extensions within existing hardware configurations to enable the implementation of new software functions.

In order to support an integrated function update of mechatronic systems, it is therefore essential to analyze the interrelations between functions and features as well as the components realizing these functions and features.

B. Focus of Research

Figure 1 highlights the problem addressed in this contribution by schematically representing the development of vehicle variants in product lines and their constituting components. The development is ongoing over time and new products are based on either existing, updated or newly developed components. To support the update of products, it is essential to understand how their components can be adapted. This question is directly linked to the time scale we present in Figure 1. Here, the first two vehicles p_1 and p_2 represent vehicles, which are already in use. Vehicle p_1 of the first generation uses three components $k_{11} - k_{31}$. Note, here k_{ij} is the component k_i used in development version j. The vehicle p_2 in the middle is an advanced development of p_1. Product p_2 uses the same component identities $k_1 - k_3$ but in development version 2, here components $k_{12} - k_{32}$. On the right hand side of Figure 1 a vehicle in development version, p_3, is illustrated. Variant p_3 uses the components k_2 and k_3 in version 3. In this case, the component k_{12} used in vehicle p_2 is reused directly, because an improvement was not necessary. Additionally, p_3 receives a new functionality, in this case a lane keeping system (LKS), illustrated by the top most component. Because of a proper executed development process of vehicle p_3, we can be certain that the LKS will work correctly in the component configuration of this vehicle. Additionally, during its own development, the previous vehicle p_2 was already tested and checked for functional correctness. In order to support the integrated update of the vehicle p_2, we are facing the question whether the LKS system of vehicle p_3 can be also integrated and which changes have to be made with regard to existing software and hardware components.

Our research is focusing on methods to model and analyze the compatibility and interaction between hardware and software components. Primary objective is to provide methods supporting estimation and evaluation of required changes of both, hardware and software, components. Furthermore, we aim to reduce the effort required for safeguarding of changed product configurations after updating these. This research will contribute to efficient upgrades of existing mechatronic systems and, therefore, the extension of their use periods. The research is guided by the following questions:

- How do we model the structure, behavior, functions and requirements of systems to identify required adaptations or updates with regard to hardware and software?
- How do we reduce test effort of a new system configuration when its functions and structure are already partly tested?
- How do we support the design of evolution friendly

system structures?

In this contribution, we describe a formalism to specify the first question. Furthermore, we state the areas to work on further more precisely. Therefore, in Section II we discuss the state of the art and basic understanding of releases and design for maintainability as well as approaches for systems modeling, both from the mechanical and the software point of view. In Section III, we define a simple formalization to describe functions, components and their connecting structure. Based on this, we introduce our approach to the stated problem in Section IV. The paper is summarized by a short conclusion in Section V.

II. Background and State of the Art

Based on the focus of research introduced, in this section an overview and definitions of essential terms are given. The focus is on basic strategies to extend the use period of complex systems and their effects on hardware and software components.

Release Management (RM) is originated from software development and describes the process and activities conducted to develop and deploy releases as a result of change requests. A major task of RM is to maintain the integrity and minimize the disruption of the original system during and after the deployment release of new features. This is done by prior planning and testing of a release [8]. A release in this context, is a collection of "one or more changes to a service that are built, tested and deployed together" [8]. At the beginning of the RM process, a subset of changes (sometimes also referred to as requirements) is selected as the scope of the release [9]. Besides the development and implementation of the release, RM also covers the estimation of effort and the resource management needed for planning, design and implementation of releases. In information technology, RM is well-established. The transfer to "hardware" products is still subject of research, cf. [10].

Design for maintainability (DfM) comprises the consideration of aspects regarding for instance serviceability, repairability or supportability, minimizing the effort during the use phase of the system to keep it in - or to restore it to - a usable condition [11]. According to the IEEE Standard Glossary of Software Engineering Terminology, maintainability is defined as "the ease with which a software system or component can be modified to correct faults, improve performance or other attributes, or adapt to a changed environment" [12]. DfM is closely linked with the modularity of products whose foundation is laid during the early design phases in form of the product's architecture [13].

There is a lot of research dealing with effort estimation in software changes, design of maintainable software systems and processes and methods for software engineering. Regarding software changes, in the last years more and more approaches were made in feature-oriented software evolution and changes. [14] proposes a feature-based software evolution with automatic traceability, analysis and recommendations. Passos et. al assume that managing changes at the level of features can help system designers in estimating costs and efforts while having a better understanding of the impacts of a change on the system.

Ferreira et. al [15] studied whether feature-oriented programming really benefits variety management in software product lines (SPL). They argue feature-oriented programming is indeed well suited for software product lines but still has drawbacks. The SPL tends to be more stable under certain aspects with feature-oriented programming. Nevertheless, feature-based software evolution does not have a general answer how new features can be integrated into whole systems dealing with both hardware and software.

The difficulty of the considered mechatronic systems and their updates are the deep interaction of hardware and software components. The software is built with a specific hardware concept in mind and vice versa. To our current knowledge there is no model or paradigm to generally address the problem of modeling a complex system to identify required adaptations for upgrade of functionalities. As a first step towards a better understanding and basis for our further research, in the following section we propose a formalism to describe integrated function updates of existing mechatronic systems. Based on the formalism, we identify further research needs.

III. Definitions

To give an idea on how we are tackling the mentioned questions, we formalize the concepts of product variants, hardware and software components as well as functions. Without loss of generality, we term hardware and software components simply as components and formalize them with the same definition. Later, a distinction between hardware and software components might become necessary. But for now, we are interested in the general idea of including new functions through new components whether hardware or software into existing products.

First, we define that every product variant consists of a restricted number of **software and hardware components** k_{ij} with i is the identity and j is the development version of component k. Furthermore, with regard to a development process we denote k_{ij-1} as the **predecessor version** of component k_{ij} and k_{ij+1} the **successor version** of component k_{ij}. So, we define the set of **all usable components** as

$$K = \{k_{ij}\} \text{ with } i, j \in \mathbb{N}$$

We define a **product variant** as

$$p_n := (K_m, v_m := K_m \times K_m) \text{ with } n, m \in \mathbb{N}$$

and the set of all possible product variants as

$$P := \{p_n\} \text{ with } n \in \mathbb{N}$$

This highlights that every product variant $p_i \in P$ consists of a subset of all usable components $K_m \subseteq K$ and a **structure** v_m. v_m describes the connections between the different components K_m to form a fully functional system. We do not differentiate the connections between components of a product variant. In case of a connection between two software components, it might be an interface usage. The connection between two hardware components might be a physical link while the connection between hardware and software are, e.g., signals.

Every product variant p_n is developed with the objective to fulfill a pre-defined set of functions taking into account specific requirements. The set of **all possible functions** can be defined as

$$F = \{f_n\} \text{ with } n \in \mathbb{N}$$

The function set $F_q \subseteq F$ denotes a subset of all possible functions. If a function set F_q is **fulfilled** by a product variant p_n we denote this as a satisfiability relation

$$F_q \models p_n$$

In the next section, we show our formalized approach to the problem described in the introduction.

IV. A Formalized Approach

If products are developed as product lines, we expect that a previous product variant p_{old} exists. p_{old} fulfills a known set of functions F_{old}. Additionally, a new product variant p_{new} exists, which fulfills F_{new}. In the proposed notation, we write $F_{old} \models p_{old}$ and $F_{new} \models p_{new}$. We now formalize our question whether p_{old} may be upgraded to fulfill the new function set F_{new} of our new product. Moreover, which changes in p_{old} are necessary to be able to fulfill the functions F_{new} completely or with limitations. We assume that a product variant called p'_{old} derived from p_{old} exists and fulfills the set of functions F_{new} from p_{new} - that is $F_{new} \models p'_{old}$. We define the product variant p'_{old} as

$$p'_{old} := (\{K_m\}, v_m : K_m \times K_m)$$
$$\text{with } \forall k_{xa} \in \Pi_1(p_{new}) \exists k_{xb} \in \Pi_1(p'_{old})$$

With other words, we are looking for a product variant, which contains for every component identity k_i in version a from p_{new} a corresponding component identity k_i in version b. Figure 2 shows the construction of the updated product based on the old and new product. The upper two product variants are the old product p_{old}, which will be updated and the new product p_{new} with a new functionality. There are components from p_{old}, which are kept in p'_{old}. Those are components not touched by the update (blue) and components, which are equal to the ones used in p_{new} and, therefore, kept (gray). Components existing in different version in p_{old} and p_{new} are updated (violet). Also, in p_{old} there are components that are removed in p'_{old} (red). Additional components for the new functionality in p_{new} are added to p'_{old} (green). The bottom product variant shows a possible outcome of the updated p_{old}, our p'_{old}.

Coming back to our initial question, we want to find a way to determine whether a new function can be integrated

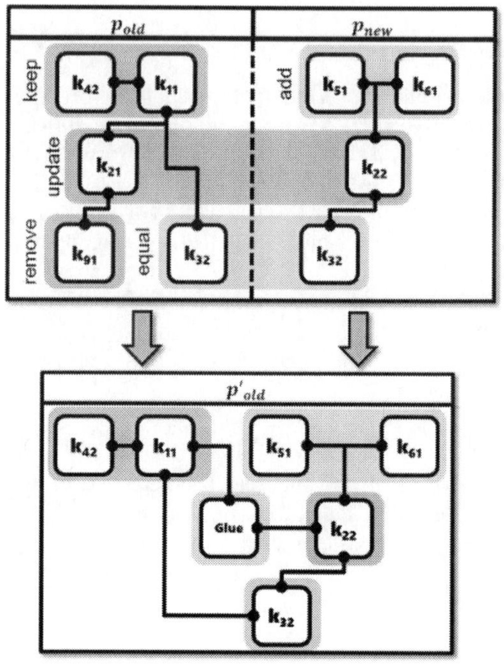

Fig. 2. Illustration of the construction of an updated product based on p_{old} and p_{new}.

into an old product and which changes to the old product are necessary. On basis of our formalization, we can now formulate essential questions regarding the necessary changes between p_{old} and p'_{old} and the changes' relation to p_{new}.

1) Which components of p_{new} are already included in p_{old} and, therefore, do not need to be changed in p'_{old}?

This questions asks for components in p_{new}, which were already used in the same version in p_{old}. Therefore, we do not need to change p_{old} regarding these components and p'_{old} remains unchanged. In Figure 2 these are the components with gray background.

2) Which components of p_{new} are not included in p_{old} and, therefore, have to be added to p'_{old}?

This question asks for components introduced with the new functions in p_{new}. These components cannot be part of p_{old} and, therefore, have to be added to p'_{old} to fulfill the new functions. In Figure 2 these are components with green background.

3) Which components k_{ia} of p_{new} are included in p_{old} but in a different version b and which version is included in p'_{old}?

This question asks for component identities, which are used both in p_{old} and p_{new} but in different versions. In other words, the component used in p_{new} is either the predecessor or successor of the component used in p_{old}. The question is, which of these version will be included in the updated product p'_{old}. In Figure 2 these are the components with violet background.

4) Which component identities from p_{old} are not included in p_{new} but in p'_{old}?

This question asks for the components in p_{old} that are not touched by the update. These components are not involved in the new or any associated functions. In Figure 2 these are the components with blue background.

5) Are there any components in p'_{old}, which are neither included in p_{new} nor p_{old}?

This question asks for components that were introduced in p'_{old} as a kind of adapter for components from p_{new}. In other words, the necessary components from p_{new} could not be added to p'_{old} because of an incompatible interface. However, an adapter component could resolve this incompatibility. In Figure 2 this is the glue component with green background in p'_{old}.

To tackle these questions we are convinced that a new modeling and engineering approach for complex systems has to be developed. Moreover, even after integrating and developing new components to construct a p'_{old} from p_{old} and p_{new}, it is not obvious that the new product will work like expected. Usually, after the integration of a new function, the entire system has to be retested and verified to guarantee that no unexpected side effects can occur. This includes testing functions without direct interactions with the new one because most side effects occur indirectly.

Naturally, it is not possible to fully test and verify already developed products in the field. Testing is a very time and cost consuming task, which is even harder to accomplish for older products that no longer have a development team. So, it is preferable that we don't need to test and verify the whole product with all its functions again. Instead, it would be preferable to just focus on parts of p'_{old}, which have changed in comparison to p_{old}.

We ask the question, whether it is possible to achieve much more simple retests for the new functions with the test results and data and control flows of p_{old} and p_{new} and the changes made to construct p'_{old}. We are convinced that these informations enable us to slice the architecture of p'_{old} in such a way that only new functions and some of their dependencies to components from p_{old} need to be retested.

V. Conclusion

We have presented the current mismatch between technical life time and the actual use period of modern products and highlighted the need for an integrated functional update approach for mechatronic systems. One of the main reasons for customers to replace a product, are extended functionalities implemented in newer product generations. In order to address this challenge, a common concept is to provide updates for existing products. Due to complex dependencies between software and hardware components, it is not an easy task to come up with these integral updates. Therefore, it is essential to understand the interrelations between the different components as well as the functions and components. We have shown that a critical improvement has to be made regarding modeling approaches for complex systems, addressing both the structure of the system as well as the functional view upon the system. While there exist methods to design both mere software and hardware systems for maintainability, the interaction of both domains in complex mechatronic systems asks for new approaches.

The formalization introduced will be used as a starting point for further research. The next research steps will be to develop an integrated modeling language for requirements, structures and components in mechatronic systems. This modeling language will be designed with the goal to identify needs for adaptation in case of functional upgrades. Another step will be the development of a method to evaluate effort of integral updates.

Our last research question is how to minimize the necessary test cases when a product was updated. Based on slicing techniques we want to reuse the results of formerly done tests to reduce the necessary retests when a product was only slightly changed.

References

[1] K. Ishii, "Incorporating end-of-life strategies in product definition," *Proc. of EcoDesign'99*, pp. 364–369, 1999.

[2] Y. Umeda, T. Daimon, and S. Kondoh, "Life cycle option selection based on the difference of value and physical lifetimes for life cycle design," *Proc. of the International Conference on Engineering Design, ICED 2007*, 2007.

[3] K. Watanabe, Y. Shimomura, A. Matsuda, S. Kondoh, and Y. Umeda, "Upgrade planning for upgradeable product design," in *Quantified Eco-Efficiency*. Springer, 2007, pp. 261–281.

[4] "Directive 2009/125/ec of the european parliament and the council of 21 october 2009 establishing a framework for setting of ecodesign requirements for energy-related products," 2009.

[5] E. Fricke and A. P. Schulz, "Design for changeability (dfc): Principles to enable changes in systems throughout their entire lifecycle," in *Systems Engineering, Vol. 8, No. 4, 2005*, 2005, pp. 342–359.

[6] A. Bischof, "Developing flexible products for changing environments," Dissertation, Technische Universität Berlin, 2010.

[7] K. Ulrich and S. Eppinger, *Product Design and Development*. New York: McGraw-Hill, 1995.

[8] "IEEE standard - adotion of the ISO/IEC 20000-2:2012, information technology - service management - part 2: Guidance on the application of service management systems," 2013.

[9] P. Carlshamre, "Release planning in market-driven software product development: Provoking an understanding," *Requirements engineering*, vol. 7, no. 3, pp. 139–151, 2002.

[10] G. Schuh and W. Eversheim, "Release-engineeringan approach to control rising system-complexity," *CIRP Annals-Manufacturing Technology*, vol. 53, no. 1, pp. 167–170, 2004.

[11] R. F. Stapelberg, *Handbook of reliability, availability, maintainability and safety in engineering design*. Springer Science & Business Media, 2009.

[12] "IEEE standard glossary of software engineering terminology," 1990.

[13] G. Schuh, S. Aleksic, and S. Rudolfs, "Module-based release management for technical changes," in *Progress in Systems Engineering: Proc. of the twenty-third International Conference on Systems Engineering*, 2015, pp. 293–298.

[14] L. Passos, K. Czarnecki, S. Apel, A. Wasowski, C. Kästner, and J. Guo, "Feature-oriented software evolution," in *Proceedings of the Seventh International Workshop on Variability Modelling of Software-intensive Systems*. ACM, 2013, p. 17.

[15] G. C. S. Ferreira, F. N. Gaia, E. Figueiredo, and M. de Almeida Maia, "On the use of feature-oriented programming for evolving software product linesa comparative study," *Science of Computer Programming*, vol. 93, pp. 65–85, 2014.

Refurbishment of Automotive Electronic Components regarding Update Capability of Applications

Nils Böcher

Robert Bosch GmbH
Business Division Automotive Aftermarket, Product Area Electronic Services
Hildesheim, Germany
Email: Nils.boecher@de.bosch.com

Abstract— **In the desktop multimedia area, modern update techniques are well known and firmly integrated. Fixed update management systems supply nearly automatically the latest software applications. In addition, the system based hardware drivers are also updated until the base system becomes obsolete and no longer supported. Additionally, functionality for data recovery, system and user settings are also given. In the automotive area, the application is based on platform package integrations and delivering states. Hereby, the application will mostly be frozen for the whole product life cycle after the end of line manufacturing process. For future Electrical/Electronic (E/E) architecture, with central functional integrations and domain centralized systems, there is a new challenge regarding the strategies over the product lifecycle. This includes update functionality in the field and after series production, for new functionalities (Car to Car/Environment (C2X) communication standards, automatic driving assistance, certificates) in consideration for latest security and safety requirements. Solutions must be developed in order to obtain a long life cycle regarding the obsolescence of the product.**

Keywords - variant management; reuse; life cycle.

I. INTRODUCTION

The refurbishment of assembly units is a common technique to be able to reuse an affected nonfunctional peripheral equipment for its target operation mode. This is mainly used in long term usage environments [1]. These methods can be sub-classified into two main areas. The first one is the individual repair, where only the functional affected root cause will be mend into a valid state. The second method is the remanufacturing. Hereby, the whole integrity of the assembly unit will be rechecked and reworked while setting the unit to a current state. This also includes software versions and constitutes software states. Today, the main focus of remanufacturing or refurbishment is still on hardware. The number of electronic modules in the cars on the roads is high and the trend to autonomous driving and Car to X communication will increase further the complexity. Customer service includes no longer only hardware exchange. Also, there is a need for software updates or system integration in car workshops. The global spare parts availability and their integration have a significant impact on success and customer satisfaction. In relation to the economic growth, in addition to the natural resource use, it is insufficient to overcome the even higher demands. This rapid growth involves increasing business risk for higher material costs, supply uncertainties and disruptions. With this background, it is necessary to improve the efficiency of the material, sustainable throughout the maintenance of the systems software components. This is especially true with regard to different life cycles for electronics and cars, long aftermarket supply obligation periods, longer warranty periods and increasing complexity of encryption and aspects related to software. Refurbishment activities have to focus more and more on the software applications.

In the future, the requirements of an application or platform development project will place new demands on the methods of a usual product creation process for a new piece of software. The software management with the accompanying support, updates and maintenance services has to be enhanced regarding update capability and long life support. As a rule, a software application for a model series - after release; it is a fixed package for serial production and additionally for spare parts in workshops. Hereby, no software updates in the entire life cycle are planned. Based on the launch management in an industrial production, the software will be specified regarding a reference architecture within the component design. After a customer software release, where additional calibration and review steps are performed, the software is packed and integrated into the product.

From Start of Production (SOP) to the stable series production, additional derivatives for certain software variants will usually be released, as shown in Figure 1. After the number of variants and quantity demands from the customer, the series production enters the stable phase. Until this section of high rate of production, usually no new software change, or engineering change to the product will be implemented.

The life cycle, which is between the End of Production (EOP) and End of Delivery (EOD) of the product, including the latest software variants, typically covers 15 years - due to post serial supply obligations. During this time, the product must be available based on a given forecast. This will reduce the impact on obsolescence due to the End of Delivery (EOD), based on a product life cycle sales forecast over time [1].

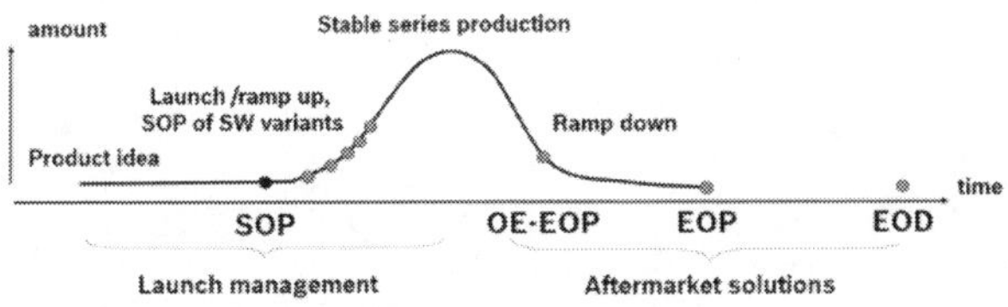

Figure 1. Product life cycle

Nowadays, a classic final stocking of finished products is cost intensive and difficult with respect to the huge model variation, which only differ by software variants within a model series. Hereby, a special software version can be used to have a bigger diversity of usable family version types. However, the product liability and requirements for protection against malicious manipulation and safety classifications in the automotive environment will affect several care strategies over the product lifecycle in the aftermarket. In case of tuning protection techniques, based on software signatures, a new target software without a valid signature is an irreversible incompatibility to the existing system - feasible despite the same hardware variant. Due to increasing security features, a software change is equivalent to a hardware change. A common security method is to fuse a complete block of defined code area in the memory area, by using a One Time Programmable (OTP) functionality of the program flash. In this area, mostly watchdog functionalities supervise the running application. This technique only makes it possible to create an updating option, by using a valid signed software. The signing technique is usually based on an asymmetric key cryptography. Additionally, new control unit cores use an internal Hardware Security Module (HSM). Besides further monitoring, runtime tuning detection regarding manipulated memory blocks and watchdog tasks, the HSM contains a program and data flash layout to store symmetric and asymmetric keys, but also data settings to handle the usage of certificates to protect public keys. This implements password handling for read/write protection, and also for open/close permissions to the debugger interface. A secure log of access entries will be written.

Future Electrical/Electronic (E/E) architectures handle the increasing complexity of the central vehicle functions, while building up a logical centralization and physical distributions. Hereby, the functionality can be partitioned into cross domain based and central vehicle functions on a multi-platform architecture [2]. The requirements for future applications and Base Software (BSW), will bring new challenges by increasing the number of features, which are activated and controlled by the software. Consumer electronic devices will be connected to the car networks, hence a growing complexity has to be expected for the in-car software and 3rd party software integration.

II. ADAPTIVE APPROACH TOWARDS INCREMENTAL UPDATE TECHNIQUES

Current software automotive standards, such as the Automotive Open System Architecture (AUTOSAR) initiative, decouple the application from the basic software package. In this case, the software is using a layer-oriented model, through the introduction of abstraction layers. These layers are separated into services areas. This abstraction opens up new possibilities for an adequate after-series supply strategy.

A suitable method for an adequate after-series supply strategy is the remanufacturing method. Hereby within the framework of the individual repair the software & spare parts can be integrated into the system. This is used to adapt function modules and software components, inside the BSW without altering/affecting the application. For this purpose, a basis must be created such as a non-volatile memory management scheme, such as in [3]. This can be, for example, a layer oriented partitioning so that updating a module in the BSW does not require a complete software container rebuild with flashing of the entire software. This also places new demands on the handling of memory allocation. This approach also requires new tasks with regard to the evaluation [4], and release procedures for hardware and software, in order to meet the latest requirements of operating approvals and aspects of vehicle safety, such as the Automotive Safety Integrity Level (ASIL) classification.

Another aspect is the individualization of the data records in future Electrical/Electronic (E/E) control units. For example this includes calibrated curves, variant coding, etc. This individualization could be used to create a basis for the prerequisite that already existing data from the field can be integrated into the supplier's production, to improve the aftermarket supply strategies. Therefore, an advanced update management is required, regarding runtime functionalities inside the control unit. This can be achieved by using version control, update history or update malfunction protection.

III. CONCLUSION

The approach, of a layer oriented base software design, provides a good opportunity to implement new requirements for automotive applications and future service solutions for update capability, in particular for increased complexity and network topology in the automotive sector, regarding future E/E architectures and its hardware requirements.

REFERENCES

[1] C. Jennings, D. Wu and J. Terpenny, "Forecasting Obsolescence Risk and Product Life Cycle With Machine Learning," in *IEEE Transactions on Components, Packaging and Manufacturing Technology*, vol. 6, no. 9, pp. 1428-1439, Sept. 2016.

[2] M. Becker, D. Dasari, B. Nicolic, B. Akesson, V. Nélis and T. Nolte, "Contention-Free Execution of Automotive Applications on a Clustered Many-Core Platform," *2016 28th Euromicro Conference on Real-Time Systems (ECRTS)*, Toulouse, 2016, pp. 14-24.

[3] J. Shin *et al.*, "A Non-Volatile Memory Management Scheme for Automotive Electronic Control Units," *2012 International Conference* on Connected Vehicles and Expo (ICCVE), Beijing, China, 2012, pp. 237-238.

[4] N. Englisch, F. Hänchen, F. Ullmann, A. Masrur and W. Hardt, "Application-Driven Evaluation of AUTOSAR Basic Software on Modern ECUs," 2015 IEEE 13th International Conference on Embedded and Ubiquitous Computing, Porto, 2015, pp. 60-67.

Memory-Map Shuffling: An Adaptive Security-Risk Mitigation

Pierre Schnarz*, Joachim Wietzke†, Andreas Rausch*
*Software Systems Engineering
Technische Universität Clausthal, Germany
Email: {pierre.schnarz—andreas.rausch}@tu-clausthal.de
†Hochschule Karlsruhe, Karlsruhe, Germany
Email: joachim.wietzke@hs-karlsruhe.de

***Abstract*—Automotive products, such as electronic control units, evolve increasingly towards adaptive solutions. From many perspectives, solutions need to be flexible with regards to the entire originating process and operation process. Here, the product development cycle, the product life-cycle and even product lines describe the dimensions a solution might have to adapt to. Certain requirements to secure the product continuously add further complexity to the aforementioned dimensions. Adversaries adapt - so the protection shall as well. However, adapting, particularly, technical solutions to products, implies the need for agnostic approaches. In this article, we propose a security-risk mitigation concept which aims to fit into the evolving automotive originating process applied to a particular class of electronic control units. Technically, the proposed approach shuffles the system memory-map of an asynchronous multiprocessing system. On the intermediate layer between the hardware and software, the assignment of memory and resources is obfuscated to a potential adversary who managed to breach one of the higher level memory protection mechanisms. As a result, the proposed mitigation adds either a further level in a defense-in-depth security architecture or fixes a structural vulnerability of certain hardware architectures.**

Keywords–Security; Mixed-Criticality; Obfuscation; Automotive.

I. INTRODUCTION

When it comes to automotive security, hardened electronic control units (ECU) are required to resist the emerging threat and attack landscape [1] [2]. Being resistant to threats and attacks is a continuous process. This is motivated by the fact that the adverse actions and methods against the system evolve over time. In other words, the adversaries change and find new methods, entry-points and tools to compromise a particular system. As a result, the risks that are related to the functionality of the system would increase. New countermeasures are necessary to limit the likelihood of an impact on safety, financial, operational or privacy aspects [3] [4]. The mentioned continuous process of reacting to the evolving security incidents has multi-dimensional impacts on the origination process of automotive products. These dimensions include: the product life-cycle including the development life-cycle and on a larger scale the product-line evolution. The technical goal of a security mitigation is the reduction of a security-risk. Besides that, the mitigations are required to fit into the aforementioned adaptive origination process. Depending on the particular phase in which a certain product faces the need for risk mitigation, the range of immutable (or static) system components might be wide. For example, changes to the hardware are nearly impossible after the start of production (SOP). As a result, changes to the software components of a product are targeted.

Adaptivity, the evolutionary environment and cost reductions are just a few arguments to move vehicular functions into a highly integrated platform (such as ECUs). The results are very powerful but complex systems. Important is the aspect of mixing functions which imply diverse system quality demands. For example, a single platform aggregates functions which on the one hand operate break-assistance features and infotainment in parallel. Such systems are usually referred to as mixed-criticality systems (MC-system) [5]. From an organizational point of view, these functions are required to operate as they did on separated ECUs before. This is particularly true for security. In particular, the separation and isolation aspects are key in such environments. It must be ensured that no interference between certain functions is possible. However, for example in security, the strength might need to be adapted over time due to the emerging threat landscape. This is even more important, since the functions will be adapted over the product-lifetime.

In this work, we propose a technical mitigation concept which is adaptable to highly integrated platforms. The concept is also driven by the evolutionary automotive product origination landscape. Technically, the mitigation approach aims to protect memory partitions, of certain functions, from exploitation. This is achieved by shuffling of address translation mappings of commodity virtualization mechanisms. Due to the obfuscated memory structure, the risk of further compromisation is mitigated. Metrics to characterize the exploitability [6] and effectiveness [7] are given.

In section V the memory-map shuffling concept is introduced and analyzed. The rest of the article is structured as follows. In section III the target of evaluation (ToE) is defined. In the following sections the threat analysis (compare Section IV) and the particular attack vectors (compare Section IV-B) are described. Section VI gives an outline of the effectiveness of the given approach. Lastly, section VII contains concluding remarks.

A. Related Work

The idea of obfuscating addresses is not new in certain areas. On application level, address obfuscation is adopted by many operating systems. Particularly, in general purpose operating systems such as *Linux*, *Windows* and *Mac OSX* this technique is actually state-of-the art. As of today, this is said to be one of the most effective countermeasures against memory exploits. Recent efforts brought that technique down to the system level, by randomizing the operating system's (OS) kernel address space [8]. In Linux, for example, the developers aimed for a significant increase of system security by making attacks into the monolithic kernel space less predictable for adversaries. In [9] Bhatkar et al. describe address obfuscation as an efficient approach to combat memory error exploits. The authors argue that these attacks require an attacker to have an in-depth understanding of the internal details of a victim program, including the locations of critical data and/or code. Therefore, program obfuscation is a general technique for securing programs by making it difficult for attackers to acquire such a detailed understanding. Kil et al. extend in [10] the idea of address space layout permutation to enable a finer grained randomization. Generally, they address one of the biggest drawbacks of current address space randomization implementations, namely the lack of a cryptographic secure entropy. Possible adversaries are able to guess the locations statistically in a very short amount of time, since the number of bits used for randomization is very limited. The permutation of address layouts facilitate to combat attacks using techniques such as buffer-overflows, format string attacks and code re-usage attacks like return oriented programming (ROP). In [11] Shuo et al. introduces a method to utilize hardware virtualization in order to prevent ROP attacks within the kernel. In [12] Rushanan et al. elaborate on the concept of malicious behavior based on direct memory access (DMA) transfers. The attacks are implemented using commodity desktop hardware. Although the implementation is not applicable to embedded hardware, the DMA issue is transferable to the attack surface of embedded system-on-chips (SoC).

II. Security of Evolving Automotive Products

The issue of securing products depends on the evolutionary state inside the product life-cycle (PLC) or outside within the product-line. Generally, the PLC is mainly focused on when it comes to security processes. PLCs of automotive products are roughly dividable into two main phases. First, in the *pre-SOP* phase, the product will be developed using a suitable development cycle, such as the v-model. Second, in the *post-SOP* phase, the product needs to be maintained. From the security perspective, two major goals are spread over these two phases. The first goal is to create a state in which the system can be treated as secure. In other words, to be aware of risks in the first place and to mitigate or accept them in the second. The second goal is to keep a certain risk threshold in which the system is still in this secure state. Most commonly, the applied method to find security requirements in the pre-SOP phase is risk assessment [3]. For every function the system has, a potential impact and likelihood will be analyzed. With respect to the particular risk, a risk treatment phase follows and the specific strategies to mitigate those risks will be defined. Those mitigations are fed as logical requirements and technical requirements into a system design. In the verification and validation phase of the v-model, appropriate security testing methods are applied to raise confidence in the absence of severe vulnerabilities. Security testing methods include fuzzing (negative testing) and penetration testing. In other words, during the development, the foundations for determining the security requirements are built accompanied by techniques to gain confidence in the derived logical and technical security architecture. During the post SOP phase, the system should be observed. If an incident occurs a proper response should be initiated. Accordingly, if this response requires a security update (software) the development of this update will traverse the secure development v-model for the new function. Limiting factors for the upcoming security mitigations are immutable components of the system which might be functional or technical. A prominent example is the hardware platform which is obviously hard to modify once it is deployed. However, this immutability is not only true for products that are already deployed, as practically within product lines the engineering strategy such as top-down and bottom-up might also imply further restrictions. For example, a hardware platform is to be integrated (bottom-up) for a certain set of software functions. Some of the functions then need to be fitted and developed onto (top-down) the hardware platform. This also implies restrictions for security solutions. This might appear in many reuse situations in automotive product line development. To summarize, security solutions need to fit into this evolving landscape.

III. Mixed-Criticality System

Mixed-criticality systems integrate multiple organizational domains (MC-domains), each of which potentially has different demands on the necessity (criticality) of the fulfillment of quality goals. Quality goals are for example dependability aspects, performance, etc. [13]. MC-domains are facilitated by combining several functional and technical components of a system. As an example, technically it might contain a software stack including OS, containers and applications. The technical implementation of the MC-system is discussed in the following section.

A. Facilitate MC-systems by Means of AMP

Where the definition of MC-systems describes a functional and logical setup, AMP refers to the technical part. In general, AMP is a system utilization paradigm which aims to control hardware elements independently by multiple operational units. As such, AMP systems can facilitate a MC-system by assigning technical means at the hardware level and software level. In other words, it is a configuration of the hardware to create the logical layers on top of it. In the following, this level is referred to as the *intermediate level*. As mentioned in Section III, the separation of functionality is a fundamental requirement to implement a proper MC-system. From the hardware level up to the application level, there are several technical possibilities to create a logical separation. Technically, each layer of a system provides means to create separated domains. For example, applications are separated most commonly in processes and threads which are provided by the OS. At the lower architectural layers, virtualization technologies emerge within the automotive environment. The aim is to combine multiple OS in one platform [14] [15].

B. Target of Evaluation

In this work, the target of evaluation (ToE) adopts the AMP paradigm and facilitates a MC-system on the intermediate level. In Figure 1 the ToE is depicted. It shows two MC-domains, *MC-domain1* in red color and *MC-domain2* in blue color. The figure indicates a software stack assigned to each of the two domains. Furthermore, the hardware layer is modeled. It shows a minimalistic set of elements of a commodity

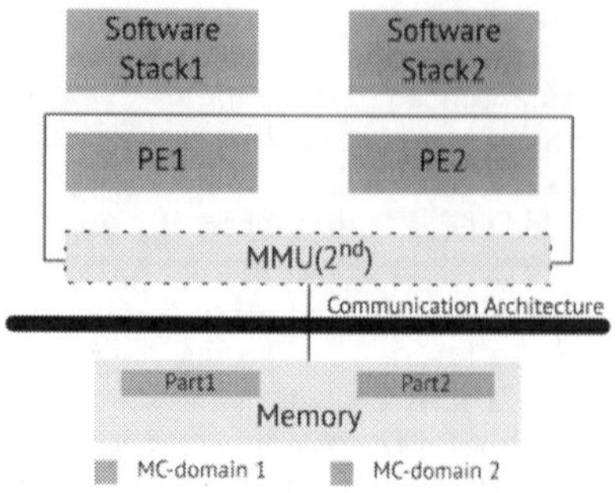

Figure 1. Target of evaluation.

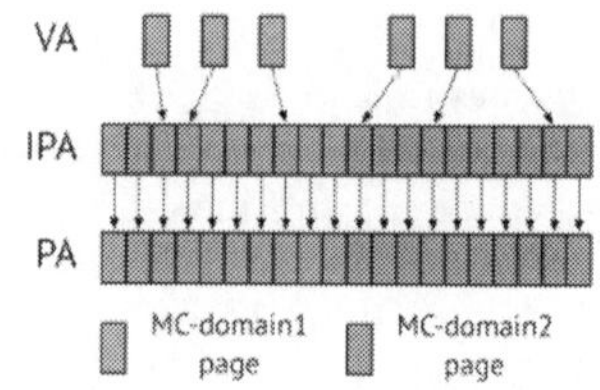

Figure 2. Identity memory-mapping principle.

SoC. The elements inlcude processor cores such as processing elements (PE) (denoted by *PE1* and *PE2*), a communication architecture and main memory. *PE1* is assigned to *MC-domain1*. Accordingly, *PE2* is assigned to *MC-domain2*. Each Mc-domain includes its own memory partitions, which are denoted by *Part1* and *Part2*.

C. Memory-Maps in AMP Based Systems

In an AMP system, typically three types of addresses are handled. First, the virtual address (VA) space at user level which is maintained by the operating system to provide horizontal memory separation of processes. Second, the physical address (PA) space which represents the address of the main-memory. Last, the intermediate physical address (IPA) space which is introduced to be able to separate the MC-domains (or virtualized OS). The translation from VA to IPA is referred to as *stage 1* translation and those from IPA to PA as *stage 2* translation respectively. Depending on the particular implementation of the PE the translation is handled by a memory management unit (MMU) in hardware. The structure which is used to identify corresponding addresses is referred to as a mapping table filled with a finite set of translation entries. In the translation process, the MMU extracts the most significant bits of the input address to index the translation table. The output address resides at the given index. In practice, those entries map to a specified amount of memory which is commonly referred to as a memory page. The granularity differs among hardware architectures. A simplified example of a typical address map is shown in Figure 2. The figure shows the entire PA space (PA) on the bottom. Above, the IPA stage mapping is depicted. The relationship between the two address stages represents the actual mapping. In this case, the so-called *identity* mapping is shown. Identity mapping means that there is no translation (or redirection) of memory addresses between stage 1 and stage 2. The MMU is only used for memory protection in this case.

D. Memory Access Control

Accesses to the distinct hardware elements is enforced by a MMU. Since this work focuses on access control, other means such as interrupt routing are not considered any further. In this type of AMP-based system, the access control is configured by the memory-map table of the particular MMU. In Figure 3 the access control principle for the intermediate level is shown. The PE are considered to be the subjects requesting access to a certain memory area. In this case, those memory areas are the partitions (*Part1* and *Part2* shown in Figure 1) and therefore the accessed objects. The MMU enforces the memory accesses. The access control policy is manifested in the memory-map. An important prerequisite is that the MMU memory-map, in this particular case a second-stage MMU, must not be accessible by any of the MC-domains itself. This must be handled by a higher privileged instance. Most commonly this is referred to as the hypervisor.

IV. Threat and Attack Analysis

Threat and attack analysis facilitates two core methods to identify and rate security risks. Threat analysis aims for structured decomposition of systems and the derivation of security threats [16]. A commonly accepted and applied threat model is STRIDE (spoofing, tampering, repudiation, information disclosure, denial-of-service and elevation of privilege) which is shown in [17]. Depending on the system element, a particular subset of the previously mentioned threats is applicable. Attack analysis is an offensive method which aims to foresee and factorize the behavior of an adversary. During the assessment, the minimum effort to exploit a specific component of the system is to be estimated. A qualitative and quantitative statement (risk) results in the exploitability estimation with regard to a particular threat. The exploitability factors which are applied in this work are adopted from the common vulnerability scoring system [6]. The ontology between the threats and attacks are adopted from the risk model given in [7]. To summarize up, the threats are a functional categorization of security risks. Whereas, attacks refer to the technical facilitation of a certain threat category.

A. Threat Landscape and Memory Asset

In the first place, our work focuses on *tampering* threats on the memory partitions of the MC-domains. With regard to the example given in Figure 3 one MC-domain tampers with the memory partition ($Part_i$) of another domain. Despite, the compromising the integrity of main memory can be the root-cause for further or even more advanced threats. It is worth to mention, that tampering might lead to elevation of privileges or one subsequent step of spoofing a communication link to another entity. Even though denial-of-service attacks can be mounted by tampering with the memory base of a system. This is motivated by the fact, that software intensive systems rely on their code and data base stored in the main memory. Tampering with that does not only compromise and modify information, but also the control flow integrity of their function. Meaning, by having the ability to deliberately change the control flow, an adversary might gain full or partial control of the vehicle's behavior. Impacts on safety and operation of the entire vehicle are severe. As a result, memory storage is an important asset.

B. Attack Vector

As it is mentioned before, the factorization of attacks gives insight on the exploitability of a particular threat. Technically, it shall be assumed that an unintended access to main memory is caused by a defect or vulnerability. Accordingly, in this section, we elaborate on potential breaches. In the following, the potential preconditions are elaborated. Ultimately, this work considers attacks at the intermediate level. However, in order to mount exploits on this level, the adversary is required to break into the system first. There must be an entry point for the attacker. In ECUs of a vehicle, this might be facilitated by external telematic interfaces, internal vehicular buses or entertainment media. A comprehensive analysis of vehicular attack surfaces is shown by Checkoway et al. in [18]. Once the adversary has successfully entered the system further exploits might be necessary to break the memory access control. We assume that the adversary needs to break several levels before he reaches the intermediate layer. For example, if he succeeded to take over an application he needs to elevate his privileges towards OS level. This might be done via a root/kernel exploit [19]. Once the adversary reached the intermediate layer the memory access control mechanisms (compare Figure 3) need to be exploited. By compromising or circumventing these isolation controls, the main memory then is fully exposed to further exploitation. As an example, in various experiments, it has been demonstrated that state-of-the-art multiprocessor SoCs running AMP-based multi operating systems imply architectural weaknesses in memory protection [12] [20] [21] [22]. This flaw suffers mostly from insufficient hardware support for throughout system isolation. In addition, the fixed and static memory layout at the intermediate system level provides a wide surface for attacks. If an adversary successfully circumvented the memory protection, the static memory configuration enables an attacker to aim for particular data or information contained in the memory. Once the memory isolation is breached, the adversary has full access to the memory. Before the attacker can manipulate the data or the code he must locate its target structure within the memory space. Since multiple MC-domain partitions are present in the main memory, the attacker first needs to determine the base address of it's targeted partition. Starting from this offset, the re-interpretation of OS memory structures can be initiated. Re-interpreting the kernel structure is a broad research field of computer forensics, for example by Andrew Case et al. [23]. By assuming a consecutive memory structure the attack can follow references within those structures until the target is found. In addition to the re-interpretation of the structures, the attacker could simply scan for specific binary patterns or so-called *magic bytes* to reach its target structure.

C. Attack Complexity

With respect to the metrics in [6] the following aspects refer to the exploitability. The required entry attack vectors and required privileges are discussed in the previous section. With regards to the complexity of the attack, the attacker does not need to conduct a target-specific reconnaissance. The system configuration is considered to be static due to the fixed memory mapping. There is no intended variation from target to target.

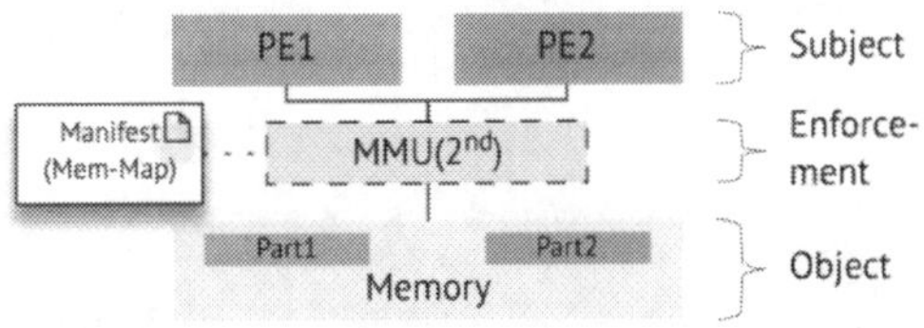

Figure 3. Access control at intermediate level.

As a result, once an adversary is able to breach the memory protection for one system, the concept is applicable to other systems in the product-line or vehicle fleet.

D. Scope and Elevation of Privilege

Due to its nature, memory protection breaches allow a wide range of impacts on security goals. In this particular case, the adversary is able to conduct control flow integrity attacks and elevate the privileges of certain functions of the system. This implies a change of scope [6], meaning the attacker is not only able to control the targeted function but also further assets from this position.

E. Impact to General Security Goals

With the herein assumed attack vectors a potential adversary is able to disclose information from the system and to tamper with the integrity of the information contained or used by the respective criticality domains. The availability is not directly affected by the given attacks. However, due to the change-of-scope (compare with Section IV-D), denial-of-service attacks might be conducted by further exploitation as well.

V. MEMORY-MAP SHUFFLING

In this work, we propose a concept to increase the effort of localizing and predicting the attack target structure in the main memory. We aim to elaborate the certain aspects with regards to concept, implementation aspects and integration. Furthermore, we discuss aspects of the effectiveness of our approach. The obfuscation of address layouts is a method to increase the difficulty of exploiting vulnerabilities. Using this technique it is more difficult for an attacker to determine the location of memory structures. Address space obfuscation, which is often referred to as *Address Space Layout Randomization* (ASLR), was originally implemented for *user-space* applications. It added an artificial diversity of the memory locations of the applications *Stack*, *Heap* and linked libraries and positions within a process's address pace. Thus, the exploitation of buffer-overflow and format-string vulnerabilities became harder.

The core concept aims to create a random permutation of a translation table. However, beyond identifying a proper permutation procedure the concept builds on certain aspects relevant to the target environment. Architectural or technical constraints are relevant as well as procedural prerequisites. In Figure 4 an overview of the causal dependencies of the concept is shown. Usually, the AMP system configuration consists of several configurations to produce the IPA system mapping. These configurations include a board support package (BSP) which describes the SoC hardware element utilization, the

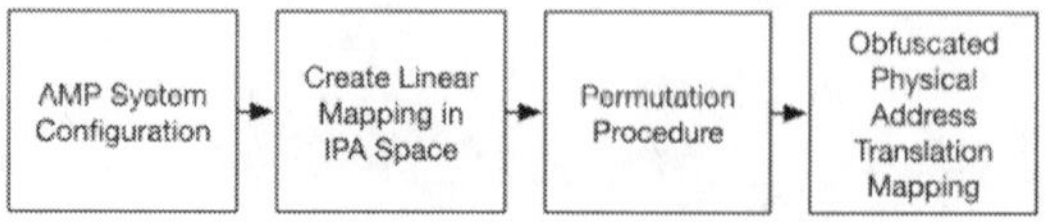

Figure 4. Overview of the obfuscation concept.

device assignments to split the peripherals, and the main memory partitions for the OS-layer instances. This information will be transferred into the suitable mapping table. This pre-initialized mapping will then be processed by a permutation procedure which outputs a random physical address map.

A. Obfuscation Concept

The concept aims to place the physical addresses in such a manner that without the knowledge of the mapping table an adversary cannot reconstruct the entire memory structure of a memory partition. That means, after the access control breach the attacker is able to jump to and access every position in main memory. Nevertheless, at PA level it cannot be differentiated to which MC-domain the memory pages belong. Furthermore, the order of pages is not sequential after the obfuscation. According to the ToE, Figure 5 visualizes the principle. To summarize up, the obfuscation takes effect in two dimensions. First, the page assignment and second, the sequential order of the pages. Our exemplary system consists only of two MC-domains. With a decreasing number of domains, the effect of the obfuscation rises.

B. Permutation Procedure

The core of the obfuscation concept is the algorithm to produce the permutation of the address mappings. The procedure of randomizing the address space can be compared to a shuffle of a deck of cards. Therefore, in order to transport the overall approach, we chose the shuffling algorithm by Fisher and Yates [24]. The Fisher-Yates shuffle is simple and fits well to produce random permutations of finite sets. In this particular case, the finite set is the translation table which was previously created by the initialization process. The translation table is denoted as a finite set TT of mapping entries E.

$$TT = \{E_1, E_2, ..., E_n\} \quad (1)$$

Each entry redirects an intermediate input address to its corresponding output address range. We assume TT is initialized with an identity mapping, which means each intermediate address is equal to the physical address *IPA* = *PA*. The entries of the set would then be arranged as follows:

$$TT = \{PA_{0x000000001}, PA_{0x0000000040}, ..., PA_n\} \quad (2)$$

The Fisher-Yates algorithm is shown in Algorithm 1. It iterates through TT and swaps the entry in the current position with a random position. The random position is determined by a randomization function which draws values out of a specified range.

Algorithm 1 Memory-Map Table Shuffle

```
for all TT[] do
    random ⇐ random number such that 0 ≤ random ≤ range
    swap TT[random] and TT[current]
end for
```

C. Assumptions and Requirements

One of the key elements of the shuffling algorithm or the permutation algorithm is a suitable random number generator. As shown in Listing 1 a discrete random number from a specified range ($0 \leq randomNumber \leq Range$) is drawn. As a prerequisite, we assume a cryptographic secure random number generation providing sufficient entropy. The required entropy depends on the granularity of page mappings of the system. In other words, the total number of entries in TT. Furthermore, we require that the generated numbers are still non-biased after truncating them to the specified range. Performance plays an important role since this approach will be integrated into a timing critical environment. Every time the system is reset the memory mapping will be randomized. Therefore, the algorithmic complexity must be kept to a minimum so the start-up phase of the device is not significantly delayed.

VI. Discussion

With respect to the characteristics given in the threat and attack analysis, this section discusses the effectiveness of the given approach.

A. Effect on the Attack Complexity

By applying the random permutation at the intermediate physical address mappings, the physical memory structure is obfuscated. Exploits like those referenced in the threat scenario would fail. However, adversaries would adapt to the newly introduced circumstances and try to de-obfuscate the memory map. In reference to crypto analysis, nevertheless, a reasonable way to evaluate the effectiveness of this kind of statistical security control is to estimate the effort to break it. In general, we assume two approaches to compromise a permuted address mapping. Either the attacker scans the whole main memory for a page he is looking for or applies statistical analysis to the permutation procedure. The former approach makes it necessary to assume that the attacker is able to scan the whole main memory. Furthermore, he needs an evaluation function that determines whether or not the current scanned page is the one he was looking for. This is what we also described in our threat scenario, however, the adversary now has to deal with the fragmentation of binary patterns. By applying this brute-force attack, the attacker needs to scan half of all left pages on average to find the next designated page. In other security fields such as cryptography, the strength of a certain function, such as encryption, is hard to define using discrete methods. Statistical analysis or complexity estimations on the randomization output forms the second approach to de-obfuscate the mapping table. This mathematical problem is comparable to the crypto-analysis of ciphertext. Concepts like *known-chiphertext* and *chosen-plaintext* attacks can reveal algebraic weaknesses of the implemented algorithms. Hence, the cryptographic secure implementation of those procedures is the key to preventing

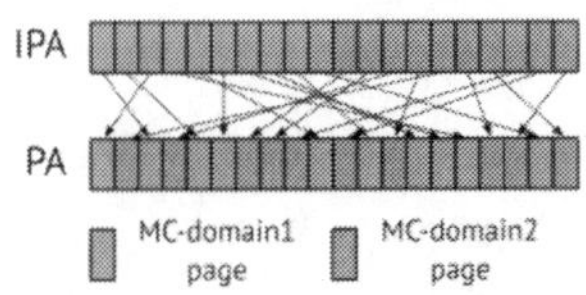

Figure 5. Principle of randomized memory assignment.

such information leakage. The proposed concept implies an in-depth target-specific reconnaissance in order to de-obfuscate the system mappings. Since the mappings are randomized on each system individually and change over time, given exploits are not directly applicable to a range of systems.

B. Change of Scope

The proposed approach does not influence the ability to change the scope (such as elevation of privileges) of the target. Once the adversary succeeds in overcoming the complexity of the obfuscation, the scope change is still possible.

C. Protection of Confidential Information

Protecting the integrity or even the control flow integrity in breached environments is the major target of the given approach. Nevertheless, the disclosure of information is also possible. Although, the adversary has increased effort to find the targeted information. Reading the data then does not further impact the system. In other words, the de-obfuscation could be done offline with increased resources and without interfering with the system. As a result, the rearrangement of data is not sufficient to protect from information disclosure.

VII. Conclusion

The evolving nature of automotive origination processes such as product-lines and product life-cycles imply special needs of the created products. This is particularly true for the analysis and definition of security mitigations. In this article, we proposed a concept to mitigate the effects of breaching the hardware memory protections of automotive mixed-criticality systems. The particular technique to implement the multiple compartments for the distinct criticality domains is asymmetric multiprocessing. This technique implies a static system configuration on runtime. In the threat and attack analysis, we identified that this can be misused to mount direct-memory-access-based attack vectors. The proposed mitigation approach aims to obfuscate the intermediate address mapping based on the introduction of random permutations of a normal, continuous memory-map arrangement. This adds complexity and raises the exploitation effort for adversaries. This approach is applicable to hardware architectures utilizing memory-maps and two-staged memory management. As such, it contributes to a through defense-in-depth security architecture applied to the automotive landscape.

References

[1] D. Spaar. (2015, Feb.) Beemer, open thyself! - security vulnerabilities in bmw's connecteddrive. [Online]. Available: http://www.heise.de/ct/artikel/Beemer-Open-Thyself-Security-vulnerabilities-in-BMW-s-ConnectedDrive-2540957.html

[2] A. Greenberg. (2015, Jul.) Hackers remotely kill a jeep on the highway—with me in it. [Online]. Available: https://www.wired.com/2015/07/hackers-remotely-kill-jeep-highway

[3] S. International, "Sae j3061, cybersecurity guidebook for cyber-physical vehicle systems," SAE International, 2016.

[4] O. Henniger, L. Apvrille, A. Fuchs, Y. Roudier, A. Ruddle, and B. Weyl, "Security requirements for automotive on-board networks," in *9th International Conference on ITS Telecommunications (ITST)*. IEEE, 2009, pp. 641–646.

[5] S. Baruah, H. Li, and L. Stougie, "Towards the design of certifiable mixed-criticality systems," in *Real-Time and Embedded Technology and Applications Symposium (RTAS), 2010 16th IEEE*, April 2010, pp. 13–22.

[6] S. Hanford, "Common Vulnerability Scoring System v3.0: Specification Document," pp. 1–21, Jul. 2015.

[7] J. Freund and J. Jones, *Measuring and Managing Information Risk: A FAIR Approach*. Butterworth-Heinemann, 2014.

[8] J. Edge, "Kernel address space layout randomization," *Linux Security Summit*, Oct. 2013. [Online]. Available: http://lwn.net/Articles/569635/

[9] S. Bhatkar, D. C. DuVarney, and R. Sekar, "Address Obfuscation: An Efficient Approach to Combat a Broad Range of Memory Error Exploits." *USENIX Security*, 2003.

[10] C. Kil, J. Jim, C. Bookholt, J. Xu, and P. Ning, "Address Space Layout Permutation (ASLP): Towards Fine-Grained Randomization of Commodity Software," *2006 22nd Annual Computer Security Applications Conference (ACSAC'06)*, pp. 339–348, Dec. 2006.

[11] H. Y. Tian Shuo and D. Baozeng, "Prevent Kernel Return-Oriented Programming Attacks Using Hardware Virtualization," *LNCS 7232*, pp. 1–12, Mar. 2012.

[12] M. Rushanan and S. Checkoway, "Run-DMA." *9th USENIX - Workshop on offensive technologies (WOOT)*, 2015.

[13] ISO/IEC, "ISO/IEC 25010 - Systems and software engineering - Systems and software Quality Requirements and Evaluation (SQuaRE) - System and software quality models," Tech. Rep., 2010.

[14] Y. Kinebuchi, T. Morita, K. Makijima, M. Sugaya, and T. Nakajima, "Constructing a Multi-OS Platform with Minimal Engineering Cost." *IESS*, vol. 3, no. Chapter 18, pp. 195–, 2009.

[15] J. Porquet, C. Schwarz, and A. Greiner, "Multi-compartment: a new architecture for secure co-hosting on SoC," *System-on-Chip*, pp. 124–127, 2009.

[16] S. Hernan, S. Lambert, T. Ostwald, and A. Shostack, "Uncover security design flaws using the STRIDE approach," *http://msdn.microsoft.com/en-us/magazine/cc163519.aspx*, 2010.

[17] A. Shostack, *Threat modeling: Designing for security*. John Wiley and Sons, 2014.

[18] S. Checkoway, D. McCoy, B. Kantor, D. Anderson *et al.*, "Comprehensive experimental analyses of automotive attack surfaces." in *USENIX Security Symposium*. San Francisco, 2011.

[19] H. Chen, Y. Mao, X. Wang, D. Zhou, N. Zeldovich, and M. F. Kaashoek, "Linux kernel vulnerabilities: State-of-the-art defenses and open problems," in *Proceedings of the Second Asia-Pacific Workshop on Systems*. ACM, 2011, p. 5.

[20] P. Schnarz, J. Wietzke, and I. Stengel, "Towards attacks on restricted memory areas through co-processors in embedded multi-os environments via malicious firmware injection," in *Proceedings of the First Workshop on Cryptography and Security in Computing Systems*. ACM, 2014, pp. 25–30.

[21] P. Schnarz, J. Wietzke, and I. Stengel, "Co-processor aided attack on embedded multi-os environments," in *International Conference on IT Convergence and Security (ICITCS)*. IEEE, 2013, pp. 1–4.

[22] J. Danisevskis, M. Piekarska, and J.-P. Seifert, "Dark side of the shader: Mobile gpu-aided malware delivery," in *Information Security and Cryptology–ICISC 2013*. Springer, 2014, pp. 483–495.

[23] A. Case, L. Marziale, and G. G. Richard, "Dynamic recreation of kernel data structures for live forensics," *Digital Investigation*, vol. 7, pp. S32–S40, 2010.

[24] R. A. Fisher, F. Yates *et al.*, "Statistical tables for biological, agricultural and medical research." *Statistical tables for biological, agricultural and medical research.*, no. Ed. 3., p. 90pp, 1949.